DATE			

Ballantine Books · New York

Directed by
JAMES
BURROWS

Directed by
JAMES
BURROWS

Five Decades of
Stories from the Legendary Director
of *Taxi, Cheers, Frasier, Friends,
Will & Grace*, and More

James Burrows

with EDDY FRIEDFELD

Published in the United States by Ballantine Books, an imprint of Random House,
a division of Penguin Random House LLC, New York.

BALLANTINE is a registered trademark and the colophon is a trademark of
Penguin Random House LLC.

Grateful acknowledgment is made to CBS Studios for permission to reprint dialogue from
Cheers, dialogue from *Frasier,* and dialogue from *Taxi.* Used courtesy of CBS Studios.

Photo on page i by Luke Fontana.
Photo credits located on page 351.

LIBRARY OF CONGRESS CATALOGING-IN-PUBLICATION DATA
Names: Burrows, James, author.
Title: Directed by James Burrows: five decades of stories from the legendary
director of Taxi, Cheers, Frasier, Friends, Will & Grace and more.
Description: First edition. | New York: Ballantine Books, 2022.
Identifiers: LCCN 2021047965 (print) | LCCN 2021047966 (ebook) |
ISBN 9780593358245 (hardcover) | ISBN 9780593358252 (ebook)
Subjects: LCSH: Burrows, James, 1940– | Television producers
and directors—United States—Biography.
Classification: LCC PN1992.4.B8957 A3 2022 (print) |
LCC PN1992.4.B8957 (ebook) | DDC 791.4502/32092 [B]—dc23
LC record available at https://lccn.loc.gov/2021047965
LC ebook record available at https://lccn.loc.gov/2021047966

Printed in the United States of America on acid-free paper

randomhousebooks.com

2 4 6 8 9 7 5 3 1

First Edition

Book design by Debbie Glasserman

This is dedicated to the one I love . . .
To every one of you who has grown up with sitcoms,
and shared both laughter and tears
with family and friends.

"This place is the closest thing I have to a real home."

Sam Malone, *Cheers*

FOREWORD

Glen and Les Charles

Our first encounter with James Burrows was in the 1970s on a soundstage at MTM Enterprises, where we'd gotten our first staff-writing position—i.e., full-time job. We'd gone to the stage to see a run-through of the week's show being directed by a newcomer, a young man, bearded and bald beyond his years. He was in the process of getting his butt chewed out by one of our show's executive producers, who was never the least bit shy about sharing his opinions loudly and publicly. The young director stood there taking it but not liking it.

We decided it was pointless to introduce ourselves to the poor bastard, because he was clearly going to be on the next plane back to wherever he'd made the mistake of leaving. If anyone had told us we'd one day partner with him in what would turn out to be the most happily successful show and production company in our careers, we'd have thought them insane.

Of course, you've guessed by now that poor bastard is the author and subject of this book. Jimmy Burrows weathered that storm and went on to become a great friend and a brilliant and incomparably successful director.

He was just starting out in his profession that day, but it seemed like he'd been destined for a career in show business for his entire life. Born to legendary writer, humorist, script doctor, and personality Abe Burrows, he'd spent hours of his life in theaters and studios and socialized with people whose names the average person only sees on a marquee. It was as if both nature and nurture intended that he become a member of the entertainment world.

But what was he to do? He couldn't act his way out of the rain, couldn't write, sing, dance, or play an instrument with any distinctive ability. He tried to yodel, do impressions anyone recognized, throw his voice, juggle plates, or saw a woman in half (volunteers for rehearsal are tough to enlist).

Then inspiration struck. Directing was the perfect job. He could do it sitting down, he could wear any clothes he wanted, and he could tell everyone what to do. And if anything ever went wrong, he could blame it on the writers.

Whatever the real origin of his career choice might have been, it has entertained millions, starting with the brothers Charles. We worked together with him on many MTM shows, then for four years on *Taxi*. Our collaboration over those years was so positive we ultimately decided to make it legal. We made some very good and some very lucky decisions together over the years, but the best one was the first. We became partners.

It seemed inevitable. We'd "grown up" together, worked out any personality kinks, and had the important things in common: We admired the same movies and TV shows, we laughed at the same things, and, most important, we liked each other. As only people who have shared hundreds of meals eating from Styrofoam containers on their laps can bond.

As excited as we were to be working with Jimmy at the time, even we, his biggest fans, couldn't have predicted how far he would go. He's simply become the greatest director of comedy in television history. And that's not just the opinion of Jimmy and his wife, though they're the only ones who have it on their bath towels. He's the greatest by any measurement: number of episodes, number of gigantic hit series, number of awards, and the amount and volume of laughter he's been responsible for. And, amazingly, when he's not working on a series, he's doing pilots for new series.

We could write a book ourselves about everything that Jimmy brings to his work. He's smart and incredibly inventive. He's in full control onstage—there's never a doubt who's in charge. Yet within the order he maintains, he makes space for people to feel comfortable to experiment and create.

He's an actor's director, as any actor who's worked with him will tell you, but he's also a writer's director. Maybe in part because of his father, he understands how writing works and why it sometimes doesn't. Most important, he knows good writing when he sees it.

First and foremost, he has the perfect temperament for the job. He's particularly well suited for directing TV, where, as opposed to film and theater, casts and crews can sometimes work together for years, as has been the case for Jimmy several times. The situation requires a special kind of personality, pretty much exactly the one he has. We've never seen him lose his temper (though we have seen him want to). He has no capital-E ego. He's supernaturally patient, calm when everyone around him is pounding on panic buttons. And he's a great audience and encourager. People want to do their best for him; they want to make him laugh.

And, oh yeah, Jimmy's funny.

One day when we were just starting to put *Cheers* together, the three of us were in our office and were presented with a huge stack of legal documents for our signatures. They were detailed partnership contracts, anticipating every possible contingency and laying out legal procedures to settle any future disputes. We stared glumly at them in silence for a moment, then Jimmy said, "I'm okay with a handshake." We shook hands and tossed all the paper in the trash. That was over forty years ago, and working with him has never been anything but a pleasure and an honor. And a hell of a lot of fun.

Ready when you are, J.B.

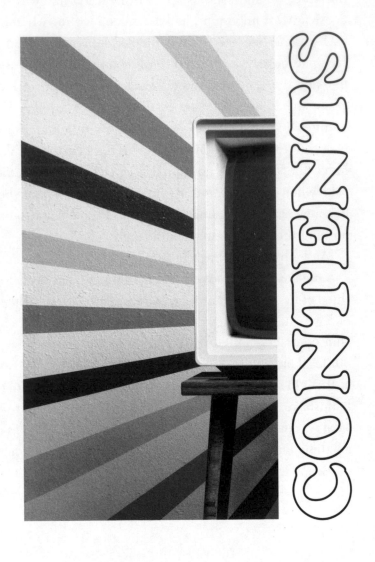

CONTENTS

Directed by
JAMES
BURROWS

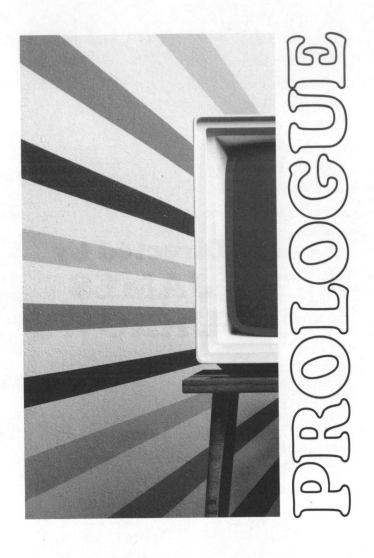

PROLOGUE

I agonize over laughter. More specifically, getting the best, smartest, character-driven laughs. I also wrestle with character. Is the character likable, believable, and sustainable? When I direct a television show, I try to reach that sweet spot where the best script meets the best performance and the best chemistry between performers. Hitting that exact moment, where these factors land in combination, results in the sweetest and most enduring laugh. Part of that means figuring out why something isn't working and how to give the actors and writers input, suggestions, and guidance as to how to make it work. The process is like sculpting clay: It must be formed, carefully and passionately. Whether working on an entire series, one episode, or just one scene, a director must be thinking about how to develop characters and have them interact with other characters who are also growing. That's what creates good comedy.

The sitcom has been a staple in American homes since the 1930s Golden Age of Radio. Over the decades, there have been extremely creative shows that were ahead of their time. Sitcoms are families that we introduce, first to American audiences and then to viewers all over the world. They are the friends and families we choose that help us connect with our own families. There are often unlikely friendships and always different circumstances at hand, but the shows are invariably about people who form a common and inextricable bond. *Taxi* featured a family of unrelated people trying to get out of a dead-end joint and into a better life. *Cheers* was a family of people that met regularly at a bar where they could share their stories. *Friends* was a formed family trying to help one another navigate young adulthood. *Will & Grace* was about people getting to choose a family that gave them acceptance and encouragement, protecting and supporting one another against a world that was at least in part prejudiced against them. With all those different bents and permutations, it is always basically about a family. And over time, they become our family.

I have spent most of my professional life developing and directing a certain type of comedy—the situation comedy, the "sitcom." Sitcom directors are in charge of the set, establish the tone and pace of the show, and elicit the performances. They ultimately communicate the vision of the writers and actors, which starts with the ideas on the empty page and ends with people at home watching and laughing. If you ask most people to tell you what their five favorite television shows are, odds are that a few of them will be sitcoms. The same goes with favorite characters. And if you ask someone about their favorite sitcom, they will likely talk not only about the characters and the comedy but also about where they were in their lives when they watched it and with whom they watched it, about who introduced them to the sitcom and to whom they introduced the sitcom. It's all about that shared experience. There is an inherent warmth to a great sitcom. A movie gets shared once. A TV show, especially a sitcom, is perpetually shared, thanks to syndication and now streaming.

People like characters they identify with. Audiences internalize sitcom characters more than any other type of character because they have gone through many of the same experiences or emotions that the character has. They have dinner, they fight with each other, they fall in love, often at the same time. Most people don't investigate crimes, go to court, or operate on patients like the characters in dramas with cops, lawyers, and doctors, but everyone eats with their family and friends, sitting and talking.

Along with stand-up, the sitcom is the best, most enduring, and most resilient form of comedy, because in its best incarnation it gets the audience to fall in love with characters, and the comedy gets delivered through the stories and character development. Sitcoms also bring a theatrical flair that you don't normally get from television, because it is a staged performance being filmed, often in front of a live audience. The best sitcoms transcend the screen and reach out and grab the audience by the throat and by the heart.

The formula to sitcom success is deceptively simple yet very difficult to achieve: Create brilliant, multilayered characters that the audience will identity with and love. Then create great supporting characters, followed by storylines that will allow the characters to grow and play off one another for successive seasons. Even though each episode is only twenty-two minutes long, you still have to tell the audience in those twenty-two minutes who all these people are and repeat it every week.

The core of the show is about the primary relationship between characters. It has to be either one character you care about who has travails with other characters or a couple of characters whose dynamic is funny but also real, and it has to be loving and it has to be identifiable. If you have that, then the jokes are attitude jokes and not necessarily jokes about just funny words or about falling down and getting a laugh. On *Cheers,* it's the response of George Wendt's Norm Peterson to Ted Danson's Sam Malone, asking him the first time he came into the bar, "What do you know?" Norm's reply, "Not enough," got a huge laugh from the first test audience. That's not a joke. It was never written as a joke. Good characters create good stories. If you have distinct characters, the humor also becomes attitudinal humor, character-driven humor. Norm saying a line is not the same as John Ratzenberger's Cliff Clavin saying one. It's a distinct character analysis. Without that, it doesn't matter what the blocking is, how funny the jokes are, the characters don't translate into what the audience cares about. You have to care about these fictional people, their relationships, and their problems in order to care about the show.

My job as director is to protect the writer's vision. Most networks try to vitiate the writer's vision. I work to guard it and enhance it by constructing a safe, creative environment that fosters the best ideas, including those no one had thought about before.

My goal is to get the writer's voice on the air and not have it meddled with by the homogenizing effect of a network, which tends to imitate what has been done before. Garry Marshall once referred to television-network executives as "people who aren't funny who are telling people who *are* funny what to do. And it's always going to be that way, because the men who are funny don't want to put on a suit and tie and sit at the networks." There are and have been exceptions—people like Grant Tinker, Brandon Tartikoff, Warren Littlefield, Jamie Tarses, and Michael Eisner, who understood not only the business of television but also the art of television, including character development and the writer's vision.

When I first started, I didn't turn down any offer. I needed the work and wanted to establish myself. In the five decades since, I've had the privilege and pleasure of working with some of the most talented people in the business. Fortunately, most of the work has held up to the test of time. The most cutting-edge and ground-breaking sitcoms were created without a guidebook, without any North Star, other than well-intentioned and creative people wanting the audience to laugh and think about life and social issues. They are a reflection of both where society was at the time and where it aspired to be. They illustrate how people evolved.

For most people, a multi-camera sitcom, which essentially is a scripted play performed in front of a live audience (as opposed to a single-camera sitcom, which is filmed without an audience), is the closest they'll ever come to live theater. For those of us in this business, there's a privilege and a responsibility to deliver a certain level of performance to viewers. Before television, I grew up in the theater, learning and developing skill sets I never realized would give me a unique edge as a sitcom director. The highest form of comedy is where it's combined with pathos, where at the moment you're watching, you don't know whether to laugh or cry. I got to come into that world at a time when audiences were not only comfortable with that mix, they expected it.

In order for a sitcom to get on the air, a pilot—a stand-alone episode that is used to sell a television series to a network—has to be shot first. A successful pilot needs characters that the audiences would want to see every week, in a location that will appear again and again, with a series of conflicts and goals that viewers would want to tune in to see resolved. What's the most important goal of directing a pilot? The obvious answer is to get the network to buy the show and put it on the air. Most pilots never air on television if the series does not sell. In the sitcom business, you can do everything right and still not succeed. Great writing, great cast, and great time slot—but if the audience doesn't connect with what you've given them, your show is canceled. For every *Cheers*, *Frasier*, and *Friends*, there are dozens of shows that don't make it past the pilot.

An artist works their entire career and life improving their instrument. A director works at improving other artists' instruments, as well as their own. I generally get hired by the writers, bridging the gap between writer and actor. When it comes to my work, my mission has been not only to be on happy shows but to help foster those happy and creative ensembles. We enjoy the luxury of getting paid for what we are good at and what we enjoy doing. I have always looked for holes in the metaphoric dikes and tried to plug them. But you don't prevent a flood with mere fingers. You need a sturdy boat with a capable crew. On my shows, we're in the boat together. If the writers and the actors are content and working together and communicating creatively, then that joyfulness is also transmitted to the audience.

I still consider every pilot I direct as if it were a Broadway show, in that you have to show the audience very early on who these characters are. Whenever I begin a new show, I endeavor to be a font of energy and enthusiasm. I try to get everybody to consider me the dad of this newly created alternative family and to trust me.

I want an actor to be comfortable enough to walk the comedic plank for me and to feel an affinity with me. My deal is, "Go out as far as you can. You may get wet, but you'll never drown. I'll always catch you. See what you discover. If there's a gem at the end of the plank, I want it to be in the show." At a certain point, and under the right circumstances, good actors will be so immersed that they will know their character as well or better than the writer or director.

You have to nurture that environment. If actors are comfortable with their role, I don't have to over-rehearse or direct with a heavy hand. I can guide and fine-tune performances.

If an actor says something funny and it passes muster with the writers and gets on the air, the director will get a glint from the actor's eye that says, "I'm part of this creative process; I'm putting my own spin on this." Once an actor finds their character, I work with them to make sure they don't lose it. Sometimes they have to dig deeper into a character and their motivations, with insight from the writers and me. Other times, results can be achieved by giving a direction as simple as "Go faster."

Positive energy in a cast and crew transmits across the screen and infects the audience. I encourage a lot of camaraderie with creativity and hard work. On my sets, everyone is free to say anything they want about anyone or anything, as well as about me. If someone doesn't like a direction I give, my house rule is "Just tell me." If they want to help out with other actors, the rule is "Just go in there and say what you want." I also encourage writers to do this. On my sets, no one dismisses the contributions of actors. That said, you have to be funny and you have to know what is funny. Like Dr. Frasier Crane, I am always listening. "Uvula" is a funny word.

Over the years, I have become both an actor's director and a writer's director. I'm very opinionated when I read a pilot script. I want to think, "This is funny, I can add to this." If I'm interested and don't already know the writers, I meet with them. All writers think they're auditioning me, when in actuality I'm auditioning them. I need to find out if they can defend their material without being defensive about it. I don't want to work with someone who says, "No, it's funny, do it." If I make suggestions that they don't think will improve the script and they can articulate why, I will never be upset by it. If they can't explain why, I won't work with them.

I constantly look for that amazing and rare combination of comedy and heart, humor and humanity. The concept is never what attracts me; it's the execution. There are lots of shows about bars, news and radio stations, cabdrivers, and shrinks. I want to see what the characters that are put into these situations do. I'm concerned about believability and the economy of the comedy, the shortest distance between the character and the laughter, and the best way to get there. When I direct an episode, I have a lot of notes. I am apt to tell writers, "Fifty percent of what I say is gold and fifty percent is garbage. It's your job to figure out which is which." I have a sense of what is funny, but I don't have a writer's logic. I will do anything for a joke. I'll sell a scene down a river for a good joke, but that may not be integral to the emotion in the piece, and where that is wrong, I will fix it.

What I enjoy most about directing is the sense of surprise that reveals itself along the way. I built my career on trying to do pilots and shows with unknown actors in them. When a known actor says something, the audience is already primed to laugh. The element of surprise is gone. When an unknown actor or unknown character says something funny, you're startled, so you laugh even harder. There's no baggage for the audience, no preconceived notions. You never know what's going to happen with your piece until an audience weighs in. You may think that you know what will be funny as hell, but then an audience watches it and says it is terrible, and you're shaking your head in dismay. I continue to find this surprise both scary and a rush. When taking a new piece and shepherding it down the creative river, it's exhilarating to see if an audience will buy it, laugh at it and embrace it, or hate it.

If you listen carefully to the audience, they will tell you everything you need to know about what you need to do to be funny. My friend and colleague Chuck Lorre, who created *Two and a Half Men*, *The Big Bang Theory*, *Mom*, and many other hits, and who started his career as a musician, said that good comedy has rhythm and pitch, tempo, rests, dynamics—all the things you normally associate with music. We both hear that music.

To date, I have directed more than seventy-five pilots that have gone to series. I have been called the Sitcom Sorcerer, the Concorde of TV Pilots, the Willie Mays of Directing, and the Obi-Wan Kenobi of Sitcoms. I was most flattered when I was called the Steven Spielberg of Sitcoms and even more flattered when, in response to that, Steven called me and told me that he wanted to be known as the James Burrows of Movies.

In 1979, *Time* magazine's Richard Schickel included me in an article about "the credits you never read," mentioning the people you don't see who work behind the scenes. With very rare exceptions, I've spent my life behind the camera. Most people wouldn't recognize me on the street (unless they've seen me on *The Comeback*). Some would recognize my name. But most people know my work. I'm very proud of and very comfortable with that. I'm also proud of all the people I've worked with behind the scenes who helped deliver these shows to the audience, some whose names flash across the screen quickly at the end of each show.

The Charles Brothers, Glen and Les (much more on them later) nicknamed me the "Actor Whisperer"; what I really do is blow in their ear and they'll do anything I want. But, seriously, it's a moniker I am both very proud of and accept with slight discomfort. People think that about me because my actors perform so well. The discomfort comes because I have been blessed with such talented performers. The ability to draw out the best in people, professionally or personally, is a skill set. It's about training a new group of actors to behave as an ensemble and respect one another. I don't start a show with matchstick figures on a page, planning out each move. I let each actor bring their gifts and show me. I initially suggest where they will be on a stage and how they will move. If anything doesn't work, we'll develop it. I expect actors to check their egos at the door, no matter who they are. Again, we're all in a lifeboat together and we're all rowing.

If I had to sum up my professional legacy, it would be that I got to work with some of the most talented people who have contributed to some of the best work in entertainment. Having directed over a thousand shows means that almost any night you can turn on your television or go online and find a show that I directed. I'm very proud of that.

I continue to direct sitcoms. After almost fifty years, I still crave having my days energized with gifted people. To me, success is not about working less, it's about working harder at jobs that I adore with brilliant, passionate people that I care about. I continue to work because I both love what I do and love and respect the people I work with.

Even though I haven't touched a theatrical stage in a long time, in my head and heart I'm still a theater director. I'm still staging a sitcom as a play and then I film it. That moment in front of a laughing audience is something I enjoy more than anything else I've ever done professionally. While every audience is different, each generates its own warmth, affection, and community that galvanizes performers. My favorite night of the week of every series is still show night, when we film. And my palms still sweat before every show night.

As much as you've enjoyed watching all these shows, I've had even more fun directing them. I've resisted writing a book for a long time. I generally hate talking about myself. But I keep staring at the at least seven imaginary bottles of lightning on my metaphoric mantel celebrating the magical shows and groups that I got to be part of. I wanted to share the joys and the struggles of that journey. This book is a celebration of the great people that I worked with and the joy and challenges we had together. From my first four episodes of *The Mary Tyler Moore Show,* to eleven episodes of *The Bob Newhart Show,* eight of *Laverne & Shirley,* nineteen of *Phyllis,* seventy-five of *Taxi,* two hundred forty-three of *Cheers,* thirty-two of *Frasier,* fifteen of *Friends,* forty-nine of *Mike & Molly,* and two hundred forty-six of *Will & Grace,* I've had the unique privilege and pleasure of directing over a thousand episodes of television, including five thousand rehearsal days, ten thousand rewrites, five hundred thousand network notes, and a million laughs.

Growing Up

If it's a girl, Phoebe; if it's a boy, Phoebo.

PHOEBE, *FRIENDS*

James Edward Burrows was born in Los Angeles on December 30, 1940, but for as long as I can remember, I was Jimmy. I'm not sure where the James came from, but the Edward was after Ed Gardner, the star of the radio program *Duffy's Tavern* and the best friend and mentor of my father, Abe. When I was five, we moved from Los Angeles back to New York City, which is where my childhood really began. We lived on the Upper West Side of Manhattan on 229 West 78th Street, between Amsterdam and Broadway, in a three-bedroom apartment. It was here that my lifelong romance with sports began. On my bedroom wall I had taped up the cover of the first issue of *Sports Illustrated*, featuring Milwaukee Braves catcher Eddie Mathews and a picture of Dick Kazmaier, Princeton's magnificent triple-threat tailback. I was a big New York Yankees fan. I loved Mickey Mantle, Hank Bauer, Elston Howard, Yogi Berra, Phil Rizzuto, and Roger Maris. I saw Mantle hit home runs from both sides of the plate. I went to Ebbets Field for a World Series game. I watched Duke Snider play for the Brooklyn Dodgers.

My grandmother, Sarah, who spoke English with a Russian accent, lived nearby on 102nd and Broadway, on her own. She would come visit us often, a sweet and supportive fixture as we were growing up. My sister, Laurie, also possessed this same kindness, always looking to help others.

We were culturally Jewish but not very religious. Both my parents were agnostic atheists. My father was bar mitzvahed. My mom's parents were Russian Jews, but religion was never an important part of their lives. They flirted in the 1930s with the whole communist movement, which was its own religion at the time, or at least a viable substitute for a conventional one. Both my parents spoke a little Yiddish. The expressions permeated and stuck with me. I heard *pisk* (mouth), *machatunim* (in-laws), *punim* (face), and *mishpucha* (family). One word always struck me as weird-sounding: *fakeft*, which means "beholden to." I remember my father using it about one person who wanted to do a favor for him. He said, "No, I don't want to be *fakeft* to him." It's a good word.

When I was twelve years old, I was asked if I wanted to have a bar mitzvah. I think if you give most Jewish boys at any point in our five-thousand-year history the choice of whether they want to put all the work into getting bar mitzvahed at that age, they'd probably decline. Which is what I did. But that's not where that story ends. My first wife was conservative, and at her urging I got on the "Shulbus" and agreed to be bar mitzvahed when I was forty-seven years old. The Charles Brothers said that I was the only man they knew who was bar mitzvahed at forty-seven and lost his hair at thirteen.

What I do remember doing when I was thirteen was seeing movies. Fifty cents got you a ticket to a double feature and a newsreel. Before the Beacon Theater on Broadway and 74th Street became a live-performance venue, it was a movie house. I went to see a double feature of *Bwana Devil*, with Robert Stack, Barbara Britton, and Nigel Bruce (Dr. Watson to Basil Rathbone's Sherlock Holmes), and *House of Wax,* with Vincent Price. His muscular assistant, Igor, was played by Charles Bronson, in one of his first roles—he was still using his real name, Charles Buchinsky. It was the first color 3D feature film from a major American studio, complete with stereophonic sound. The glasses were a novelty. The wax-covered bodies scared the hell out of me.

I started playing golf at sixteen. I would ride the subway to play public courses throughout the city. I was self-taught and loved the game. Over the years, my swing has gotten good but not as consistent as I aspired to. Occasionally I hit the ball square. There's the old joke about the gorilla who hits the ball four hundred yards and then goes to putt and hits the ball another four hundred yards. Sadly, my golf game bears too close a resemblance to that joke. (These days, I like to play with my friend Al Michaels. He'll often bring along two younger guys for a foursome. After they see me hit a couple of drives, they'll ask me how old I am. When I tell them, their response is usually "No way!," which always makes me smile.)

Growing up, I had a set of Lionel electric trains and a reel-to-reel tape recorder. I recorded all the groups that were ushering in the new form of music on the radio, rock and roll, including Bill Haley and His Comets, the occasional Elvis Presley. I fell in love with the rhythm-and-blues and rock groups: Danny and the Juniors, the Cleftones, the Drifters, Little Anthony and the Imperials, Frankie Lymon and the Teenagers, and all the doo-wop singers. Groups of guys would cluster at every street corner and sing harmony. Wonderful sounds emanated from those corners, because the music we were singing—all within four chords—was accessible to us. Music became a crucial part of my life, especially because of its inextricable connection to comedy.

I was a reticent kid. Quiet in school, often playing stickball with a small circle of friends. On a good day, I could hit the ball for "two sewers," the length of half a block. We also played stoopball and pitched pennies. I played basketball and baseball in Central Park. I drank vanilla egg creams (milk, vanilla syrup, and seltzer), ate penny candies, the dots on the white paper, and Borden's vanilla ice cream.

My mother, Ruth Levinson, was the first person who instilled within me a sense of social awareness, politics, and social conscience. Every year, she had my sister, Laurie, and me march in the May Day parade downtown, which celebrated labor groups and trade unions. She was very left wing and did a lot of social work, including at the Hudson Guild, which helped the poor, and at the West Side Tenants Union. In 1951, she went across the street from our apartment building to Harvey's Coffee Shop and put enough nickels into the pay phone to reach the White House, begging for clemency and a pardon for Julius and Ethel Rosenberg, who were tried and convicted for espionage. She came back and told us that she made the call to endorse her feelings but didn't want to do it from home, because she didn't want her children to be unfairly tarnished by her beliefs.

My dad, Abe Burrows, was the legendary writer, playwright, director, and producer. Born Abram Solman Borowitz, he grew up in Brooklyn, went to New Utrecht High School and then New York University. He first worked as a Wall Street runner, then as an accountant. In 1938, as Abram S. Burrows, he started writing jokes for nightclubs and radio broadcasts. Abe never aspired to be a writer. The only professional aspiration came from my grandmother, who wanted to be a doctor's mother. Abe once wrote, "The only reason I started to write is that the Depression was on. I was out of work, and I found out that there were many comedians who needed jokes as much as I needed money."

While they were good parents, my mom and dad's marriage was far from storybook. I remember being eight years old, sitting on a fence at Floyd Bennett Field, right after my father flew back to Los Angeles to live and work. My mother told me that they were divorcing. "Mothers and fathers stop loving each other but never stop loving little children," she said. I knew that things between my parents weren't perfect, but there was rarely any yelling or screaming. Neither my sister nor I saw this coming. As I sat on that fence, I thought about how they were separating but wasn't quite able to figure out why. I couldn't wrap my head around it.

I didn't know many kids whose parents weren't together. That said, my parents did a good job raising us, even after the breakup. They were always attentive to Laurie and me and were cordial to each other as we shuttled back and forth between them. The lack of confrontation and communication was a shock for me that took a long time to get over. Beginning in my thirties, I spent more than two decades in weekly therapy sessions and eventually learned that I struggled with the divorce because I didn't understand the animosity between my father and mother. Their parting came as a complete surprise to me because they never fought openly.

On the positive side, those events also contributed at least partially to my success as a director. Because I didn't have that stability growing up, I've tried hard to provide stability with family, friends, and colleagues. My hypersensitivity made me a good read of people and talent, quicker to sense and manage tension on a set, a good listener, able to get people to work together constructively, and a facilitator of constructive and creative communication.

Missing being close to his children, Dad moved back to New York in the late 1940s. I don't think he could have loved Laurie and me any more than he did or have been more nurturing, but he did feel guilty about leaving the family. As a result, he became what was later called a Disneyland Dad, trying to compensate for not being around all the time by being "the fun one." The division of parenting was clear: Dad did dinner, plays, sports (on my sixteenth birthday, in 1956, Dad and I went to the championship "sneakers" game between the New York Giants and the Chicago Bears at Yankee Stadium. It was twenty degrees and icy, so the Giants wore sneakers instead of cleats and won 47 to 7. Frank Gifford was on the field and Vince Lombardi was coaching. I got to meet quarterback Y. A.

Tittle. What a memorable time). He was the hugger in the family, as am I. Mom covered the major and mundane everyday parenting work.

Upon returning to New York, Dad eventually lived in a floor-through apartment at the Beresford, on Central Park West and 81st Street, which he bought for fifty thousand dollars in 1954. Lauric and I would see him at least twice a week, on a weekday and every weekend. After dinner, he'd put us in a cab home. We'd meet him at the theater before dinner break. We'd eat at Gallaghers and Henry Stampler's, where he'd order steaks for everyone, and Sardi's, which was the center of the theatrical universe and home to so many parties. Everybody had spies there, looking at the *New York Times* writers to get ahead of a review that could make or break a show. Eventually the producer would get a call from the *Times* before the review was printed. There was either excitement or gloom.

As a kid, I wasn't a big reader, mostly comic books and sports magazines. My brain would get too distracted. I still don't absorb a lot through books, as opposed to my father, who was more innately intelligent and crudite. He seemed to be able to swallow a novel whole in ninety minutes, and it would sink in. He knew the classics, Greek mythology, and Shakespeare. He gave me an old edition of Charles Dickens and made me read *Oliver Twist, David Copperfield,* and *Nicholas Nickleby.* I loved it.

In New York City at that time, theater was the preeminent form of entertainment. As the son of a Broadway playwright and director, I had access to so many great productions, including *Finian's Rainbow* with David Wayne and Ella Logan, who were amazing; the stage play of *Peter Pan* with Jean Arthur (before Mary Martin starred in the musical version); and *Where's Charley?* with Ray Bolger, the Scarecrow from *The Wizard of Oz.* These were among some of my favorites from childhood.

My first personal exposure to the entertainment business came when I was in the sixth grade. Two people from the Metropolitan

Opera came to my school and asked if anybody could sing "My Country 'Tis of Thee." (It's now "Happy Birthday.") I got up and sang and was summarily inducted into the Metropolitan Opera Children's Chorus. I fell in love with opera and, as with doo-wop, that love affair has lasted throughout my life. It was a totally different theatrical experience from watching my father work, because now I was part of the performance.

For the next five years I was in Bizet's *Carmen, La Gioconda, Cavalleria Rusticana, La Bohème,* and *Boris Godunov.* We'd sit around during rehearsals at that beautiful facility on 40th Street and Seventh Avenue and soak up the atmosphere while also playing hide-and-seek. We would get three dollars a performance. *Pagliacci* and *Cavalleria Rusticana* were shorter and always done together. In the latter, where we were supernumeraries (extras without lines), we got two dollars a performance. We would show up right before going on, so we wouldn't have to be there all day. In *Carmen* we were only in the first act, very early on. We'd tease Don José and then go home. We were not afforded a sink to remove our makeup, so we all had urchin makeup on as we rode the subway back home. I'd walk into our apartment, my face covered with soot, and teach my sister all the songs. To this day, I take Laurie to the Hollywood Bowl every summer to see and hear classical music.

The opera was mesmerizing for me. The music, the costumes, the pageantry, enthralled me. Most kids didn't get to be in this theater of music. There were only thirty of us. I felt like a kid in a candy store. At the old Metropolitan Opera House, I listened to the magnificent orchestra and these beautiful and extraordinary voices and heard the audiences cheer, yell, and scream in adulation. At eleven years old, this was a new and exciting world.

After five years, my voice started to change, and I could no longer be in the Children's Chorus. But because of my involvement, I was able to get into the Fiorello H. LaGuardia High School of Music & Art. The school was founded in 1936 by the New York mayor, who wanted to establish a public school in which students could hone their talents in music, art, and the performing arts. It was located in Manhattan at Convent Avenue and 135th Street, right next to City College. Alumni included Steve Bochco, Tony Roberts, Hal Linden, Richard Benjamin, Liza Minnelli, Dom DeLuise, Suzanne Pleshette, Ving Rhames, Billy Dee Williams, and, much later, my future colleague and good friend Jennifer Aniston.

Music & Art had kids from all over the city. It was at this point that I began dating, which involved travel. Depending on where you lived, you could be deemed "GU"—geographically undesirable. I went out with a pianist, Gina Raps, who lived in Brooklyn, Naomi Tessler from Riverdale, and Roz Schreiber from Parkchester. Half of the dates were spent going back and forth on a train and a bus.

Television became part of everyone's lives by the late 1940s. I remember watching *Captain Video and His Video Rangers,* the first kids' science-fiction show, which aired on the DuMont network. Like most of America, I loved *Lucy* and then, years later, *The Dick Van Dyke Show.* Westerns were very popular, including *The Rifleman, Bat Masterson,* and *The Life and Legend of Wyatt Earp,* which starred Hugh O'Brian (with whom I later would work). *Maverick* was a legitimate Western that also made fun of every aspect of the Western formula. James Garner's Bret Maverick wasn't your typical cowboy. He was a professional poker player, a self-proclaimed coward, and a reluctant hero. A funny rebel with a great smile. Unlike other cowboys, whose hats were pulled down over their foreheads, Maverick's was back on his head. Tipping the hat back made all the difference in the world—an early lesson for me in the subtle touches that define a character.

During that time, I also discovered Steve Allen, the host of *Tonight Starring Steve Allen,* which became *The Tonight Show.* Steve was saddled with the unenviable pressure of getting an audience to stay up and watch this new format when they needed to be at work at eight A.M. On his first show, in 1954, he bravely went into the audience and asked an older woman if she wanted to say hello to anyone at home; she replied, "Everyone I know is sleeping." Steve was a genius. He had a brilliantly funny mind.

Nat Hiken was a founding father of the sitcom. He spent a year with Phil Silvers developing the character of Master Sergeant Ernest G. Bilko, a fast-talking con artist, who ran the motor pool at Fort Baxter, Kansas. Bilko had one weakness—a heart of gold when it came to his men and the Army. Originally called *You'll Never Get Rich,* it later became *Sergeant Bilko* and then *The Phil Silvers Show.* Nat followed that five-season hit with *Car 54, Where Are You?,* about the misadventures of bungling but lovable cops in a New York City police precinct in the Bronx. Both were character-driven comedies and among the first shows on television with integrated casts. Nat also was the first not to do pickups (reshooting scenes to correct small mistakes in dialogue), which made the show seem even more realistic. Years later, when I was a director and a producer, we'd occasionally call up a plot of *Bilko* and say, "This is how they did it then. How can we change it a bit and make it different?"— still using Nat's ideas but making them our own.

All these shows were recorded on film in front of a live audience. Film made it look better. It gave the show the patina of Hollywood, one generation removed. All these people that I encountered either directly or on TV were teaching me important skills. I was starting to learn through osmosis.

After high school I attended Oberlin, which was and still is a very liberal institution, fully in sync with how I was raised and what I believed was right. Hopefully, college is the time where you figure out who you are apart from the daily influence of your parents. My mother's liberal values were now independently mine.

And while I was at an institution of higher learning, my education came mostly from outside the classroom. We had huge lunches and dinners where everyone talked about ideas and current events.

I was obsessed with John Glenn and cut classes to watch him go into space. One of my biggest contributions at the time was sharing with the group Mel Brooks and Carl Reiner's newly minted *2000 Year Old Man* and Bob Newhart's *Button-Down Mind* albums, which my dad had sent me. My small single room became the hot spot for kids to come listen to and get blown away by the cutting-edge comedy. My self-esteem and my ability to communicate with people grew exponentially as a result of all these interactions. I was becoming an adult, but I still didn't know what I wanted to be when I grew up.

Abe

> When I was a young man about to go out in the world, my father says to me a very valuable thing. "Son," the old guy says, "one of these days in your travels, a guy is going to come to you with a brand-new deck of cards and offer to bet you that he can make the Jack of Spades jump out of the deck and squirt cider in your ear. But, son, do not bet this man, for as sure as you are standing there you are going to wind up with an ear full of cider."
>
> SKY MASTERSON, *GUYS AND DOLLS*

My dad was always very present in my life, offering helpful advice and telling me stories about his early years in entertainment. He had come to L.A. in the 1930s, where he started out selling jokes and then became a full-fledged radio writer. His first big hit was on *Duffy's Tavern*, a situation comedy with eccentric characters set in a bar (it was either coincidence or prophetic that his son would find his own success four decades later with a comedy set in a bar: *Cheers*). Beginning in 1941, my dad was head writer for the first five years of *Duffy's* ten-year run. He was careful about writing and casting. He implemented a program where writers got paid for submissions that he liked and created a path for the best ones to get jobs. One of the best of his discoveries was Larry Gelbart, who later went on to write for Bob Hope, develop *M*A*S*H* for television, co-write *Tootsie,* and co-author Broadway shows, including *A Funny Thing Happened on the Way to the Forum* and *Sly Fox.* Larry said of my father, "He was the best of us and the one we always wanted to be." Abe also mentored Nat Hiken and Dick Martin.

Dad understood a key tenet of casting, the element of surprise. He wrote for two legendary dramatic actors, Charles Laughton and John Barrymore, whom he added to his list of great comedians because they surprised the audience with their comedic chops. Finding dramatic actors that the audience doesn't expect to be funny and is pleasantly surprised by has been one of the cornerstones of my career as well.

Dad also had a second career as a songwriter, which led him to play the piano and sing at Hollywood parties. He played by ear—he couldn't read a note of music, one of the only things I can do that he couldn't. What he lacked in formal training, he made up for in a joyfulness that matched the lyrics. He endeared himself to Hollywood because he would come to parties and sing his songs and play the piano, along with Robert Benchley, Groucho Marx, Danny Kaye, and Johnny Mercer.

He composed "type" songs, named after "Scotch type" whisky, which was being peddled during World War II as a poor substitute for the real thing when shipments from England stopped. His parodies included "I'm in Love with the Girl with the Three Blue Eyes"; "How You Gonna Keep Them Down on the Farm after They've Seen the Farm"; "I'm Walking Down Memory Lane without a Single Thing to Remember"; "I May Be Sick in the Hospital but I'm Not Sick of You"; "You Put a Piece of Carbon Paper under Your Heart and Gave Me Just a Copy of Your Love," which he wrote at Ira Gershwin's house; "I'm So Miserable without You It's Almost Like Having You Around"; "I Know I'm Going to See You in My Dreams Tonight, which Is Why I'm Going to Stay Awake"; "When Your Hair

Turns to Silver, I Will Love You Just the Same Through All the Other Colors"; "Everyone Has Someone, but All I Have Is You"; and "Every Time I Kill Myself, I Die a Little."

Louis B. Mayer, the head of Metro-Goldwyn-Mayer during the era when studio heads were referred to reverentially as "moguls," summoned/invited Dad to perform at a party that included Frank Sinatra, Danny Kaye, and Jimmy Durante. Abe became good friends with Danny's wife and collaborator, Sylvia Fine. My grandfather raised his son with music in the house, so when Dad met Charlie Chaplin, the two hit it off singing English dance-hall numbers and became friends.

The combination of Dad's writing and performing success led him to nightclubs, including doing a gig on a cruise ship with Bing Crosby, whom he adored. When they finished singing together for the first time, Crosby said to him, "If the ship's foghorn ever busted, we'd always have you." He also starred on a number of radio and television shows, including *Breakfast with Burrows*. On *Abe Burrows' Almanac,* he was billed as "The bald-headed baritone from Brooklyn." It was on one of the shows, *This Is Show Business*— where a panel of celebrities solved problems that were presented to them—that he got to know George S. Kaufman.

Dad owed much of his theatrical success to Kaufman, the legendary comic writer (for the Marx Brothers, among others) who penned or directed at least one play on Broadway in every season from 1921 through 1958, including *Guys and Dolls*. In 1955, the two collaborated on the Oscar- and Golden Globe–winning film version of Kaufman's play *The Solid Gold Cadillac,* which Kaufman had co-written with Howard Teichmann.

I got to meet George Kaufman. He was very tall, surly, and acerbically witty. For over a decade he was the drama editor for *The New York Times,* while his shows ran simultaneously on Broadway. He avoided a conflict of interest by not having his shows reviewed by the *Times*. According to legend, a press agent once asked, "How do I get our leading lady's name in the *Times*?" Kaufman replied, "Shoot her." He hated love scenes and would exit the theater during the scenes in *Guys and Dolls* between Sky Masterson and Sarah Brown, leaving Dad to direct them. Kaufman was known for being blunt. During that show's run, he once wrote a note to Stubby Kaye, who was overdoing his scenes: "I'm watching your performance in the back of the theater. Wish you were here."

The character Nathan Detroit ran the "oldest established permanent floating crap game in New York," a perpetually down-on-his-luck mug. Sam Levene was the original Nathan Detroit on Broadway, but he couldn't sing. Dad's partner and close friend, songwriter Frank Loesser, was pulling his hair out. When Frank Sinatra was cast as Nathan in the film version, they put a couple of extra songs in for him. Frank Loesser also complained that Robert Alda sang out of one side of his mouth and that the other half of the theater couldn't hear him. At the premiere of the movie version of *Guys and Dolls,* which was directed by Joseph L. Mankiewicz, Orson Welles came over to Dad and me after it ended and said, "Joe Mankiewicz just laid a little turd over all your lines," and walked away.

Dad learned a lot about directing from Kaufman on *Guys and Dolls.* Contrary to the image of the old-school Hollywood writers, who were affectionately known as "schmucks with Underwoods," Dad hated the typewriter; he wrote all his scripts in longhand on big yellow legal pads. Evelyn Green, his longtime assistant, would type everything he wrote. He also wrote on his feet while he was directing. I wound up doing a lot of changes on my feet as well. Seeing the actors and watching the script in real time, you can immediately see what works and what doesn't.

When he was directing, my dad always said that when the other actor does a joke, your reaction shouldn't be slapping your knee; you shouldn't screw up your face. The way you react to a joke is to pretend that you have three holes in the top of your head and you have three balls. And as you're trying to react to the joke, you're trying to get the three balls into the holes. Less is more.

In my teens, I would go to rehearsals with Dad, including for *Guys and Dolls*. I'd like to say that I absorbed every creative moment that I was exposed to. I did not. I was a kid. This was my dad at work. During the rehearsals of *Guys and Dolls,* I snuck up to the empty balcony section and ran around. When you're a kid, your dad's fame doesn't mean that much. I had no "eureka" moment or any epiphany that theater or television was what I wanted to do with my life. If anything, the more I became aware of my father's legendary reputation and abilities, the more I knew that the theater was the one arena I did *not* want to go into. Abe cast a long shadow.

Despite my consciously not wanting to pursue a career in theater, I couldn't help but pick up on some of my dad's techniques. One involved him standing behind the scenery and listening to what was going on, rather than watching. He cared about dialogue more than anything else. He went crazy if there was no noise. If he heard silence and no laughter, he assumed it was because somebody was taking too long or that the dialogue was not right. I am also about listening first, before anything else. To this day, I often close my eyes during rehearsals and tapings, to focus on the rhythm of the comedy. If your audience can close their eyes and still see and hear the characters in their head, you're a success.

After *Guys and Dolls,* Dad directed *Two on the Aisle,* with Bert Lahr and Dolores Gray. He wanted to put a treadmill downstage, so they could move across the stage that way. He called George and said, "I'm thinking of putting a treadmill downstage. What do you think?" George said, "Depends what they say while they're on it." That's how important the written word is. I've told that story in every writers' room I've ever worked with.

Frank Loesser began collaborating with him in the 1940s. Their Broadway alliance resulted in *Guys and Dolls* and *How to Succeed in Business Without Really Trying.* (In what is now part of show-business lore, Frank's first wife, the temperamental Lynn Garland, was referred to as "the evil of the two Loessers," a play on "the lesser of two evils." Apparently, Lynn once asked someone, "Why do people take such an instant dislike to me?" The immediate rejoinder was "It saves time.")

It seemed like Dad knew everybody in show business and everyone wished to know him. He was very social and was famous for his parties, particularly his New Year's Eve bashes. It was at those parties that I got to meet Thornton Wilder and the team of Howard Lindsay and Russel Crouse, who wrote the books for *Anything Goes* and *The Sound of Music.* His social circle extended beyond actors to the New York literati, including Truman Capote; Ed O'Connor, who wrote *The Last Hurrah*; Betty Comden and Adolph Green; *New Yorker* writer Alfred Kazin; John Steinbeck; and Cole Porter, who worked with Dad on *Can-Can* and *Silk Stockings.*

I was not as impressed as I should have been, because at the time I really didn't know who most of these people were. I saw them through the lens of simply being my father's friends. I kind of knew about Steinbeck. He got drunk at one of the parties and started railing about the bad reviews that Kazin had written about his books, unaware that Kazin was just a few feet away from him. "I hate him, I hate him!" he said, almost in tears. Aunt Shirley, Abe's sister, turned to him and said, "How can you hate him when you don't even recognize him?" The wit was definitely in the gene pool, which always gave me hope. Another time I was sitting at a table with an again-inebriated Steinbeck, who took the speech for the Nobel Prize he won for literature in 1962 from his pocket and showed it to me:

> The writer is delegated to declare and to celebrate man's proven capacity for greatness of heart and spirit—for gallantry in defeat—for courage, compassion, and love. In the endless war against weakness and despair, these are the bright rally-flags of hope and of emulation. I hold that a writer who does not passionately believe in the perfectibility of man has no dedication nor any membership in literature.

Someone whose fame I appreciated immediately was Groucho Marx. One time Abe took me to Chasen's, a famous L.A. restaurant (and now a famous Bristol Farms supermarket), and we saw Adolph Zukor there—a mogul who had retired as chairman of the board of Paramount Pictures. As the elderly Zukor was shuffling through the restaurant, Groucho was yelling, "Adolph, *hasta mañana!*" beckoning him to come over. It was certainly good for a chuckle.

In the 1950s through the 1970s, Dad was a fixture as a panelist on television programs including *This Is Show Business, What's My Line?,* and *To Tell the Truth.* My sister and I loved watching him on these shows. *What's My Line?* was the most popular show in the country and was on at ten-thirty on Sunday evenings. While we weren't allowed to stay up that late to watch it, I did get to go with him to CBS and see him tape the show.

In 1961, Abe Burrows was the frequent Ed McMahon to Mike Wallace's Johnny Carson on the talk show *PM East/PM West,* which Group W Television created to compete with Jack Paar's *Tonight Show.* The one time I went to see the show live, they had a novice nineteen-year-old singer from Brooklyn, Barbra Streisand.

Edward R. Murrow had a show called *Person to Person,* where he would sit in the studio in a leather chair and interview celebrities in their homes via a large television screen, which seems very commonplace now, especially with Zoom, but was a technological marvel back then. I had my television debut when he interviewed my dad. When Ed asked me, "What do you want to do when you grow up?" my more-nervous-than-illiterate response was "I haven't made up my decision yet." Not the most auspicious beginning.

Dad was a natural and intuitive mentor as well as a willing and diligent student to anyone that mentored him. He was grateful for the guidance he got in his own life and respected people who were passionate and worked hard. Like any good father, he felt the need to ensure I had a career. He was additionally worried about me both because his own career path was circuitous and uncertain in the beginning and because I showed no initial aptitude or drive for any particular trade. He was just looking for me to have a stable professional path as well as the same passion he got from doing something he loved. If I had gone to him during college and said, "I want to be a lawyer," he would have been just fine with that.

He had me tested to see if I was suited for anything specific. When I was twenty-one, I took a career test at NYU and a Rorschach test. Dad wrote a letter trying to get the results directly so he could interpret them without the doctor's filter. The NYU Testing and Advisement Center said that I had "superior intelligence, an overall ability to reason, and a passion for theater" but was inconclusive in its results. At the time, I was laconic and had no inspiration for any career. My only discernible passion was for sports.

My dad and I were similar in many respects. We both loved people. He had an affectionate way of working and was amazingly calm and focused. He told *The New York Times,* "I never worry. What could happen? So the curtain comes down." He was incredibly kind to performers as he was putting a show up on its feet. Kindness informs the way you deal with people. I've always tried to be the same way.

Dad was once asked, "Abe, why don't you direct drama?" His response was "I do direct drama—they just happen to be funny." I feel the same way about sitcoms. In their best incarnation, they are dramas that just happen to be funny, and the comedy is character-driven. Abe taught me about the comedy "rule of threes," that the reaction is just as important as the joke, and how to shave. He once pointed to his glasses and said to me, "Most people look at the world this way." He then skewed his glasses on his face and said, "I look at the world this way." I wound up developing the same philosophy, even though I've never worn glasses.

New York City was Abe's town. For years, if I wanted theater tickets, I could make one phone call, let them know I was Abe's kid, and house seats would be waiting for me at the will-call window. I used to know most of the guys who worked at every box office on Broadway. For many years, the only way people saw me was as

"Abe's kid." That's how I got my *nachas* (Yiddish for joy), because I adored him. That said, it's understandable why I had no designs for a career in theater. I wasn't interested in competing with my father, who was a verified N.Y. legend.

Dad's fame, success, and all the perks that came with it wouldn't have meant anything to me if it didn't come with the love we had for each other. But as much as I adored him, as a writer, producer, director, and script doctor, he cast too big a shadow for any son. I grew to love what he did but was always determined not to follow in his footsteps. I thought it would be too big a burden to even reach his level of success, much less exceed it. I didn't want to be the son in the family business, and I didn't want to compete with his talent. I desired my own business and my own place in the world. Through luck and hard work, as well as directly because of Abe's generous soul and nurturing temperament, I wound up in a similar place. We both served audiences. His home was the Broadway stage. Mine became the sitcom soundstage. And I couldn't have been happier about that.

My Early Adventures in Theater and Television

Theater at its best creates a culture and community. It's a gathering of people who crave being touched emotionally. They want to laugh and cry and be moved, but, more important, they want to do that together. Theaters were built to look like palaces but also to look like cathedrals, because if everyone does their job, that ensuing magic brings groups of people together on an emotional and spiritual level in ways that nothing else can. Broadway is an amalgam of everything, from feel-good shows like *Wicked* and *The Lion King* to very serious and heady pieces like *The Lehman Trilogy* and *Oslo*. Regional theater can be a little more esoteric, but summer stock and dinner theater are more self-selective—the audience is there to have a pleasant time and laugh.

During college, I spent two years in summer stock. I worked at the Barter Theatre in Abingdon, Virginia, the longest-running professional-equity theater in the United States. Bob Porterfield ran it. The joke about the rural theater was that if you didn't have cash, you could bring a sheep and trade it in for two tickets; hence the name Barter.

I was an intern, moving scenery, building sets, and sometimes filling in for the actors. I was in eight productions, including *Make a Million, Subways Are for Sleeping, The Young Abe Lincoln,* and *The Fantasticks.* I hadn't studied acting, so I had no idea about the craft. In the second performance I decided that I needed to try to forget who I was and immerse myself in the part. I was so scared. I was living a life that fell into the category of "don't try this at home." A trained actor pulled me over later and explained to me, "When you're in the space, you have to be able to control it." I learned that lesson the hard way.

After I graduated from Oberlin, I had no real direction, but the Vietnam War did. Young people were being called up to serve overseas. Like many others, I didn't want to be part of what I thought was an unjust war. I needed to matriculate in order to qualify for an education 2-S deferment. Dad suggested that I apply to the Yale School of Drama. It was also another way to expose me to the world that he loved.

Yale in the early 1960s attracted great and unique talent. My classmates included future playwright John Guare and future film director John Badham. The brilliant comedian and actor Robert Klein became, and still is, one of my closest friends (it amazes and pleases me that fifty-seven years later I got to direct him on *Will & Grace* as Grace's father). At school we were in *The Visit,* the Swiss play by Friedrich Dürrenmatt about Claire Zachanassian, the world-famous billionaire who returns home to her impoverished village and says she will pay a billion dollars to whoever kills her former love, who spurned her. And, yes, it's a comedy. Bob and I played village people. I tried to get Bob interested in golf, but as he said, "I perfected the game quickly and became bored. The challenge was gone when I could consistently get the ball through the elephant's trunk and onto the waterwheel."

I also worked as an assistant for Julius Monk, who produced revues in New York. He was like Mr. Blackwell: a gay man from North Carolina, well-dressed, polished, and very esoteric. He had early success with a revue called *Four Below* and established "café revues" in New York.

While I was there, Julius did *Dressed to the Nines*. He had performers like Imogene Coca, Pat Carroll, and Alice Ghostley and great sketch writers like Ronny Graham, Sheldon Harnick, and Tom Poston to create revues. Performers in tuxedos would do pieces and songs. William C. Brown did a great piece called "The Old Testament Rag." I totally ripped them off and performed a lot of the Julius Monk at the Hofbräu Haus in New Haven when I was at Yale. I cast Bob in the production, during which he was spotted by a William Morris agent and signed. They got him into Second City, and that was the beginning of his remarkable career.

Bob was one of the first of the modern comedians who told funny and insightful stories. He went to and talked about college. He wasn't going to be a riff-joke comedian like many who preceded him, who were very funny but didn't bring much pathos to the art form. Bob would experiment with new stuff and go out and constantly refine it. Stand-up comedians' brains are going the entire time, storing ideas and pulling them out at the right time. They're constantly developing and refining them. For every idea that lands, there are many that don't. You can see their skill as they create, riff, and ad-lib. There is both riskiness and excitement about that corner of the creative world.

In 1964, I got a job as a production assistant on the *Ford Presents the New Christy Minstrels* show, an NBC summer replacement for the sitcom *Hazel*. The group were folk singers and one of the first to do protest songs before Bob Dylan's broke out. Larry Ramos later became a member of The Association. Barry McGuire went on to sing "Eve of Destruction." Buz Kohan was one of the writers. Young and energetic, he passed along his sweetness and talent to his kids, who became an important part of my life decades later.

We worked out of Jackie Gleason's offices at 56th Street and Seventh Avenue in Manhattan while he was on hiatus. There were postcards with Jackie's picture all over the office. I worked on an episode that was shot at the Unisphere at the World's Fair in Flushing Meadows, Queens, where the Arthur Ashe Stadium is now. It was the only World's Fair I was ever at. It was hot, crowded, euphoric, and fun.

My job was to go to different pavilions and try to get people who worked at the exhibits to be in the audience for the show. I was getting paid very little, so I hired Bob to work with me. We both knocked on pavilion doors. I got a few dates out of it with a woman who lived in the Rockaways, which was in the flight path to the newly renamed John F. Kennedy International Airport. Every time I'd visit her house, the vibrations of the airplanes taking off and landing would reverberate throughout, shaking the walls. Bob met a woman at the German pavilion, Elizabeth Schmidt, and got a long-term girlfriend as a result. "How ironic that a Jew ended up with a German," he mused. Somewhere I still have a Jackie Gleason postcard.

While it's certainly clear now, at the time I didn't realize how much my dad did for me professionally. I used to go to rehearsals without fully recognizing that he helped me leverage that into a graduate degree. At Yale, as a playwright, you have to take directing classes. I studied with Nikos Psacharopoulos, who was a famous and talented director. He co-founded the Williamstown Theatre Festival in Massachusetts and claimed to have organized his first theatrical troupe at age fifteen under the Nazi occupation of his homeland.

I got hooked on directing and spent three years at Yale as a playwright. I wrote a play that was just awful, because I didn't have a writer's logic, the nuanced mindset that gives writers the ability to organize, process, and create. For my entire career, whenever I've gone to a writers' room and had a question about something going on onstage, I've hung around for a while. For talented writers, every word has an intent and a purpose. There is a big difference between "Are you coming home?" and "When are you coming home?" I don't get that. It's in their ear, not in mine. I don't see the purpose in every word. I put in my interpretation of what it means. For me, there's a certain way a joke is said that's the correct way.

Because of Nikos, I had my epiphany. I thought, "Oh my God, I can do that!" I never realized that's what my dad did as a writer–director. When I watched him work, he was always rewriting; he wasn't giving direction or blocking scenes. What I did learn was that I was good at discerning quality writing and executing on that writing/script to bring the product to market, to bring the vision to completion. In my directing career, my job is to get it to the finish line. Complete the play. Tinker to Evers to Chance. Over the years, there have been times when I'm doing a show, a joke comes down, and I don't get it. I'm not foolproof that way. I'll attribute my ignorance to either the early onset of dementia or not getting into the weeds to think about why. I'll ask others. If someone else gets it, I'm fine. If a joke gets a laugh, I'm okay with it.

Nikos was never particularly happy with his lot as a professor. His greatest ambition was to be a Broadway director. I acted in a couple of productions that Nikos directed, and he was very good. He was all about the vision. For him it was about the picture, what it looked like. When the train was coming, the visitors in the town had to be in exactly the right position. He worried more about vision than about what was going on between the two actors. I'm completely the opposite: The relationship—the people talking—is the most important part of the piece. I also don't see certain things going on in the background.

Years later, when I'd run into Nikos on the streets of New York, I'd stop him and say, "Thank you so much for what you've done." He was one of the great inspirational teachers. So many of his students acknowledged that. He appreciated the adulation but valued even more what he was able to do to change his students' lives.

While I learned a lot at Yale, there is only so much one can do in school, regardless of how good the program is. The rest comes from trial and error and figuring out how talent and skill sets work in combination with other sets. All this exposure and training allowed me to fall into the right hole—a job that I could do really well.

When I graduated from Yale, I got my first sitcom experience, but it wasn't exactly directing. *O. K. Crackerby!* was a show that Dad co-created with Cleveland Amory, based on Cleveland's book. It ran for one season on ABC in 1965. It was a fish-out-of-water series hoping to capitalize on the success of *The Beverly Hillbillies*, with stories about the battle of wits against snobbery.

Burl Ives played the title character, a rough-and-tumble man from Oklahoma who was also the world's richest. Burl was best known as a musician and folk singer. He was big and gruff and perfect for the part. When it got picked up as a series, I came out to California in the fall, as Burl's dialogue coach. The coach runs lines with the actor, helps them memorize their part, and often helps them with something specific to the role, like a French accent.

From there I worked as an assistant on *The Patty Duke Show*. I was the gofer for director Stanley Prager. I got to observe. It was 1965 and Patty was already a big star, having played Helen Keller in *The Miracle Worker* with Anne Bancroft. For the TV show she played two roles, Patty and her identical look-alike cousin, Cathy. The camera had to stay locked down so she could talk to herself, and they would reshoot as she repositioned herself as the other character. It wasn't my kind of sitcom. It didn't have the depth of *Bilko* or *Dick Van Dyke*. It was too light and silly, but it was exposure.

By December I was out of work, so I spent four months in Los Angeles looking for a job on set. When nothing materialized, I went back to New York and got a job with the Broadway producers Guber, Ford, and Gross (Lee Guber, Frank Ford, and Shelly Gross).

For many years, Guber et al. were among the biggest buyers of live entertainment in the country. They had a lucrative suburban entertainment chain that included the Westbury Music Fair on Long Island, the Valley Forge Music Fair outside Philadelphia, the Shady Grove Music Fair outside Washington, and the Painters Mill Music Fair in suburban Baltimore. I was hired as a show tech, who works on a Broadway show's tour. I was the guy that rented the truck, took the sets apart, loaded the sets onto the truck, and drove said truck to the next town after each Saturday-night performance. I did a run of *My Fair Lady* with Michael Allinson and Anita Gillette. I sat in the aisles watching rehearsals. For the first time in my life, I thought, "What the director is doing isn't the right way to do that." I never said anything. I still have the cast picture, where I lay down in front of them on the ground with my head crooked on my hand. I signed the picture and wrote, "Without me, everyone rolls down the hill." It was such a great company. I got to be very friendly with the gypsies (the members of the chorus, the singers and dancers who are part of the ensemble and travel from show to show). After every Saturday performance, we loaded up the truck and drove to the next port. It was very hard work but very fulfilling.

During this time, I became a huge fan of Edward Albee's work. On one of his productions, I was the lighting man—not to be confused with the lighting designer. I was pulling on the handles. I watched the productions for *The Zoo Story* and *The Sandbox* every night, and I was amazed at the dialogue.

A few years later, when Albee's *Who's Afraid of Virginia Woolf?* opened on Broadway, I called Dad and said, "The guy who wrote *The Zoo Story* is opening a play; do you want to go?" He was initially ambivalent. Abe had a visible twitching nervous tic in his face and had a lot of trouble sitting still. He was restless, a fidgeter. *Virginia Woolf* ran for three hours and fifteen minutes. The audience was enraptured by the play. Abe didn't move a muscle. He didn't look at his watch once. It was a busman's holiday for him and a historical evening in the American theater. No one knew what to expect. Uta

Hagen was phenomenal as the lead character, Martha. There was a picture in the *New York Post* the next day of Dad, Albee, Uta, and me. Years later I got to tell Uta that story backstage in a show she did with David Hyde Pierce.

The Broadway community in the 1960s was amazing and intimate. The creative energy was palpable. It was thrilling to be around. There were so many nightclubs and restaurants. When I worked as a stage manager, I'd go out after the show, getting to bed at two A.M. and waking up at eleven. So much of New York was happening after the theater. I stage-managed on Broadway in 1966, then went on the road, and was back in town from 1968 to 1969.

It was hard to go to the theater when you worked there, because your shows were on at the same time as most of the others. If I wasn't working, I'd see four plays a week. While I was the stage manager of *Forty Carats,* I'd run over to watch the end of *Company* on nights when our show ended early. I could access the theater through the back of the house. I'd watch Donna McKechnie do that amazing dance at the end of the show. She had extraordinary and sultry movements and could sing. She also did the "Music and the Mirror" number in *A Chorus Line*. I first met Donna when she was in the chorus of *How to Succeed*. She became one of the great loves of my life, and we dated on and off for nine years.

Dad always believed you can't learn how to be funny; you have to be born with the gene. But that gene must be nurtured and developed, through study, hard work, and trial and error. I inherited some of his funny genes and worked really hard to develop them. He took me to rehearsals and productions and instilled within me a sense of what worked and what didn't. Early on, he let me make suggestions. Some he took and incorporated into his work. I was always working, even though I didn't have an agenda or a mission. That would soon change, as I started to fall in love with the art and mechanics of the theater.

Dad saw something in me long before I ever did. While he loved his work, he never pushed me into the business. He subtly encouraged me, exposing me to great art and great people. He was teaching me long before I knew I was learning.

My first job on Broadway was as the second assistant stage manager of the musical version of *Breakfast at Tiffany's,* which was based on the Truman Capote novel and the 1961 film about free-spirited Holly Golightly, starring Audrey Hepburn and George Peppard. The stage manager is the person who is in charge of running the show every night, making sure the actors are there by a half hour before curtain, making sure the cues are called, and making sure the curtain goes up at five to ten minutes after eight. They're in contact with the front of the house and rehearse the understudies. The assistants help the stage managers.

On *Breakfast,* my job was to take care of Mary Tyler Moore, Richard Chamberlain, and Sally Kellerman, three Hollywood people doing their first Broadway show. Dad was both the playwright and director.

The scenery was on winches, so it could be pulled up without stagehands. One evening the stage manager called the cue, but the motor to pull the bar didn't work. I said, "What are we going to do?" He said, "Dance out and move it." I danced out and moved it. It was my first appearance on a Broadway stage. For my second appearance, they needed a way to get the entire cast, which was onstage for a song called "The Party People," off. Dad said, "You get onstage and say, 'There's a party at Pearl Mesta's,' and then all the characters will run offstage." I burst onstage and there was wild applause. I thought it was for me, not for the dancers. I said, "There's a pearly at Party Mesta's." And everybody ran off.

The stage manager also writes a weekly report and calls the director when an actor is "putting in improvements"—deviating significantly from the script—and can't be politely dissuaded. During *How to Succeed,* Dad would come and sit in the back. Bobby Morse would amplify. He'd add filigree. To make notes in the dark at the time, script doctors and writers carried the same penlights that medical doctors used to look down patients' throats. When Bobby was "improving" his lines, Dad flashed the penlight. Bobby got the signal.

My job on *Breakfast* was literally to ensure that Mary and Richard made all their entrances and exits. As the gofer, I also took care of their basic needs: I brought them coffee; Mary loved the hamburgers from Gallaghers. I became very close to Mary, who was going through a tough time. Coming off the success of *The Dick Van Dyke Show,* she was trying, relatively unsuccessfully, to figure out what her next career move was going to be. Her husband, then–NBC executive Grant Tinker, was in Los Angeles, and the geographic distance was also very tough on her. She leaned on me a lot.

Breakfast at Tiffany's opened out of town, in Philadelphia, and had a two-million-dollar advance ticket sale in New York. People wanted to see the two actors they knew as Laura Petrie and Dr. Kildare. David Merrick was the producer.

There were problems with the production from the very beginning. It was not my dad's greatest work. There was a pretty good score by Bob Merrill. Michael Kidd, of *Guys and Dolls* and *Seven Brides for Seven Brothers* fame, did the choreography. Merrick fired Abe and replaced him with Edward Albee, who had no experience in musical comedy. Joe Anthony, who directed both the stage version and the later film version of *The Rainmaker,* with Geraldine Page and Katharine Hepburn respectively, was brought in to direct.

It was around this time that my dad's drinking started to affect him. While his professional life was wildly successful, he was struggling personally. In the 1940s, he'd begun to drink at parties and at nightclubs, as that was part of his life and the culture. It never affected his work or his mood. Intermittently he would stop drinking, but my sister and I still often found a bottle of Scotch stashed somewhere. And while he was never surly with anyone, drinking did eventually affect Dad's brain. Over the years, the nerve damage from alcohol deteriorated his brilliant mind and his sharpness. He started to get confused. In the late 1960s, I traveled to London with him. He asked me to go to Paris as well. I uncharacteristically said, "If you stop drinking, I'll go to Paris with you." He did for a while. Finally, in 1969, after pressure from family and friends, and self-realization, he checked into Silver Hill, a rehab facility in Connect-icut. He found sobriety and never drank after that, but he never achieved the creative successes he had earlier.

After Merrick fired him, Dad asked me, "What do you want to do?" I said, "Is it okay if I stay on the *Titanic*?" I was still too naïve in show business—or any business, for that matter—to realize that I was the enemy for no reason other than being Abe's kid. I just wanted the experience.

Edward Albee remembered me from the summer-stock days and was very sweet to me. I would go downtown to his loft, where he was furiously writing and rewriting pages. In that era before fax machines and scanners, I'd pick up new pages and run them up-town. Edward brought a lot of dark elements into the show, includ-ing a misguided attempt to spice up the comedy with Holly's abortion. Another of the many changes was revising the show's title to *Holly Golightly* in Philadelphia and then back to *Tiffany's* in New York.

Breakfast at Tiffany's became the hottest ticket in town because of the two stars and because word got out that it was such a disaster. It played for four performances in previews, beginning on Decem-ber 12, 1966, at the Majestic Theatre. It never opened. There were lines outside the stage doors, waiting for glimpses of and autographs from Mary and Richard.

It was the most excruciating show I've ever watched or been in-volved with on a professional stage. There were hoots and hollers from the audiences. Mary came offstage and fell into my arms after every performance, in tears. She was a wreck. We held the wake for the show on a Wednesday night at Sardi's. Mary was sobbing un-controllably, so despondent over this bad career move. I sat with her for three hours, until Grant was able to fly in from Los Angeles. I've always both been grateful and found it ironic that my successful television career was born of a connection made from the ashes of such a miserable theatrical experience.

Cactus Flower was another one of Dad's successes. It ran on Broadway for years before it was adapted by I.A.L. Diamond into the 1969 film directed by Gene Saks that starred Walter Matthau, Ingrid Bergman, and Goldie Hawn. The Merrick production—which Dad both adapted, from a play by Pierre Barillet and Jean-Pierre Gredy, and directed—opened at the Royale Theatre on December 8, 1965, with Barry Nelson as Julian, Brenda Vaccaro as Toni, and Lauren Bacall as Stephanie.

From the moment she starred in her 1944 debut film, *To Have and Have Not,* with future husband Humphrey Bogart, Lauren Bacall was a star. Initially, she had a small role, but it kept getting rewritten and expanded until she was the co-star, where she had the iconic line, "You know how to whistle, don't you, Steve? You just put your lips together and blow." Betty, as her friends called her, was mesmerizing. *Cactus Flower* is about a plain woman who blossoms into a beautiful woman, but Betty was already a beautiful woman. All they had to do was tone her down for the first act.

I was initially the assistant stage manager on the production. Betty was tough and often difficult. Dad was pretty much the only one who could talk to her. That said, I really liked Betty. She was very nice to me—except for the time I got my baptism by fire. To prepare to become the stage manager for the road company, they let me run one scene of the Broadway production. That night I called the cues for a scene where the telephone rings twice. After it was over, Betty walked offstage, turned to me, and said, "The first telephone bell was early, and the second telephone bell was late!" And she stormed off. She didn't care that I was Abe's or anyone else's son. She really let me have it.

I got to go to London to stage the show. Stephanie was played by Margaret Leighton, a famous and accomplished British actress, who had won Tonys for *Separate Tables* and *The Night of the Iguana.*

Tony Britton played Julian. It was not lost on me that I was still this *pisher* (Yiddish for inexperienced) Jewish kid from New York directing Ms. Leighton, but I was following Dad's blueprints, which worked on Broadway. The biggest challenge was that Ms. Leighton did not have Betty's beauty. It was hard for the audience to accept her transformation from a plain woman into a beautiful one. All Lauren Bacall had to do was start out plain-looking. When Margaret blossomed, she didn't blossom enough.

For the 1966–67 season I went on the road with *Cactus Flower* and was the stage manager of the production in Chicago with Hugh O'Brian, TV's Wyatt Earp. During the run, he was living in the Playboy Mansion, before Hugh Hefner moved the entire operation to Los Angeles. O'Brian was very good as Julian and great to work with. He also bit his fingernails to the quick, which was hard to reconcile given how calm and what a quick draw he was in the Old West on television.

There was an energy in Chicago in the 1960s that drove theater and entertainment. Our theater was very close to Rush Street, which was one of the centers of nightlife and entertainment and included Mister Kelly's, a venue that showcased many great comedians, from Bob Newhart to Richard Pryor. The Ambassador East Hotel on the nearby Gold Coast housed the famous Pump Room nightclub, which Sinatra, Bogart, and Judy Garland patronized.

During a run of *Cactus Flower* on the road, the show was re-reviewed with a new cast, and I got a nice compliment in the local newspaper. I was happy about it but not overly excited. I knew I was still a work in progress.

One of the venues I got to direct the show at was the Framingham Dinner Theater in Massachusetts, one of three Chateau de Ville Dinner Theaters (the others were in Randolph and Saugus), which most people came to as much for the ornamental chandelier in the lobby as for the productions. Between summer stock and regional dinner theater, I was laying the groundwork for my television career. I started to learn my directing stagecraft in earnest. I remembered things that Dad said and did and drew on that. I was on my own for the first time. When a play was running in New York, Dad would often show up. On the road, I had to develop and rely on my own sense of what worked and what didn't work and when one performer was upstaging another. It was tough to give notes as a stage manager, because I still didn't have the director's clout. I had to find ways to make peace between two competing actors.

I also got to stage-manage *Forty Carats*. When her car breaks down, Ann, a forty-year-old American divorcée on vacation in Greece, gets help from Peter, a twenty-two-year-old man. Their brief affair gets more serious when the young man shows up at her Manhattan apartment to take her seventeen-year-old daughter, Trina, on a date and complications ensue.

The play opened at the Morosco Theatre on December 26, 1968, and starred Julie Harris, future *Jeffersons* co-star Franklin Cover, Glenda Farrell, future *The Graduate* co-star Murray Hamilton, future *Lou Grant* co-star Nancy Marchand, Marco St. John, and Michael Nouri. Julie Harris, who won the Tony Award for Best Actress, was a legend in the American theater. She was an absolute pleasure to work with. I learned early on that insecurity often brings out toughness and anger as a way of keeping people at a distance. If you're comfortable in your own skin, you generally get along well with others in any collaborative environment.

Forty Carats initially got lukewarm reviews. Walter Kerr, who was the Sunday critic for the *Times*, called my father and said, "I'm gonna give you a rave review." David Merrick bought a full-page ad in Monday's *Times*. In those days, you didn't have to write "advertisement" on top and you didn't play Sunday night. So Merrick's ad on Monday seemed like it was a brand-new review.

When I went to work on Monday, the line for tickets was around the block. That was Merrick's marketing genius. For another of his shows, *Subways Are for Sleeping*, Merrick found guys who had the same names as the big theater critics; he placed ads with pictures of those guys and their names underneath, endorsing the show.

During that time, I got to know Woody Allen fairly well. He was also on Broadway with one of his first hits, *Play It Again, Sam*. Woody was a distant cousin by marriage. When he was starting out, he reached out to Dad, who was so impressed with his comedic skills that he introduced him to some celebrities who were looking for talented writers.

Woody and I, along with cast members Tony Roberts and Diane Keaton, would go out after our shows. We played softball together in the Broadway Show League. The casts of *Sam* and *Forty Carats* were combined to form a terrible softball team called Schlissel's Schleppers. Jack Schlissel was Merrick's "bad guy." He was in charge of the money and had perfected every way in the book of saying no. Fortunately, I never had to deal with him, because I was getting Broadway minimums. When you're making the minimum, you can't fall off the floor.

After Julie Harris left the *Forty Carats* run, June Allyson took over as lead, which was a traumatic experience for me. For decades, June had developed this "girl next door" image in film and was the natural heroine for Van Johnson in a number of pictures. She wasn't such a nice neighbor to me. To this day, I have saved a quote from her from an interview she did in the mid-1970s, during a run of *No, No, Nanette,* and she mentioned that she had worked on Broadway in *Forty Carats,* "with Abe's kid, Jim, and the man has no talent whatsoever."

The person who truly launched my stage career was Zsa Zsa Gabor, the Hungarian American actress and socialite, who is infamous for having had nine husbands, one more than Elizabeth Taylor. Zsa Zsa came on board *Forty Carats* in 1969. When Merrick asked her to replace June, Zsa Zsa was understandably nervous. But she learned the role, and New York turned out for her opening night. She brought an entirely new interpretation, making it more frivolous. She managed to fill the house most evenings until the play closed. Thousands of her gay fans flocked to see her, hoping to witness a performance of high camp.

She needed me. Having been with the show from the beginning, I knew the ropes, figuratively and literally. I knew where she had to be; I knew where she had to go. A lot of times she would miss her cues because she cared more about how she looked than about making a cue on Broadway, which was criminal. I would have to go into her dressing room, and she would complain about how she looked. I would throw her out onstage no matter how she looked.

When multimillionaire building contractor Hal Hays was pursuing Zsa Zsa, he gave her a twenty-five-carat diamond engagement ring after only two weeks. It cost him two hundred fifty thousand dollars (three million dollars today). "I couldn't return a ring that valuable," she said, "so I agreed to marry him." She later claimed that the ring weighed forty carats. She really enjoyed that experience.

Zsa Zsa and I wound up developing a very warm and platonic friendship. Virtually mother and son. After *Forty Carats,* whenever I came out to California, I stayed at her house. I cherished that side of her and the friendship. She told me about every one of her husbands, referring to each by his respective number. "Number six cheated on me," she'd say.

I understood who Zsa Zsa was. I wound up becoming someone she trusted and relied on to get her through shows. I was more than just her wrangler. I could get her to do a show; I could get her to rehearse, perform, and not go off on a tangent. I traveled the country, directing either *Forty Carats* or *Blithe Spirit,* the other play she did. Producers wanted her because she drew an audience.

I got to direct my first Broadway show in 1970. *The Castro Complex* was a play about an American woman who has a compulsive crush on Fidel Castro and meets a real-life Cuban revolutionary seeking refuge from the CIA. Not the greatest premise to begin with. The woman was played by Marian Hailey. She beat out Diane Keaton and Dianne Wiest for the part. A young Raul Julia played Paco, the Castro character, who was based on Che Guevara. The play also starred Terry Kiser, who is now best known for playing the deceased gangster in *Weekend at Bernie's,* and who at that time was famous for an Alka-Seltzer commercial.

I was hired by producer Jeff Britton. There were fourteen performances. The creative lightning bolt had not struck me yet. I couldn't wrap my head around it. It wasn't especially funny. It needed work, and I was not at that stage in my career where I could do justice to it. The opening was a little creepy, so I put in Blood, Sweat & Tears "Variations on a Theme by Erik Satie," which opens the self-titled *Blood, Sweat & Tears* album. *The New York Times* wrote, "There are occasional farcical elements in the production, which can perhaps be attributed to the director, James Burrows. If so, he should have restrained himself." Fair enough. I wasn't discouraged, because I knew I had done the best I could with what I had.

My fingerprints were then all over Neil Simon plays in the 1960s and '70s. I directed *The Odd Couple* five times. I love that play. I liked the film version, except for the scene where Felix is in a hotel room contemplating suicide. I think he might have talked about it but would never have gone that far. I felt that it hurt the character and it hurt the farce.

Neil's plays were funny, and he was funny in person. He had a dry sense of humor. I liked Neil a lot, and we were in and out of each other's lives for many years. I learned quite a bit from his work. There were tragic undertones to all of Neil's comedies but structured with brilliant comedic lines. The minute any play went far down the dark road, he could pull you out. He said, "I never really wanted comics in my plays, with the rare exception of a Sid Caesar, or a Bert Lahr, if I could have gotten him on the stage. He would have been incredible in *The Sunshine Boys.* I wanted first-rate actors who could play comedy, the reason being that you never see the comedy coming. You're watching what you think is basically a serious play and suddenly you find yourself laughing your head off."

When I directed *Guys and Dolls* in San Diego, where I was artistic director of the Off Broadway Theater, I had two pianos. We cast John Saxon, Art Metrano, Maureen Reagan, and Eileen Brennan in the lead roles. Eileen played Sarah not like an ingenue but like a woman who had been around but chose the missionary because she'd been around. Dad came to see it and had only one note, about a character who had an interaction with Big Julie. He thought the actor didn't believe the line when he praises Big Julie. I felt great that he watched my work so intently.

I could now do summer stock and dinner theater and go everywhere, because I had the skill to put up a two-hour play in eight days. I could also rewrite or punch up a script and put some jokes in. I worked quickly and efficiently. My philosophy was "Get it done." Get the basics in there and, after that, tweak it and make it better; think about how to generate nuances that would enhance the show. I knew that doing nuances right away was like building a house and putting the couches and the curtains in before laying the foundation. This was literally how my directing career began. I was doing well, but I still felt I was getting other people's laughs, not my own.

By early 1974, I had directed fourteen dinner-theater and summer-stock productions in addition to my Broadway work over the eight years. The more I did, the more I added pieces—a joke, a physical move—which you're not allowed to do. I started seeing the audience laugh at things that weren't in the original script, at what I added. I was also facile and could amuse the people eating roast beef. It was during this time that I turned on the television and there was *The Mary Tyler Moore Show*. I was watching it and had one of my other life-changing epiphanies. "They're doing a play!" I thought. "I'm doing two hours in front of a live audience every week. I can do a half hour on television! And I know Mary! I know and really respect that woman. And she was sweet to me. Maybe I could do that!"

I immediately started writing a letter to Mary:

I think it is time for me to attempt to make a move, take a giant step, change keys, or, to put it delicately, get my ass in gear and involve myself in television. So I thought I would go right to the top, to the best, and ask if there is any opening in your operation, small or smaller, that I can fill. I think my training in theater will be valuable to me in TV. However, right now nothing can be as valuable as being where the action is, and as far as I'm concerned the action is where you are.

After a few more weeks of directing theater on the road, I returned home, where there was a letter waiting for me from Mary's husband and business partner, Grant Tinker: "We received your letter; we're very interested in theatrical directors." The next and defining chapter of my career was about to begin.

The Mary Tyler Moore Show

BOB
Have you ever thought of getting out of show business?

MR. PLAGER
But all you need is one hit show!

THE BOB NEWHART SHOW

I came to network television in 1974, during the Second Golden Age of Television. In 1971, Norman Lear's *All in the Family* had premiered. It was the show that broke the mold. Before Norman, sitcoms were largely idealized and homogenized portrayals of how America was supposed to look. Rather than follow this formula, Norman created shows where the characters looked and sounded like most of the people who were watching them. They represented a cross section of America, including race, class, and gender. Norman almost single-handedly revolutionized the format. He turned the mirror around and showed America as it was, with all its differences, biases, and hopes. Norman's sitcoms, including *All in the Family*, *Maude*, *Good Times*, *Sanford and Son*, *The Jeffersons*, and

One Day at a Time, offered characters on American television that began an important ongoing dialogue around social and political issues. Like most people, I was becoming aware of the changes both in America and its reflection on television. As an up-and-coming director, I was lucky enough to have a front-row seat for that experience.

Norman was always very astute as to what was happening in the world, and thus his shows were overtly political. He has an inherent sense of comedy that allowed him to see what could work in America. He's an inveterate lefty and has never backed down from advocating for social causes. Norman calls himself a bleeding-heart conservative, believing that the most conservative thing in America is to be devoted to the First Amendment, to the Bill of Rights, to the notion that we are all created equal under the law and we must find a way to ensure equal justice. The Mike Stivic character on *All in the Family,* played by Rob Reiner, was Norman's surrogate and alter ego.

Ever since Norman's characters started discussing social and political issues, sitcom characters have been a platform for audiences' reflections about what goes on in their lives and for discussion with family and friends. A well-crafted sitcom can have more of a social impact than almost any other form of entertainment. You can take viewers down a road to discuss sensitive issues like race, religion, civil rights, sex, or substance abuse, because you can bring the audience back with a joke. The laugh takes the "curse" off; it softens the edge and the stigma. When you're poignant, when you go to the depths of a sensitive discussion, the audience doesn't want to be left there. As an artist, you never leave them there. You lead them down one road and then you give them joke #75 so they can come back feeling happy, fulfilled, and smarter. That kind of road is complex and dangerous, because if you take them too far down the road, you may not be able to bring them back.

When I started out in sitcoms, CBS had a number of successful ones, including *The Beverly Hillbillies, Petticoat Junction,* and *Green*

Acres. While popular, they failed to appeal to a younger audience. They were eventually canceled all at once to make room for a lineup that had cross-generational appeal. *The Mary Tyler Moore Show* (*TMTMS*) premiered a week after *Petticoat Junction* was canceled, in its coveted Saturday-night time slot.

Sitcoms were now a vehicle for changing both the social and political landscape, with some sitcoms even more impactful than the news and documentaries. They certainly advanced the feminist movement. Taking a single woman and putting her at the center of a TV show was unheard of at that time. But *TMTMS* became one of television's seminal sitcoms. It also spun off *Rhoda* and *Phyllis,* sitcoms about strong, capable single women. As Garry Marshall said, "If you made people laugh at the same time you sent the message, it was more powerful and palatable."

In May of 1974, after receiving Grant Tinker's invitation to direct one episode, I headed out to Los Angeles. There were no handbooks or "bibles" back then, as a lot of shows have now, with compiled historical data that allows any new writer or director to get caught up on background and backstories quickly. At that time, you learned by watching other shows being directed so you could get your turn at bat. My deal was that for every week I was out there as an apprentice, I would get a stipend of $400. For that first show, they let me keep the $2,200 director's fee. For every subsequent show I directed, I had to pay back $200 of the weekly stipend. In 1974, with the stipend plus the fees for the few shows I actually directed, I made $12,000, which was a good living at the time.

MTM had four sitcoms running simultaneously: *TMTMS, The Bob Newhart Show, Rhoda,* and *Paul Sand in Friends and Lovers.* Paul was a very charming, yet offbeat character. He was trained by Viola Spolin from childhood, who created techniques to help actors be focused in the present moment, to internalize, and to find choices improvisationally. He worked at Second City and won a Tony Award for Best Performance by a Featured Actor in a Play in 1971 for *Paul Sills' Story Theatre.* He had a part on an episode of

TMTMS as an IRS agent sent out to audit Mary's taxes and who falls in love with her. The MTM folks all wanted to find something for him.

In *Paul Sand in Friends and Lovers,* Paul was cast as a cellist in the Boston Symphony. The show co-starred Michael Pataki as Paul's brother and Penny Marshall, in her first regular sitcom, as his sister-in-law. The cast also included comedian and pre–*Barney Miller* Steve Landesberg, and Craig Nelson (the one without the T). Paul couldn't learn lines by repeating them. He had to learn gestures and physicalize his lines. I would go to his house on the weekends and work with him, my second time as a dialogue coach. I later directed an episode. As affable as he was, Paul was not a series lead. He was too ephemeral and asexual to have the appeal a sitcom star needed at the time. Also, creators James L. Brooks and Allan Burns were spread too thin between their other sitcoms and weren't able to nurture the show and give it their focus and the "oomph," the magic that might have saved it.

As part of my apprentice program, I observed rehearsals. I watched from the top row of the bleachers of the soundstage, where the audience sat during shoot days. The soundstage is a sound-proof, hangar-like structure, building, or room for producing a tele-vision show and is usually on the studio property. With any show, it begins as a cold, large, empty shell; ideally, the producers, directors, and actors turn it into a show's home, filled with warmth and laugh-ter. Every week, the audience fills the bleachers of the soundstage and the show is taped in front of them.

My confidence and eagerness were metaphorically tied to my progression down the MTM bleachers to the soundstage. Every week I sat one row down from where I was the week before, until I got to the front row. Eventually, I would spend my professional ca-reer behind the camera. I've gotten to be part of a number of shows where the soundstage was transformed into a home and the place where the magic happens.

The first show I got to observe was *The Bob Newhart Show,*

which started shooting earlier in the season than other shows be-cause Bob's deal with MTM Productions allowed him a break in June to perform in Las Vegas for a month. I was also mentored dur-ing that time by Robert Moore, a director I knew from New York; he went on to direct the film version of *The Boys in the Band,* which helped launch the gay-rights movement.

Robert was rehearsing a scene; when he took a break, I walked down to say hello. I said, "I don't know why, but I think it'd be fun-nier if Newhart was over here when he said that." It was not a criti-cism, just a suggestion. I don't think it was retribution, but Robert later tapped me to be in an episode of *Rhoda* as Mike Brock, a sketchy literary agent trying to close a book deal during a funeral. He also cast himself in the same episode. It was the first of many small acting roles that I didn't audition for or particularly want. MTM would draw on people who worked there to play minor parts as needed, saving the time and expense of outside casting. It was part of paying my dues and being a team player in order to become a director.

When I was on set, I would often see Grant Tinker in the back row with his leg up on the chair in front of him, watching and enjoy-ing everything that was going on. He was a great inspiration to everyone who worked at MTM, because he was so positive and encouraging, advocating for creators. He would collect all the com-ments the network executives had, many of them critical and nega-tive, and selectively pass them along to the writers and showrunners. With so many hits on the air at once, he had a lot of power at the network, which he utilized judiciously and respectfully. His good nature seemed to be reflected in his physical features. A very hand-some man, he resembled the hood ornament of a Pontiac. He and Mary looked like they belonged together. We were in each other's lives until his passing in 2016. He would always remind me to "stop and smell the roses."

The legacy of MTM Productions was impressive. Not since Sid Caesar's writers' room—which included Mel Brooks, Carl Reiner,

Neil Simon, Larry Gelbart, and Woody Allen—had there been such an impressive incubator for future talent. At MTM, in addition to James L. Brooks, Allan Burns, David Lloyd, Steve Bochco, and Glen and Les Charles, the family tree included Tom Patchett and Jay Tarses, Gary David Goldberg (*Family Ties, Brooklyn Bridge*), and Hugh Wilson (*Frank's Place, WKRP in Cincinnati*). The latter two and I were brought out to L.A. as interns. Grant gave us money to live on. It couldn't have been a warmer, more nurturing, or more encouraging community. The MTM writers' program was known as the Harvard Law School of Television Comedy, despite the fact that Harvard lawyers have never been that collectively funny, on television or anywhere else.

TMTMS starred Mary as Mary Richards, a thirty-year-old woman who moves to Minneapolis after a broken engagement and begins a brand-new life. Mary gets an apartment, with landlord and friend Phyllis (Cloris Leachman) and a new best friend, New York transplant Rhoda (Valerie Harper). Like *The Dick Van Dyke Show,* *TMTMS* balanced the comedy between home life and work life. Mary gets a job as an associate producer at television station WJM, working for gruff Lou Grant (Ed Asner) and with sweet and quick-witted news writer Murray Slaughter (Gavin MacLeod) and dim-witted anchorman Ted Baxter (Ted Knight). Later regulars included Betty White as Sue Ann Nivens, the promiscuous host of *The Happy Homemaker,* and Georgette (Georgia Engel), Ted's equally dim-witted and very good-natured girlfriend and later wife.

A single professional woman in a metropolitan environment, living in the moment with all its opportunities, was a beautiful and winning formula and a template for future sitcoms. Combining a great cast with a great writing team, it was also created by James L. Brooks and Allan Burns, produced by Mary and Grant, and was the first in a long line of television hits that included *Rhoda, Phyllis, The Bob Newhart Show, Hill Street Blues, St. Elsewhere, Newhart,* and *Remington Steele.*

Originally, the character of Mary was a divorcée, but there was concern that the audience would think she was divorced from Dick Van Dyke. In the early 1970s, divorce wasn't taken lightly, by either the couple or the audience. The theme song, "Love Is All Around," which played during the opening credits, ended with Mary tossing her hat in the air—a metaphor for emancipation, self-actualization, and the optimism of a bright future.

Mary Richards was television's first feminist icon and an enduring character. The respect that Mary Tyler Moore got for her talent and demeanor was well deserved. She was extremely professional and gracious. She set the tone and was the heart of the show. Mary became one of television's most beloved women on camera and one of the most important television producers off camera, along with Lucille Ball. Lucy and Desi Arnaz founded Desilu Productions, which was responsible for not only *I Love Lucy* but also *Star Trek* and *Mission: Impossible*. After their divorce, Lucy took over the studio. She was a star in front of the camera but didn't have the management experience. "I had a big talk with myself," she once told her close friend Carol Burnett. "And I knew that I could do it, because I learned a lot from Desi. I went in and became tough, you know. A guy can be tough, but the woman being tough was a different thing then. That's when they put the 's' on the end of my last name."

My first and greatest mentor on television was Jay Sandrich, a gifted director. Jay directed 119 out of the 168 episodes of *TMTMS*. He started his career as an assistant director on *I Love Lucy* and specialized in sitcoms, directing more than ninety different shows, including *Get Smart* and *The Odd Couple*. I followed in his footsteps.

There were weak and bad directors out there, people who succumbed to pressure and/or didn't know what a scene or a show needed. Jay was the opposite. He said, "The first ingredient in becoming a director is trying to find good writers to work with good actors who know how to perform the material. Your job is then to create an atmosphere in which the actors can do their best work.

The director is one step closer to the performers and therefore more able to shape the script to the actors' needs and to come up with small bits of stage business." I watched Jay battle tooth and nail with Jim Brooks over what they both wanted for the show. It was often a loud yet healthy and constructive exchange. It emboldened me because I learned about how a passionate exchange could get you to a great episode. Writers want you to do the script, but sometimes what works in the writers' room doesn't work on the stage. Jay would say, "I'll do it your way, but I'm not sure it's the right way. Let me show you what we can do." That empowers the actors to feel like a larger part of the creative process.

Coming from the theater, I was schooled in how to talk to actors. Working in film gives you more technical expertise than you realize. In a film, you're mostly shooting isolated scenes out of order. I don't think you can learn how to talk to actors, but you can hone and perfect that skill, get more experience and tell better, more insightful stories. Being a psychiatrist is definitely part of the skill set. You have to learn how to manage both the performers and the audience in the best way possible. In a sitcom, there's the communal feeling of a play, where everybody is together all the time in that lifeboat.

I knew I had a funny bone. I had watched my dad work for years and would often pitch lines, some of which would make it into his shows. My father was a tailor. He taught me how to make a suit. At MTM, I had the ability and opportunity to make a suit. I also knew how to direct and encourage actors and block scenes. My steep learning curve was in understanding the technology. To cover the work I needed to do, I had to quickly learn how cameras operated. I paid careful attention when the cameras came out and asked the camera coordinator a lot of questions. I also went into the editing room and asked what the team needed to capture on camera to put together a final cut of an episode.

Jay patiently answered every question I asked. He taught me that if you have a group of people sitting at a table, you want to match your shots. You don't always need a close-up, but make sure there's a master shot that always carries the person who's talking. Mary and the rest of the cast were also open to my questions. But even with a good friend and lots of mentors, there are only so many questions you can ask. If you want to be a leader, you first learn from others and eventually jump into the lion's den and figure it out for yourself. I learned best by doing.

I watched *TMTMS* for three months before I directed anything. I especially remember seeing the episode where Mary goes to jail for not revealing a source and shares a cell with two prostitutes. One turns to Mary and says, "What'd they get you for, impersonating a Barbie doll?" I also saw the episode where Lou dates a woman who tries to shake things up by getting him to wear a turtleneck. "I feel like a turtle," he says. Lou Grant was a very well-defined character.

Mary's gift was that she was both beautiful and funny. In her first regular television role, she played Sam, the sexy-voiced telephone operator on *Richard Diamond, Private Detective,* with a pre-*Fugitive* David Janssen. They never showed her in her entirety. You would see glimpses of her lips and her beautiful legs. The producers created a sexy mystery character that was unbilled but very popular.

Mary was not a jokesmith, but her reactions were amazing, and people wanted to be her. You don't find that combination very often. She was an amazing center, a great reactor, and had an ensemble around her that was really funny. She was extremely approachable, sympathetic, and funny. She listened to and validated the wacky people around her. Mary could go from one extreme to another, and where Lucille Ball's comedy was broader, Mary's was understated and elegant. She was skilled at both comedy and drama. As with Lucille Ball, people felt comfortable around her. Like *I Love Lucy,* the show could easily have been named *Everyone Loves Mary.*

Most sitcoms have a center—a character that the audience is going to like, trust, respect, and enjoy, despite any flaws or neuroses. It helps if they're good-looking or otherwise compelling. It's the rational center of the show. Centers are all sympathetic characters—

not just by nature but often by a profession that, at their best, requires them to be good at listening and intuitively and inherently generous. Mary Richards is a news producer; Bob Hartley, a psychologist; Alex Reiger, a cabdriver; Sam Malone, a bartender; Frasier Crane, a psychiatrist; Harry Stone, a night-court judge; John Lacey, a teacher; Will Truman, a lawyer; Mike Biggs, a cop.

Amid a group of eccentric characters, the center is the least-crazy person in the room. Physically, the center is always in the middle of the set, so they can look and react both ways. It's much easier to shoot. It's not as funny as looking left and then looking further left. If one person is sitting hard left, the definition isn't as accentuated. The more accentuated the take, the better and funnier it is.

For a center, trusting a character is a significant part of believing in them and is crucial to a sitcom's development and evolution. Alex Reiger was flawed and vulnerable but a very decent person. You want a friend like Alex. You need to touch on that in a show, on the character who's got the eyes that become the windows into the soul of the show. Alex, like Will Truman, is a character of amazing integrity. Sam Malone could talk to a Martian, and if Sam believes he's real, so will the audience.

Your center can also be subtly benevolent or sympathetic: *Two and a Half Men*'s Charlie Harper is a perpetually drunk womanizer, but, with little hesitation, he opens his beach home to his newly divorced brother and nephew. On *The Big Bang Theory,* Leonard Hofstadter is a socially awkward scientist who has trouble communicating feelings, but he protects his roommate and best friend, the even more socially awkward and brilliant Sheldon Cooper. Some shows have no center at all. In *3rd Rock from the Sun,* all the characters are eccentric and play off one another.

In the beginning, the characters must be appealing and compelling. Networks want characters to be appealing all the time. But that's ultimately terrible for storytelling, because there's no journey. There's no redemption if there's no sin. There has to be some dimension. The challenge is in figuring out how to grow and nurture characters carefully so that the audience will continue to accept them.

I got to direct my first episode of *TMTMS* the middle of the fifth season. The plot of "Neighbors" has Lou tired of living alone in his big house with things constantly breaking down. Mary suggests that he downsize. Phyllis's daughter, Bess (Lisa Gerritsen), innocently says that Rhoda's apartment is still vacant, and to Mary's dismay, Lou moves in. Mary is concerned about living so close to her boss and friend. I read the original script nine times, and it got worse each time. I wasn't the only one who noticed.

In sitcoms, the first time a script is read aloud in a group is called a "table read." The cast, director, and writers sit around multiple tables combined into a huge square. The cast speak their parts, trying to get familiar with the new script. The director guides the cast, with the writers and everyone else trying to figure out how to stage it, produce it, and how to fix anything that is not working.

The next table read of "Neighbors" was as disappointing as I thought it would be, as were the subsequent rehearsals, which we had to re-rehearse after revised and improved script pages came in. I had neither the experience nor the gravitas and clout that I would develop later. And at that point, even a good idea would still have been one coming from the "new guy."

In any working environment, you have to prove yourself and earn trust and respect. That's especially true with a talented group that has been together for a while, but it didn't stop me from trying. From the moment I start reading a script, I think about how I can add to it, make it funnier. This time I'd exhausted all I had in my creative bag of tricks, much of it taken from my theater experience: staging and creating pieces of business to try to make things funnier; comic bits; Stanislavski method. I even invoked Anton Chekhov. In the last scene, as Lou is packed up and ready to leave the apartment, I directed them to sit on Lou's suitcases and pretend they were leaving the cherry orchard to go to Moscow.

LOU

I'm used to it here.

MARY

You were only here for two weeks.

LOU

Yeah, but it seemed like three or four.

I could have brought a pony into the room, and it probably wouldn't have helped. I turned to Arthur Price, one of Grant's partners, and said, "In a sea of Danishes, I get a bagel." In those days we rehearsed right after reading, even though the script was being rewritten. It was very frustrating. Mary was yelling, "Why are we doing this?" I was getting very nervous.

John Chulay, the assistant director, was a whiz with cameras. Often, when *TMTMS* and other shows had new directors who weren't quite accustomed to cameras, John would help them, and he asked if I wanted help with my cameras. I thanked him but said that I had to do it myself. Grant asked me if I would still share the directing credit with John, and I answered yes immediately. I said, "Look, that's fine. But I'm getting my shot."

In preparation for a Friday shoot, I worked all of Wednesday night on "marking." I went through the script, line by line, putting letters A, B, or C next to the dialogue. The letters identified which of the three cameras would cover what the actors were saying during the shoot. When I got to the set, I made further revisions to what I thought might not work. I also improvised a bit.

When cameras came on Thursday, I was petrified—not only because the script wasn't that great but because I was convinced the only reason I was hired was that I was "Abe Burrows's kid, so we're giving him a shot." Not because I was talented, worked hard, and showed promise.

At the time, there were only three cameras and very few pickups. Without the all-important fourth camera to capture the nuances and with limited pickups, I came to a moment in a scene where Mary was gesturing wildly with her arms. I had the close-up camera on her, and I asked if she could not be so animated, if she could change a gesture. She said, "No. Don't crowd me. Don't make me change my emotions."

I had to figure out a way to cover the gesture. I took the master shot and excluded Ed Asner, so it was a full shot of Mary. When the line was finished, I included Ed in the following master. By reconfiguring, I had a close and a wide shot to see all the hand gestures. Those are the kinds of decisions that the audience should never think about or realize and only do when something is very wrong. That is the television director's technical craft. It sounds and is complicated at first, but you work backward from what the audience has to see and what you want them to see, and then you figure it out.

I started at nine A.M. and finished at five-thirty P.M. on Thursday. I was exhausted, but I knew we had made progress and that the episode would work. I came back the next day, freshly showered, in a pressed suit and tie (I didn't wear jeans to a shoot day until decades later, on *Will & Grace*). We had a final run-through. Everyone wished me luck. I don't remember when I started to sweat through my fancy duds, but it was early in the day. I was both nervous and excited. I knew that this moment could make or break me as a television director.

Mary had a trailer on the stage. Just before we shot the episode, Mary came over to me and said, "We feel our investment in you has worked out." That was both Mary's and Grant's blessing. I had impressed Mary, and she was the person I needed to impress. When she said that to me, I was through the roof. If I had a hat, I would have thrown it up in the air the way Mary did during the opening credits of every episode. In my head, I was throwing up a bunch of hats! Afterward, I thanked her and walked away as quietly and respectfully as I could. I was and still am a very emotional person. I cry when I'm sad and I cry even more when I'm happy. As soon as I was out of anyone's field of vision, I teared up.

I got through it. It turned out to be a good episode. During filming, something happened that I will also never forget: There was a scene where Ted enters the office and says his line and Murray responds. Murray screwed up his line. I said, "Okay, let's take it from Murray's line." Suddenly there was a voice from the loudspeaker on the ceiling: "No, take it from Ted's entrance." My first thought was that God was helping me. I then looked up into the control booth and saw Jay Sandrich. I didn't know he was going to be there, because he didn't want me to know he was coming. He was looking out for me and, in that instance, protecting me. He knew that I couldn't edit/cut the show effectively the way I was directing it. As a director, you try to back up to the last usable line. As an experienced director, Jay knew exactly where that was.

When Lou tells Mary, "I'll take it," Mary does her best to discourage him, including calling out how small the apartment is and that he has seven rooms full of furniture. Lou tells her that he will get rid of most of it and put the rest on wheels and roll them out as needed. When he asks Mary if she has wheels on her bed, she replies, "I don't need wheels on my bed, Mr. Grant. I never go anywhere in my bed."

I thought it would have been better if when he said, "I'll take it," he walked out and Mary ran after him to bring him back in. But I was just starting out, so I acquiesced to the writers. Also, while rewatching the episode recently, I realized that when Lou comes in to see the apartment, I didn't shoot as wide as I should have, even though I got all the reaction shots.

Word traveled fast about how I turned the episode around, and, soon after, I started to get a lot of TV work, including two episodes of *The Bob Newhart Show* and episodes of *Rhoda, The Bob Crane Show,* and *Phyllis.*

I was able to turn a B- script into a B+. Another first-time director was brought on to do an episode of *TMTMS*, and it won an Emmy. Despite that, he was never asked back. When I talk to aspiring directors, I always use that example. In my mind, the other director was not asked back because they didn't like the quality of the work he did. He had a great script and I had a terrible one, but they liked what I did with mine and how I did it. When you get your shot, you have to be ready for it. If you're not ready, the second shot is much harder to get. You have to work hard and show skill in order to earn the right to be asked back.

Probably 80 percent of sitcom directors are akin to traffic cops in that they move the process along without ever injecting any creativity into the process. They listen to the writers and get the scenes done. You see it in the work and in the performances. I've never been that director, even before I had the power and experience that I have now, and especially after that. I was never a martinet: I never beat up any actor till I got the performance I wanted out of them. My sets have always been relaxed, cooperative, and collaborative. I compliment where I feel compliments are deserved and offer constructive criticism. It's all about trying new things, creating multiple options, and taking creative risks. "Maybe we can do it this way" should be something everyone on a creative set is not only thinking but feels comfortable sharing.

These directors do what the writers and actors tell them to do. There are five life lessons Jay Sandrich left me with: First, express yourself, say what you feel. Second, don't be intimidated. Third, do not worry about your next job; if you're good at what you do, the jobs will find you. Fourth, good sitcom directors are not traffic cops; we have stuff to say and things to do. And fifth, and most important, is the lesson that became the cornerstone of my directing philosophy for my entire career and what I have tried to teach other directors: Die with your boots on. You have to try to impress, both yourself and others. You have time when you're not subject to writers' opinions. You have time with the actors to score your points and make your mark. Add a leaf to the tree.

I directed three more episodes of *TMTMS*, and I got my Danishes:

In "Mary's Insomnia," Mary gets hooked on sleeping pills. It was a poignant look at addiction through comedy. Lou is angry over Mary's addiction.

At night in bed, Mary is tossing and turning, flipping a coin as to whether to take the next pill. She drops the pill down the neck of her pajamas and dances around until it drops out. I directed a lot of physical business. First, a worried Lou, unable to reach Mary on the phone, breaks into Mary's apartment, followed by Murray and Ted. She's in the bathtub. Mary is now iconic for bathtub scenes: In *The Dick Van Dyke Show,* Laura Petrie plays with the faucet in the tub and gets her toe stuck. In our show, Ted accidentally drops his reading glasses into the tub. As he smiles and prepares to reach down into the tub, he tells Mary, "This won't take more than an hour." Mary screams, "Don't you dare!"

In "Mary, the Writer," Mary writes a story and submits it to *Reader's Digest* for consideration.

Murray loves Mary's piece, but Lou hates it. He pulls out Raymond Chandler's short story "Red Wind" and reads from it to show Mary what great writing is. Mary gets even more upset:

LOU

Y'see, Mary, Ted's writing is lousy. Even worse than yours. But when you brought yours to me, I respected you enough to tell you the truth. Would you have rather I treated you like I treated Ted? Huh? Would you prefer that I treated you like some idiot? Shower you with empty compliments? Pump up your ego like you were an empty-headed brainless boob? Is that what you want?

MARY

God, yes!

Gavin, Ted, and Ed had never done comedy. They all played heavies on *The Untouchables* and other dramatic shows. Really bad guys. If you cast actors who you've never seen do funny and they are funny, you'll get bigger laughs. People just don't expect it. When you hire an actor, especially a dramatic actor, who doesn't look funny, their jokes are more explosive and impactful. They carry that cachet forever.

Both onstage and off, Gavin and Ted were as nice and good-natured as they seemed to be and were great to work with. The insults from Murray to Ted were at the core of the show and a consistent go-to laugh:

Ted is intrigued and considers writing himself:

TED
Maybe I should write a book.

MURRAY
Ted, you would be the first person to write a book
without ever having read one.

There was a lot of Lou Grant in Ed Asner. He was gruff and had a reputation to maintain, especially in front of the fledgling director. I played by the rules. I was respectful and I wasn't affected by his gruffness. Lou was not an angry character. It was frustration. He could walk that fine line—he looked like he could kill you. Shelley Berman was the first choice to play Lou, but Ed turned out to be the right choice. In "The Happy Homemaker Takes Lou Home," Lou and Sue Ann finally go out on a date. After dinner in Sue Ann's apartment, they sit on the couch. Sue Ann kisses Lou hard, and they are literally wrestling as he pries her off him. Lou is uncomfortable with her aggressive style. In a poignant scene, he explains to her that she should give men a chance to find out how terrific she is, that "the treasure shouldn't do the hunting." Sue Ann replies that she's been accepted by lots of men but didn't feel as good as she just did from his rejection.

Betty White was fabulous, particularly in the couch struggle. There was a scene where Sue Ann comes into Lou's office. Most of the time when a character went into Lou's office, they'd go upstage of the desk, around to the right. I had Sue Ann come downstage and go left, where you were able to see all of her. It felt more seductive. Jay told me I was the first one to do that move. He was always watching.

My early successes didn't make me any less concerned about what was going to happen next. I was trying to navigate the sitcom world with the goal of making a living and eventually getting my own show. I succeeded in my early years because of my demeanor and lack of antipathy. I worked hard, listened to everyone's suggestions, plus I offered my own ideas, based on my theatrical experiences, which often worked. I didn't have the ability to choose the scripts I got to direct or to modify them, and I had no authority over the larger creative direction of the show. I was a journeyman. The life lesson was that if you get on a show, don't try to change the pattern; instead, try to find the way to put your own "stink" on the show, think about ways to leave a creative mark that shows you were there and made the show better.

My nineteen *Phyllis* episodes began with the third one, "Up for Grabs." When Phyllis's never-seen husband, Lars, suddenly passes away, Phyllis and Bess move back to her hometown of San Francisco to start a new life. They move in with her mother and stepfather (Jane Rose and Henry Jones). She gets a job for a photography agency run by Julie (Liz Torres). Her co-worker, the dull-witted Leo, was played by Richard Schaal, a veteran sitcom actor.

In that episode, I played the Telephone Repairman—another part I didn't ask for but was pulled into by the writers. I had to remember my lines and direct Cloris at the same time. Phyllis's mom hangs Phyllis's dry cleaning on the phone line, and I hold up the line as the plastic-covered dress slides into the closet.

I was physically beaten on that show. Cloris would playfully slap me across the face as a way of emphasizing her points, something that you pretty much can't do anymore, and you probably couldn't do then either. She was not mean-spirited. She just had nine ways of doing a joke and I was ready to move on after the third version. In addition to her *TMTMS* Emmy awards, Cloris was an Oscar winner, winning Best Supporting Actress for *The Last Picture Show* in 1972. Despite her talent, *Phyllis* never really worked as a spin-off, for the same reason that, later on, *Frasier* did work. The self-absorbed, narcissistic character that worked on *TMTMS* wasn't re-aligned for a starring role, whereas *Frasier*'s creators rewrote the Frasier character to enable him to play the lead and deliver the comedy as well as the pathos. They filled the gap with a brother character, Niles, who resembled the *Cheers* version of Frasier. With Cloris, they never augmented the character and centered her the way they did for Frasier.

That said, there were fun and funny moments that showcased Cloris's chops. In "Phyllis and the Little People," Bess announces to Phyllis that she wants to marry a kid whose parents are little people (referred to as midgets, in that pre–politically correct world). I was in the room when Stan Daniels and Ed. Weinberger were rewriting the script. Cloris came in and said, "Bess wants to marry a boy whose parents are midgets." Stan pitched a line: "Has she found one yet?" I thought we were going to die of laughter.

In the final version, Phyllis tries to explain the situation to Leo:

LEO

What's with her?

JULIE

Oh. She's got a problem.

LEO

What's the matter, Phyllis?

PHYLLIS

Bess—she wants to marry a boy whose parents are midgets.

LEO

Has she found one yet?

PHYLLIS

Leo. Bess has a boyfriend. And his parents are midgets.

LEO

Well, what's the problem?

PHYLLIS

The problem is she's too young.

LEO

How old do you have to be to marry a midget?

PHYLLIS

She's not marrying a midget.

LEO

Poor kid. She wanted to so badly.

PHYLLIS

The boy is not a midget. His parents are.

LEO

If Bess wants to marry a midget, she should
hold out for the real thing.

All exaggerated and no sense of reality, but wonderful reaction shots from Cloris and Liz.

By contrast, *The Bob Newhart Show* was rooted in reality, and that was its genius. It centered on Chicago psychologist Dr. Robert Hartley, who, like Jack Benny, played it straight against every other character in the ensemble. As Jack did on radio and then television, he could turn to any character and get a laugh. There was Bob's schoolteacher wife, Emily (Suzanne Pleshette); next-door neighbor and airline navigator Howard Borden (Bill Daily); best friend and orthodontist Jerry Robinson (Peter Bonerz); receptionist Carol Kester (Marcia Wallace); and a plethora of patients, notably the neurotic Mr. Carlin (Jack Riley), Mr. Peterson (John Fiedler, who was later at the bar in *Cheers*), and Mrs. Bakerman (Florida Friebus, who played Dobie Gillis's mother). You had everything you needed for a great sitcom: the wacky neighbor, the eccentric secretary, the crazy best friend, and an assortment of crazy patients, many recurring and some one-offs. Bob Newhart was a rock-solid center. He was the ticket. He was the kind of guy you would love to sit down and talk with.

During the pilot, the show was running a little long. When producer Lorenzo Music came over to him and said, "Bob, could you stammer a little less?" Bob's now-legendary reply was "That stammer paid for my house in Beverly Hills."

During my first time as an observer in the bleachers, I definitely felt like I was being tested by Bob and his close-knit team, to make sure that I was right for the show and up to the job. I always got there early enough to see the "warm-up" comedian, who appears before the show to get the audience laughing. Desi Arnaz was the first performer to do the warm-up for his own show on *I Love Lucy*.

Bob would do his own warm-up for every show. He'd come out and take the mike. He would tell the same parrot joke—it never missed: This guy gets a parrot from the pet store. After two days, the parrot was lethargic, lying down. He wouldn't do anything. After two weeks, he found him gasping for breath at the bottom of the cage. He brings him back to the store. The store owner says, "The parrot can talk, ask him what's wrong." When he asks what's wrong, the parrot says, "Food!"

Bob eventually retired that parrot joke and put a new one in his repertoire: There's this magician on a cruise ship, and he does the same show every night in front of a different audience. But the captain has a parrot. And the parrot's seen the magician's act 100 times, and he'd be giving all of the secrets away to the audience. The magician would do a trick in front of the audience and the parrot would yell out, "How come the deck is all the ace of spades? The flowers are under the table! It's a new hat!"

The cruise ship hits a storm. It gets really bad and the ship sinks. The magician is in the ocean, hanging on to this piece of wood and the parrot is hanging on to the same piece of wood. And they don't talk for four days. Finally, the parrot turns to the magician and says, "Okay, I give up. Where's the ship?"

During the MTM years, writers David Lloyd, Jay Tarses, and Lorenzo Music also warmed up the audiences. On *Taxi*, we had writer–director Earl Pomerantz and Bob Perlow. We even had a little jazz band entertaining the crowd. The warm-up comic was a function of necessity, both to get audiences ready to laugh before the show and to keep them laughing during the show's taping. As a taping got longer, maintaining that energy level became even more important. My dad once mused about how directors were created out of such necessity. In the earliest days of Greek theater, there was a writer and an actor, Theseus and Orestes. Orestes turned to Theseus and said, "You're not in the next scene; go into the audience and tell me how I look."

Bob Newhart was an accountant and advertising copywriter who broke into comedy with a series of hit record albums right at the time when record companies realized that people would buy records of comedy, not just music. Bob, along with Shelley Berman (and George Jessel decades before), specialized in bits where he seemed to be talking to someone on the phone. The "phone pieces," one-sided conversations with an unseen character, allowed them to set themselves up for their own punch lines.

His reactions were amazing. He was one of the first stand-up comedians to transition successfully to a great actor. I have always preferred actors who are actors. I worry whether I am going to get enough depth from a comedian. Also, you're not sure if a comedian is going to fit into an ensemble. I'm directing dramas that happen to be funny. I prefer an actor who is funny. Having said that, Kevin Pollak and Ray Romano both began as stand-up comedians and have now done some of their best work in dramatic roles.

There is a big difference between drama and comedy for performers. Dramatic actors usually can't make it in comedy, unless they're born with it. If you don't have innate comedy chops and you're playing against seasoned comedy performers, you'll likely be written around or recast, as the audience will figure out your shortcomings immediately. If a dramatic actor does have those chops, it's a comedy gold mine. Whether it's Ed Asner, Gavin MacLeod, Ted Knight, Nicky Colasanto, Judd Hirsch, Danny DeVito, or Chris Lloyd, the audience is completely surprised. It's much easier for a comedy actor to do drama—because they are trained as actors.

I was amazingly lucky in the eleven *Bob Newhart* shows I got to direct: A number of them were among the most beloved episodes of the series and were some of my own favorites as well. The first of many Thanksgiving episodes that I directed over the years for different shows was "Over the River and Through the Woods," or the "Moo Goo" show, as it is affectionately referred to. In it, Bob is reluctant to accompany Emily to her parents' in Seattle. He comes home and tries to discuss it with the angry Emily:

BOB

Emily, sit down.

(Emily doesn't move.)

BOB

Good.

When Bob finally decides to join Emily in Seattle, he can't get a flight. He wins a turkey raffled off by the orphanage where Jerry grew up, so he and Jerry decide to watch college football, cook the turkey, and drink—a lot. They are joined by Howard and Mr. Carlin.

Bob Newhart plays the greatest drunk in the world. His secret is simple: "All people who play drunks fall over. I try to stay upright." In one of Bob's nightclub routines, called "The Retirement Party," he is Charlie Bedlow, who, after fifty years, is given a retirement party and a watch. When Charlie gets up to speak, he's blasted, drunk. And he explains that it's the only way he could have gotten through this lousy job. And because he's drunk, he's able to tell the truth about what he really thinks. Sometimes in his act, Bob would do his iconic driving-instructor routine, playing the calm and collected character first and then segue into becoming instantly drunk. There were certain tricks he learned, so he knew exactly how to play somebody who was drunk, because somebody who's drunk thinks he's the only one that knows he's drunk.

When Bob, Jerry, and company find out that the frozen turkey won't thaw in time for dinner, they decide to order Chinese food. The inebriated Bob struggles to pronounce words:

HOWARD
You said, "Moo goo goo goo"!

BOB
Maybe I'm ordering Chinese baby food!

CARLIN
I'll have the sweet-and-sour pork.

BOB
Make up your mind, Mr. Carlin!

Bob keeps ordering the same dishes, reminiscent of Groucho in the stateroom scene in *A Night at the Opera*. He puts the phone on the floor and tries to hang up the receiver by slamming it down on the desk.

Emily misses Bob and returns from Seattle early. The oven timer goes off, and the hungover Bob grabs his ears. When Emily asks what's in the oven, Bob replies, "The turkey." When Emily says, "Bob, there's no turkey in the oven," Bob frantically responds, "Emily, whatever you do, don't look in the dishwasher!"

The show's success was also due in large part to the late Suzanne Pleshette. She was a woman of incredible skill and comic timing, who was able to share a stage, playing a second banana, and bring humor, not just do setups for Bob. That relationship was really strong. They were a sexual couple and one of the first sitcom couples to sleep in the same bed. One recurring bit was that she never made breakfast. She was one of the first sitcom wives to disagree with her husband. When talking about her character, she said, "You could hear me quietly stick my foot up his ass." Suzie had this great combination of the foulest mouth and the sweetest character.

She cheekily (pun intended) complained about her butt: "I used to get every job I ever got walking out of the office. It was my best feature. But gravity does take its toll. I don't want you seeing it down around my ankles now." She could have easily been a leading lady. I directed her again in *Good Morning Miami*, where she played the grandmother, in *The Boys Are Back*, where she and Hal Linden starred as empty-nest parents who are frustrated when two of their three adult sons move back home, and in *Will & Grace*, where she played Karen's mother. She was always a delight.

I was excited and more than a little intimidated to work with Bob Newhart. I had all of Bob's albums. As a guest director, I had to inveigle my way in, play by their rules, stick to a strict schedule—because people on a successful show expect to get out early—and still put my own imprint on a show. Bob insisted on an efficient set. Shows were wrapped within two hours, and after that, he and his friends hit the Scotch to get drunk for real.

The Bob Newhart Show had rotating directors, including cast member Peter Bonerz and comedian Dick Martin, of *Rowan & Martin's Laugh-In* fame. Dick and Dolly Martin were very close to Bob and his wife, Ginny. Dick started his career writing on *Duffy's Tavern* and sat next to me in the bleachers to learn about the shows he was going to direct, the same way I did. Bob had no affinity for any particular director; on Bob's sets, the director's job was to keep it fun and keep it fresh. I rehearsed a scene twice. When I asked if I could rehearse it again, he said no. Because of his stand-up training, where there were no second chances, he got everything right quickly.

Bob did yell at me once, but it was in character. In "Halls of Hartley," Bob is having a terrible day. His car antenna was ripped off, his office door won't open, and the coffee machine drips coffee on his shoes. When he presses the elevator button to escape home, the maintenance man slaps an out-of-order sign on the door. Bob yells, "What do you mean, out of order? I just used that elevator!" To which the man responds, "Oh. You're the one that broke it!"

I played the maintenance man. The provoked Bob says, "Look. I want the elevator fixed and I want it fixed right now!" As I disappear into the stairwell, I say, "It can't be done," to which a further-incensed Bob says, "It can be done, it must be done, it will be done!" It was so fun to play straight man to Bob's ire.

I also directed "The Way We Weren't," which introduced Howard's older brother, the game warden. Warden Gordon Borden (William Redfield) always took everything from his brother growing up, and now he's making a play for Howard's girlfriend, Bob's sister, Ellen (Pat Finley).

In addition to the great cast, the show was produced and run by Tom Patchett and Jay Tarses, who also wrote a number of episodes. The moment there was a problem with a script, they identified and quickly fixed it. On a strong sitcom, there are rarely bad scripts. Both Bob and Suzanne would ask me questions during shoots, and I'd answer them. I impressed them because I was right more than I was wrong. I learned another valuable lesson: Take a stand. I could say, "Bob, do this; I think it's going to be funny." If an actor ever asks you which version of a take will be funnier, don't say, "I don't care." Pick one. Pick one even if you don't know. If you're wrong, say, "Jesus! I was wrong. Let's try the other one." The minute you equivocate or are perceived as someone who doesn't know what they're doing, no actor will walk the comedic plank or take any risks for you.

In the *Rhoda* spin-off of *TMTMS*, Valerie Harper's character moves back to Manhattan for a new job. She falls in love and gets married. In 1974, eight episodes into the first season, fifty-two million people tuned in to watch Rhoda's wedding, in an expanded hour-long episode. It was the highest-rated television episode until *Roots* aired and is the second-highest-rated sitcom episode, after the birth of Little Ricky on *I Love Lucy* in 1953. During the episode, Phyllis asks for the opportunity to drive Rhoda from Manhattan to the Bronx, where the ceremony is being held. Phyllis forgets, and Rhoda is forced to take the subway. Valerie running through the streets of Manhattan and the Bronx in her wedding dress and veil is one of the most memorable moments in sitcom history. Right after the episode aired, Howard Cosell welcomed his *Monday Night Football* audience back to the Atlanta–Pittsburgh game, where he quipped that he had not been invited to the wedding.

Valerie was a pleasure to work with, and she captured the pathos as well as the comedy. Like Paul Sand, she had come from Second City and Viola Spolin's training. She was one of the few actors I ever worked with who needed a reason to cross the room in a scene. She would always ask why. And I would answer her, as I was still a novice director. When we worked together later, on the pilot of *Valerie,* with Jason Bateman, I'd smile politely when I gave her the direction to walk across the room: "Because I'm the director."

Consistent with the Frasier/Niles formula, as Rhoda moved from support to center, the very talented Julie Kavner was cast as sister Brenda. Julie, who also later played Tony Danza's sister on *Taxi,* has had a great career since, as the voice of Marge on *The Simpsons.*

Nancy Walker already had a successful career in movie musi-
cals, including being the comic relief to Mickey Rooney and Judy
Garland, before her second successful career, in television comedy
years later. Nancy was a hit from the moment she guest-starred as
Rhoda's mother on *TMTMS*. I got to direct Nancy on *Rhoda*. She is
one of the people I have worked with over the years that I refer to
as a "heat-seeking missile for a joke." Whatever was in the script,
she could make it significantly funnier, whether it was a punch line
or setting someone up for one:

IDA

I have enjoyed being your mother.

RHODA

And I have enjoyed being your burden.

In "The Job," Rhoda and Brenda visit Ida in her Bronx apartment. The sisters are chasing their mother around the living room,
with Rhoda and Brenda turning on lights while Ida turns them off,
as they comfort her on the loss of a friend. Nancy could be both
funny and poignant at the same time:

IDA

You invest forty years in a friendship and then
she up and dies on you.

While at MTM, I directed my first pilot. *Bumpers* was a comedy
about auto workers, which starred Richard Masur and Stephanie
Faracy. It was created by Dave Davis. Dave had the idea to "feather
the set," which meant that, like in the old movies, the wall was ta-
pered. So rather than reset when the camera moved from set to set,
you just followed the actors into the other room. It was an interesting artistic choice. I was honored to be chosen to direct the pilot—
and also pretty intimidated. I read the script over and over. By 1977,

I already had three years with the cameras, so I literally knew all the angles.

Bumpers was also one of Brian Dennehy's first television roles. In the pilot, Richard goes to a bar. Brian takes two sips of beer and Richard asks him what time it is. In the age-old routine, Brian would flip the glass over to check his watch and pour the beer on himself. There's a saying that there are only thirty-nine jokes in the world and that it's both the writer's and director's job to freshen the humor, to add a new spin or permutation. In our variation, Brian acknowledges the bit and says, "You want me to lift the glass and do this?" and turns the glass over on himself. I used that bit again years later on *NewsRadio*. In "Bitch Session," Bill (Phil Hartman) tries to trick Matthew (Andy Dick) into spilling the coffee he is pouring into his cup by speaking loudly over the microphone in the broadcast booth. Matthew laughs Bill's prank off and is feeling very smug. Beth (Vicki Lewis) walks by and asks him what time it is, and as he looks at his watch, he flips his mug over and spills coffee on himself.

It was during the MTM training that I figured out what I was saying and what I was giving the actors. I don't know what I would be doing if I hadn't ended up there. I'd have probably continued to be a stage manager and theater director, perhaps directed Off Broadway plays, and likely been unsuccessful. It's a very hard road in that world: If you direct a Broadway play, you don't have the same ability to nurture and cement the characters that you do with a sitcom. My dad said, "If you have a hit on Broadway, it doesn't matter when you open. If you have a flop, it also doesn't matter when you open." A play is static. You're stuck with the script. If it's not a good play, there's not much you can do. And a bad *New York Times* review will kill you.

In a sitcom, there is a lot you can do to embellish the characters over the course of the first thirteen weeks, which is usually the amount of time the network gives a new show. You can try to finesse certain things. Introduce a new character and start to write to that person. It's still hard to capture the audience if people have turned you off after one or two shows, but it's not impossible.

I was now in regular demand as a sitcom director. I directed four episodes of *The Tony Randall Show.* Fresh off the success of his iconic performance as Felix Unger on *The Odd Couple,* he was cast as a Philadelphia judge. Tony was sweet, nice, and respectful. In the first scene he would deliberately forget a line, so he could say, "You can forget a line, but you can't say shit." The audience would go crazy with laughter.

There were two primary "schools" in the 1970s and '80s, where actors and writers learned to create sitcoms and then moved on and created other shows: the MTM school, which begat *Taxi, Frasier, Cheers, Wings,* and *Family Ties,* and the Garry Marshall school, which begat *The Odd Couple, Happy Days, Laverne & Shirley,* and *Mork & Mindy.* To be MTM-pedigreed in those years was a seal of approval. You still had to prove yourself, but it helped you get in the door. There was also a shorthand between people who worked together on similar projects.

I became good at creating fertile arenas for both actors and writers to work and play together to create comedy. I encouraged suggestions and quickly came up with ideas and bits. I also realized early on that I could devise a safe and nurturing environment where actors became comfortable trying different ways of doing the same thing, facilitating their best performance and enabling their creativity.

Garry Marshall's *Laverne & Shirley* was a very successful spin-off of his sitcom *Happy Days.* Penny Marshall and Cindy Williams played best friends who worked at a beer factory in 1950s Milwaukee. Comedian Phil Foster played Laverne's father. Michael McKean and David L. Lander played the wacky neighbors and friends, Lenny and Squiggy, and Betty Garrett was their landlady.

Mike and David, whom I loved, based their characters on two they had already developed as part of a Los Angeles comedy troupe called the Credibility Gap; Lenny and Anthony were modeled on people they knew from New York. ("We woulda been here on time, but we was late.")

They were hired as junior writers and helped integrate their characters into the cast. Their entrances were always timed to an incongruous moment where someone would say something like "Someday your prince will come," and the front door would swing open and, in their nasal voices, the two would say, "Hello!" They have become part of the sitcom vernacular. When a line is followed by someone coming through the front door and saying hello, it's referred to as a "Lenny and Squiggy" move.

The gift of *Laverne & Shirley* was Penny and Cindy, specifically their rapport and their ability to do schtick. It was a sillier, more juvenile show. The two women were not the most advanced when it came to relationships with men. It was a lower-class comedy than *Taxi*. Penny and Debra Messing are the two greatest physical comedians I have ever worked with.

I directed eight episodes, starting in the first season. There was tension on the set from the get-go. Co-star Penny Marshall was the sister of creator and producer Garry. Their father, Anthony, and sister, Ronny Hallin, were also producers. Cindy felt that the show was too Marshall-heavy and counted how many lines she was assigned versus Penny. The two started having problems with each other, which went public. I was on the set when the shit hit the fan and the entire writing staff, whom I loved, was fired—Mark Rothman, Lowell Ganz, and Marc "Babaloo" Mandel.

Garry Marshall was a great comedian, musician, actor, writer, and producer and then became a great film director. He played a drummer in the background of an episode I directed. He was always evenhanded and funny and never got upset. One of his greatest gifts was generating the sentimental moments, especially in his movies, including *Pretty Woman* and *Overboard,* the "aww" moments. More recently, we shared season tickets next to each other at the Hollywood Bowl. We were big huggers, especially with each other.

Garry wanted me to take over *Laverne & Shirley*. He took me to Nickodell's restaurant on Melrose (it was literally built into the side of RKO Studios, which became Desilu, then Paramount). It was there that Garry tried to convince me to take over the show as director. I politely declined. There was too much turmoil. I wasn't interested in all the drama; I was interested in the work. It was now 1976, and I already had a reputation as a sought-after sitcom director. I had some cachet going into the show, so I felt okay turning Garry down without hurting my career.

Penny Marshall was married to Rob Reiner, and they became a power couple in the 1970s, even making the cover of *People* magazine in 1976. In 1978, I directed them in a TV movie called *More Than Friends*, a sweet love story set in the Bronx, which Rob co-wrote with Phil Mishkin. Billy Crystal's brother Richard was also in it. It was the only time I was credited as Jim Burrows.

After *All in the Family*, Rob Reiner, who became a brilliant film director and friend, created and starred in a sitcom called *Free Country*, about immigrant Jews on New York's Lower East Side in the 1900s. Rob's wife was played by Judy Kahan. As a new immigrant, she was afraid to leave her tenement apartment. She was alone and trying to get the courage to go out. She couldn't open the door. I told her to grab the high-backed chair with determination to go out the door. She grabbed the chair, opened the door, and took the chair with her, which got a big laugh.

Directing the two episodes of *Free Country* wound up catapulting my career to the next level. In those years, the sitcom community was much smaller—there were less than thirty shows on television. Everyone in that world knew one another. Rob and Penny built a big house in the Valley and had amazing parties, which everyone in that microcosm went to. When Rob got a call from Jim Brooks asking, "Where'd you get that chair moment?" Rob said, "It came from Jimmy." And that's how I got to direct *Taxi*.

Taxi

ELAINE
I'm only going to be working here part-time. I'm not really a taxi driver.

ALEX
Oh yeah, I know. We're all part-time here. You see that guy over there? Now, he's
an actor. The guy on the phone, he's a prizefighter. This lady over here, she's a
beautician. The man behind her, he's a writer. Me? I'm a cabdriver.
I'm the only cabdriver in this place.

Being a New York City cabdriver is one of the toughest jobs in
the world. Turns out, so is directing a sitcom about New York City
cabdrivers. When I think about working on *Taxi,* the word that immediately comes to mind is "difficult." Having said that, I would not
have changed any of it. When you get an opportunity to work with
the best writers and the best actors, or the best and most talented
people in any profession you're in, don't think about how hard it's
going to be. It will be amazingly difficult. Just do it. MTM was sitcom college for me. *Taxi* was graduate school. I was still learning my
lessons and earning my stripes.

James L. Brooks, Ed. Weinberger, Stan Daniels, and Dave Davis
formed a production entity and named it the John Charles Walters

Company. Based on their success on the MTM shows, Paramount gave them a three-show deal, which wound up being *Taxi, The Associates,* and *Best of the West,* all of which I was involved in.

Jim Brooks was one of the greatest, if not *the* greatest, sitcom writers in history. He started out at CBS, writing for *My Three Sons* and *The Andy Griffith Show.* He then spent two years working at CBS News, which may initially seem incongruous but was actually great training for the new type of realistic comedy that was to come. He and Allan Burns co-created *Room 222,* a groundbreaking series about a high school with a black teacher as the main character. At MTM, they were part of the rise of the writer-producer auteur, the idea that writers were as important on a sitcom as the performers. Jim brought that ideology with him to *Taxi.*

He later went on to write and direct *Terms of Endearment, Broadcast News,* and *Spanglish,* and co-create *The Simpsons.* During the early days of *The Simpsons,* when scripts were still transmitted by messenger as opposed to email, a script was delivered to his house. The messenger knocked on Jim's door. Jim opened it and the messenger handed him the envelope. As Jim signed the receipt, the messenger looked into the house. Jim saw him looking in and said, "Nobody's happy here."

Jim Brooks could pitch a scene off the top of his head. It was amazing to watch. His lines are so unexpected. They're not jokes as such. He doesn't do bada-bums, but he writes interesting characters who say interesting things. He's one of the funniest guys I've ever seen pitch on his feet. When the character Latka on *Taxi* introduces the liquor Brefnish, from his country, he explains to Alex how strong it is. Alex takes a swig and falls backward off his chair. Jim Brooks then pitched the line of dialogue for Reverend Jim (Christopher Lloyd): "The line forms behind me."

Jim is extremely meticulous. He can do movies because he has a sense of what Shirley MacLaine's home should look like in *Terms of Endearment,* what books would be in her bedroom, what shape and color the Afghan rug would be. I don't see the world that way. I've always hired someone to do that. Generally, that kind of detail doesn't belong onstage or in a sitcom, but in a movie you can see all the details, the accoutrements of what's on the set. In a sitcom, the sets are looser, less detailed, because you focus on the character primarily and often exclusively through dialogue and interaction. Over multiple episodes, backdrops become a constant and a source of familiarity and comfort rather than something that drives the narrative.

Ed. Weinberger (short for Edwin, and yes, the Ed. has a period after it, which is also very tough on spell-check) has written for Bob Hope, Dean Martin, Johnny Carson, and Dick Gregory, and in addition to the MTM shows, he also co-created *The Cosby Show.* Ed. led a unique life. A lot of episodes came from things that happened to him. He hit on the answering-service lady, who was the basis for Alex's "Blind Date" on *Taxi.* The *Frasier* episode "Miracle on Third or Fourth Street," where Frasier goes to the diner, forgets his wallet, and the diner patrons think he's broke and chip in to pay his tab, was based on Ed.'s actual experience. He then drove away in his fancy Aston Martin.

Writers came in at the beginning of every season and shared personal stories that formed a basis for scripts and the arc of the season. Garry Marshall said that when he worked on *The Dick Van Dyke Show,* Carl Reiner would go around the room and make all the writers recall the most embarrassing moments in their lives. A number of those stories wound up in scripts.

In addition to being a great writer, Stan Daniels was a great musician and pianist. Dave Davis was one of the first people I met when I came out to California in 1965 for *O. K. Crackerby!* Dave was an associate producer. When I came out again in 1974, he was the first person to talk to me. He and Lorenzo Music were writing *The Bob Newhart Show.* He initially edited all the *Taxi* episodes, but he left the show and retired early. Dave still lives on Shelter Island with longtime partner Julie Kavner.

When the creators of *Taxi* asked me prior to launching the show if I wanted to be the resident director, I said yes even before they could finish the question. *I Love Lucy* had pioneered the resident-director concept, as it pioneered so many novel concepts that became staples of subsequent shows for the decades that followed. I wound up directing seventy-five of the one hundred fourteen *Taxi* episodes, beginning with the first show.

While not an official title, the "resident" director is the person who helps develop the tone of the show, while protecting the writers' vision and helping the actors develop their characters. Resident directors advance and help shape the show. It makes the work easier. Rotating directors who know the ropes and where the bodies are buried are also very important, unless you have writers who do not want their work criticized and, in some instances, made better.

One of my favorite professional terms is "shorthand," where everyone involved develops such a close relationship that they often know what others are thinking and are still considerate and sensitive enough to listen to what everyone is saying. Like on Groucho's *You Bet Your Life,* if you say the secret word, the duck comes down and you win a hundred dollars. A resident director is optimal for a show, to provide continuity and represent the producers to the cast and the cast to the producers in constructive, nonabrasive ways. It was my job on *Taxi,* as well as all the other shows I've worked on, to make the actors "director-proof": able to function on their own and come up with their individual identities. My general practice is to help develop the characters and translate them from the page to the stage. I see the complete picture when I see it "on its feet." It takes on a different life during rehearsal. I get an indication of not only how the writing is working but how the actors work with the material and whether the ensemble is working together. Then I can find pieces of business, physical bits, and different ways of doing things. Marilu Henner (whom I nicknamed "Lu") called them my "goodies, my bag of tricks," which essentially was and still is "Try it this way, do this," and getting them comfortable experimenting with their own characters.

On successful shows, actors become incredibly proprietary

about their character—they want to invest their emotion in the character. They suspend who they are for the power in front of an audience to portray a character—they're living and breathing the character, so they know what's normal. If they don't think something is right, they'll tell the writer, and the writer will respect that. You have to value what the actor says, because they're immersed in the role. It's incredibly appealing and fulfilling. If you can infuse an actor and a cast with that sense of confidence and freedom, that extra energy is communicated directly to the audience. I've been lucky enough to work extensively with at least six ensemble casts that are among the greatest in television history. When everyone knows their character, you never have to "write away" from anybody to make something work. If a joke doesn't land, you know that it's not the actor's fault, it's the joke's fault, and it needs to be changed.

The only time a good actor goes crazy on a set is when there's a dramatic problem with a scene or story and they don't know how or have the creative ammunition to fix it. On a well-written, well-directed show, an actor won't get crazy, because the good writing will only get better each time. As a director, you also learn how to put jokes into the mix. The formula I've always used to direct and train actors is to first do a scene as written and then say, "We have a joke or piece of business we want you to look at." Getting actors to know their characters cold is great for a show, but it also can be very tough on any new director. A good cast will appreciate the strength of the ensemble and welcome anyone new with skills and ideas. I directed the first sixty episodes of *Taxi,* missing only one to do *The Associates* pilot. After three solid years, I was able to embolden the cast.

Taxi was based on a 1975 *New York* magazine article that Jerry Belson, Garry Marshall's brilliant former writing and producing partner, brought to Jim Brooks's attention. It was called "Night-Shifting for the Hip Fleet," by Mark Jacobson, who himself moonlit as a cabbie. During those economically lean years, people became cabdrivers to make ends meet, and those on the eclectic night shift at the red-brick Dover Taxi Garage on Hudson Street in Greenwich

Village ranged from a former window dresser to chess-playing actors between gigs to someone booking ski tours. According to the article, "A college education is not required to drive for Dover—all you have to do is pass a test on which the hardest question is 'Where is Yankee Stadium?'—but almost everyone on the night line has at least a B.A."

The show was set at the fictional Sunshine Cab Company and was about a disparate group of drivers who became good friends. With two exceptions, none of them wanted to be where they were. They were driving cabs to support themselves while chasing other careers/dreams: Bobby Wheeler (Jeff Conaway) wanted to be an actor; Tony Banta (Tony Danza) was an unsuccessful boxer; Elaine Nardo (Marilu Henner) wanted to own her own art gallery. Dispatcher Louie De Palma (Danny DeVito) and driver Alex Reiger (Judd Hirsch) were the only ones who actually wanted to work there—Louie because the garage was his domain, the only place in his life he'd have any power, and Alex because he was happy being a cabdriver. His complacency set him apart from the other characters. He did well for his means, lived comfortably, and found joy in that. He thought of himself as someone who was there to help people through being a cabdriver, and that became a dynamic we could work with. For some people it was a way station; for him, "I'm the only cabdriver in this place." If he was as consistently frustrated as the other characters, he could not have been as benevolent.

I was there for a lot of the auditions. Judd Hirsch was on Broadway in Neil Simon's *Chapter Two* and was first choice for Alex. Judd had become a successful theater actor and was hesitant to go back to television, where he'd had limited success. He initially turned down the role but then agreed to do it. Judd was one of the greatest sitcom centers; his eyes and persona were the windows through which the audience saw and processed everything. Alex is the warden, sitting with all the lunatics in the garage. He is sympathetic to their problems and issues and tries to help them, which gives the characters credibility. He especially has to deal with the lunacy of

Louie. I told Stan Daniels, "We need to find a scene between Louie and Alex about Louie's inability to make friends."

In "Louie's Mother," after his mother moves out of the apartment they shared to a nursing home, Louie throws a party. Alex is the only one from the garage whom he invites. Louie gets three guys who were with him on a New York street, watching a guy have a heart attack, to show up. When the guys get up to leave, Louie says, "Where are you going?" and they tell him, "We got another party." Alex gets Louie to open up about how lonely he is. When Louie explains that it was his mother's idea to move out, Alex yells at Louie to drop everything and get her to move back in with him. "If I come home, will you be nice to me?" his mother asks. "For a while," Louie replies, as he takes her home.

Judd is a chameleon and a great reactor. He can thrive in any creative environment. We developed a unique shorthand. Judd can explain a problem in a way that you might not completely understand but you know you have to fix. I could say to Judd, "When you hear the line, give me a forty-two." Our shorthand was based on the idea that there are one hundred types of expressions. It worked because Judd knew what to do. He just needed to be guided and needed to trust his colleagues.

Another type of complex ensemble character is the villain. The challenge is to make the villain unlikable but sympathetic enough that audiences will still laugh with and at the character. On *Taxi*, the original incarnation of the character Louie De Palma, the angry cab dispatcher, was someone who would never have left the dispatcher's cage, just announcing his lines, barking orders to the cabbies. Danny DeVito made the part a lot larger. When Danny came in to read for the network, he walked in, threw the script on the table, and said, "Who wrote this shit?" We knew we had found our Louie.

It was crucial that the audience find Louie repulsive and hysterically funny at the same time. They could be horrified that he'd walk out of a restaurant and casually pocket a waiter's tip and simultaneously laugh about it. The Louie character is fascinating. He's walking pathos. Short and irritable, he has an enormous chip on his shoulder because that's what life has dealt him. But he wields power. He has his small domain: in the dispatcher's cage and the garage. He enjoys controlling people. Initially, we were going to have Louie come out of the cage early on, but it made more sense to let people know his angry character first, so that when he finally stepped down out of the cage, his lack of height had a big impact.

On *Taxi,* the core relationship was between Alex and Louie. It was not a romantic relationship—not even a friendship, per se. They were two people who genuinely cared about each other, but not always in an obvious way. Louie is a despicable human being, and Alex is a generous human being. The reason Alex communicates with Louie is that he's sympathetic to his plight. You feel sad for him because of his stature, appearance, and demeanor. He had to be reprehensible but with characteristics that made his actions forgivable, as well as infrequent moments of redemption. There were attempts to make Louie a little more human, a little sweeter, but never too nice. It was a constant struggle between making him redeemable and not going too far. We had the same challenge with Carla (Rhea Perlman) on *Cheers.* Louie did have romances and noble moments, and those episodes were very successful because they were infrequent and showed a lot of character growth. You don't necessarily need that with your center characters, because emotionally they are fully formed. They are the caretakers for the other characters.

(Little-known fact: The same way Louie took bribes from the cabbies for a good cab, Danny developed a little cottage industry taking bribes from the company, including me, to announce the names of family and friends when he was dispatching cabs. He had a good side hustle going.)

The part of Bobby was originally offered to Robin Williams, who was still busy with *Mork & Mindy.* Had he taken it, I could have directed Robin, Andy Kaufman, and Chris Lloyd, all on the same stage. If I had, I'm sure I would have liked my stay in the Directors' Home. They also wanted Mandy Patinkin, whom Jim Brooks knew but who didn't want to get tied to a series at the time. I've always adored his beautiful lyric tenor voice.

Jeff Conaway had played Danny Zuko, the lead in *Grease,* on Broadway and later played Kenickie in the film version, opposite John Travolta's Danny. There was concern at the beginning that he wasn't as capable as the rest of the ensemble. During the first show, Jim and Ed. kept rehearsing a scene with him. They didn't think he had the chops that everyone else had. Their concerns were mollified during the fourth episode, "Bobby's Acting Career." Bobby gives himself an artificial deadline: If the phone doesn't ring by midnight with an offer for an acting part, he'll quit acting completely. Alex tries to talk some sense into him:

BOBBY
Don't worry, Alex. I just explained to you why I'm going to
get a call before midnight.

ALEX
Bobby, we gotta be rational here.

BOBBY
The only way that phone's not gonna ring before midnight is
if I'm not good enough. And you're not gonna tell me that.

ALEX
Maybe you're not that good. Yet. Doesn't mean that with a little
more experience you couldn't get there.

BOBBY
All right, just stop it, all right. Now you've said what you have to
say. Now let me talk, all right? When I was six years old, Alex, my
father died. And I never had any older brothers. Had a couple of

older sisters. Till I met you, I don't think there was ever a man in my life that I felt was on my side. I mean, I had lots of friends and everything, but I always felt that there was something special between you and me. You knew that, Alex. You knew how, how I looked up to you, and respected you, and counted on you. . . . What you just said just now, it would have been okay coming from a friend. Not from somebody I felt about, the way I feel about you.

I don't know how to tell you, but you just hurt me now, Alex.

Except to say that it feels like my father just died again . . . I needed you and you let me down. There's only one thing that I want from you right now, Alex. That's for you to get outta here.

I don't want to see you again. I don't want to talk to you.

I don't want to know you, man.

As the dejected Alex slowly walks out, Bobby grabs him around the shoulder and says, "Still say I'm not such a good actor?" Alex smiles, realizing how good an actor Bobby really is and then they both dissolve in laughter. It was a poignant scene to direct.

Marilu Henner—Elaine—was a gifted singer and dancer. I saw her on Broadway in *Over Here!* She was also in *Grease* and *Pal Joey*. A born vegan and earth mother, she was rock-solid and always one of my favorite people.

Lu was dating John Travolta when we started the show. She went to Europe with him for the international premiere of *Grease*. While she was gone, *Taxi* premiered, and she too became a household name. Upon her return to the United States a couple of weeks later, people were yelling "Elaine" at her in the street.

Tony Danza was a Golden Gloves champion and had done a movie for ABC. As he would say, just a short time earlier he was "a pug (slang for boxer) selling swag out of the back of his car." He was a natural performer and was basically playing himself on the show. We made him feel as welcome as we could. Tony brought a lot of mischief to the group. He stole Fritz the security guard's golf cart, as well as Fonzie's motorcycle from the *Happy Days* set. He'd walk onto the set, grab a fire extinguisher, and pick up a table. At which point I'd turn to the rest of the actors and say, "Is Tony here yet?"

The first episode was great but incredibly overwritten. The cabbies find out that the garage pay phone is broken and they can make long-distance calls for free (decades before cellphones and unlimited-calling plans), so they all make their fantasy phone calls. Alex finds out that the daughter he hasn't seen since she was a baby, fifteen years earlier, is changing planes in Miami to go to private school in Portugal. He and his buddies commandeer a cab and drive from New York to Florida. I liked the relationship in the first show between Alex and his daughter. He's this poor guy who's trying to reconnect with his daughter and deal with some bad decisions he made earlier in his life. I was excited about working with Judd Hirsch. I really didn't have a sense about the other characters yet, but I knew how good the writers were, so I believed that whatever didn't work would get better.

Also, managing seven characters without a tether is difficult. A few years later on *Cheers*, the characters would sit at the bar and be a permanent fixture. *Taxi* initially didn't have that firmament. I immediately added the table and chairs that the characters sit at in the garage to anchor my act somewhere. That also marked the beginning of my infatuation with different levels on sitcom sets. The *Taxi* set had different corners we could shoot in and steps to a level with an office. As a theater director, I relish a stage with levels and permutations that give you more creative opportunities. Will's kitchenette on *Will & Grace* is eighteen inches higher than the adjacent living room. *Cheers* has steps up and down, which is more interesting than a flat set like the one in *Taxi;* we got a lot of shots of feet coming in and out of the bar, which drove storylines. The *Wings* set had an upstairs piece, which I helped design. On *NewsRadio*, the broadcast booth was set higher than the office floor. *Frasier's* beautiful living room had steps up to the terrace doors.

I believe this is all due to my training from the stage. Your eye is not watching one plane. In theater, you have people walking across one another, and that kinetic movement keeps the audience engaged. In television, cutting from one actor to another serves that purpose.

Directing *Taxi* was the toughest job I ever had, because I was between two amazing groups: one of writing geniuses, and one of brilliant and eclectic actors with diverse training and styles, all of whom gave and demanded perfection. It was everything I could do to give that show and the ensemble cohesion.

For the opening of the show, we shot the actors in cinema verité mode as cabdrivers. We had them each talking about what it means to be a cabdriver, cutting to allow enough time to get all the opening credits in. Dave Davis didn't like it, so we wound up using the shot of a taxi going over the 59th Street/Queensboro Bridge. It was set against the music of a beautiful Bob James score, "Angela," which had originally been purchased to use in the show and became the theme.

The show was complicated from the beginning. There were lots of outside sets and stunts. Big things happened. It would have been a hard show for anyone to direct. It was especially hard for me, as I was just coming into my own and trying to find my way. Doing this huge show was a challenge from every perspective.

Taxi was originally envisioned as a one-camera show shot on tape. At that time, four film cameras were sometimes used on pilots. *All in the Family* had four cameras and was the first sitcom that was recorded on videotape. Carroll O'Connor was in your face. Filmed shows never had four cameras, but because the *Taxi* set was so enormous, it made more sense. I was one of the first to direct a four-camera show on film rather than tape.

The additional camera provided the ability to shoot a joke and its reaction simultaneously. Equally important, it meant you could capture the live audience's genuine, spontaneous response to each joke. The challenge lay in the fact that film was very expensive, so we had to be judicious. We rarely shot a scene multiple times, as is commonplace now with digital stock featuring reusable memory cards and without film costs required to reshoot. Now every director on a modern show does at least two takes of every scene. On some pilots I directed, especially ones without a live audience, the amount of takes got crazy. I once had eight takes of the same scene, because we couldn't gauge the laughter without the audience and didn't know whether we had what we needed to move on to the next scene.

In *The Honeymooners,* Ralph Kramden was unhappy with his lot in life. He didn't want to be a bus driver. His life was sad and hysterically funny. *Taxi* was similar. The garage was supposed to be a stepping-stone for people on their way up and out to something better professionally. The show went from very broad to very poignant comedy. In Greek mythology, Sisyphus was punished by being forced to roll an immense boulder up a hill, only for it to roll down every time it neared the top; he repeated this action for eternity. Similarly, the moment someone was about to have a big break, it didn't happen. However, they weren't losers, because they had their dreams and they had one another.

Taxi was farcical, with a lot of physical action for a group of cab-drivers. We had a few episodes with Tony boxing, where I got to stage the matches. I was still green and didn't fully know what I was doing. I had my Martin Scorsese moment, where I filmed Tony first working the heavy bag and then tracking him around the ring. It was unusual to film that way in a sitcom; you would normally just pan around the set and come to the person. No one had done a pullback shot like that. Steadicams weren't around yet, so the B camera was used to make the tracking shot work.

We had Reverend Jim, with Alex as his first passenger, backing up and crashing a cab through a wall (to which his response was "That'll be ninety cents"). We demolished sets. A wrecking ball went through Jim's apartment. In "High School Reunion," Louie doesn't want to go to his reunion, because he was embarrassed and taunted during high school:

LOUIE

So, I went to my high school senior prom alone.
The theme was "April Love."

JOHN

April love?

LOUIE

April love is for the very young. The only reason I went to the prom was because even though she was with another guy, I just wanted to see what Sheila looked like on prom night. That's how hooked I was. So I walk in, I say hello to a few people. Hello, hello, hello. I tell them my date was delayed. She couldn't make it until after her Broadway show's curtain came down.
I had to make up stories like that.

ELAINE

So what happened then?

LOUIE

I kept on looking for Sheila and this guy comes up to me. Stanley Tarses. He comes up to me and he says, "Hey, Louie, how'd you like to sit at a table with us and Sheila?" I smiled at him. I didn't want nothing but to just sit where I could look at her. So I walked through this crowded gymnasium. And I see Sheila. She looks so beautiful. She looked just like a beautician. And I can see she's smiling big and everybody said, "Hey, Louie, come on over and sit next to Sheila." And I figured, boy, I lucked out. And I moved over to the other side. And I saw they had a high chair there. I says to them, "Okay, you did it. You got me good. Enjoy yourselves." They sure took my advice—they were still laughing when I left. I went home and I swore to myself then that one day I'd come back a big shot with all the money there was, and I'd walk into one of their high school reunions and make them all eat crackers, if you know what I mean. And now, twenty years later, I'm not sure being a taxi dispatcher is enough to do the job.

JOHN

Well, why don't you just go in there and lie? Everybody lies.

LOUIE

It's too big a job. It's got to be done great. I'm not a good enough actor.

BOBBY

You know, I can't believe you just said that, Louie.

LOUIE

It's true.

BOBBY

I know, but it's incredible with what I was just thinking . . .
Now, the important thing is that they're convinced that
you turned out great, right?

Bobby does a great impersonation of Louie at the reunion and is the life of the party. He gets even with Stanley and is dancing with Sheila. Alex and Louie show up to see how Bobby is doing. Louie says, "All these momos trying to learn how to do my steps, wishing they were with my girl." Though Alex discourages him, Louie just wants to touch Sheila's hair. When he does, she turns, and it sets off a chain of events that topples the entire structure of the banquet room, destroying the reunion. It was a scene we could do only once. I had a crane set up. At the end of the shot, you could see the crane pulling back. We tried it once in rehearsals. It worked fine. In the show, Sheila bumps into a waiter carrying a punch bowl. For some reason they were at a different part of the stage, five feet from the pillars that were supposed to collapse. The waiter carrying the heavy bowl had to do a pirouette, a 360 turn, to keep the momentum that topples each of the decorated pillars, causing a chain reaction: The tables collapse, the food and drinks and people fall onto the floor, and a cascade of multicolored balloons falls from the ceiling, destroying the party. Louie, the only one left standing, exclaims, "I don't know about anyone else, but I'm really enjoying myself!" It was nerve-racking until it came together.

I was now at the first point in my career where I had the experience and confidence to try new things. I decided that I'd rather be fired for doing my job than for just being there. When I read a script, I immediately thought of different ways to stage a scene and make it funnier. I always introduced pieces of business, different ways of saying lines and staging, to enhance the comedic moments.

When they didn't work, the writers glared at me. I experienced my first real pushback when one of the writers reacted to something I had done with displeasure and said, "WTF?" To which I responded, "You know, sometimes I have to fail in order to succeed." It was that pivotal moment in any successful career where you own your work and stand up for what you believe in. After that, I had everyone's trust, and when something I tried succeeded, everyone was happy.

In sitcoms, panning (moving the camera across the screen) is generally frowned upon, because it takes away from the already limited time to tell a story, plus there's the extra cost of scoring music to accompany the pan. Despite that, on *Taxi* I did a lot of pans—it was easier to establish the scene that way than through a big master shot. It allowed for the person in the back, farthest from the camera, to not look like a moth on the wall. To avoid the need for scoring, I'd have an actor start talking during the pan. There was also no video feed at the time, so I couldn't tell whether the scenes were bumpy or uneven. Other than for the pickups, which I could actually see when we were shooting, I relied on the camera guys to tell me whether the scenes looked even.

At the time, it took me eight hours to block four cameras on the huge set (now I can do it in three). By the end of a camera-blocking day, my eyes were red and beady. Danny DeVito nicknamed me "Beads," which he calls me to this day. At the end of the series run, Danny and Rhea Perlman, who had married, gave me a neon sign that reads BEADS, which I still display prominently and proudly in my office.

Every script had to go through outline, then first and second drafts, then be sent to the producers for review. In its final form, it went to mimeo (photocopying), then to the table read. If there was a flaw in the script at any point, it would go through a rewrite. We'd start rehearsing and I'd block scenes, unless the script was a complete disaster.

Rewrites often went well into the evening, based on the complexity of the script. Directors are not normally welcome in writers' rooms, but I insinuated myself into the process early on. I did it for my own edification. I wanted to know what they were thinking so that when I met with the cast at nine A.M. the next day, I could share it with the actors. *Taxi* was such a difficult show to manage and execute, I felt I had to get a leg up.

While in the room, I'd also make suggestions and pitch my own ideas. Some of the writers panned them, literally booing me. David Lloyd would cut me up good with insults. But I also got ideas accepted. During the end of one episode, the cabbies were going to go to a new bar. Tony said, "I can't wait to go tie one on." I suggested that Jim follow with, "I love Chinese food!" That made it in. I had more rejections than acceptances, but I ingratiated myself to them.

I sat in on *Cheers* rewrites as well. On *Will & Grace,* we would shoot a scene and then rewrite, with the writers gathered around a podium, pitching jokes. I would in turn tell them my issues and concerns. We'd do it again in run-through. If you're a young director developing your craft, it's essential to spend time in the writers' rooms. Sitcoms are a writer-driven medium. In addition to the scripts, writers also produce, cast, edit, and look at scene designs. Directors are there to help them and make it better in every way they can.

During the week, comments are delivered on the stage after each run-through. The writers and producers usually sit at the edge of the set in directors' chairs. On show day, during dress rehearsal, the cameras are already on set, so everyone sits in the bleachers. There is a clarion call on sitcoms, "Cast to the rail," where notes are delivered from the bleachers. Unlike some other casts, the *Taxi* cast would run to their spot enthusiastically. Everyone was eager to make the performance as good as it could be.

One of the greatest rewards of *Taxi* was reconnecting with my future partners and still-close friends, Glen and Les Charles. For the rest of this book I will refer to them as "the Brothers," not only for brevity but because over time they also became my brothers, and that is the way I feel about them. Two huge brains, one bigger heart. I first met the Brothers while directing *Phyllis*. They were story editors. On *Taxi*, they were the producers, head writers, and what later became known as showrunners.

From the moment I met them, they were sweet men, with no ego, and they still are, which is probably why we get along so well. We meshed and worked constructively together. Glen was an advertising copywriter and had gone to law school for a year, and Les was a substitute schoolteacher. Les is more of the story man, more logic; Glen is more of a jokester. They decided that they wanted to write for television and, during the course of one year, produced spec scripts—noncommissioned and unsolicited pieces—in the hopes of having them optioned and eventually purchased by a producer or studio. They wrote for almost every show on the air in the early 1970s, including *M*A*S*H, The Bob Newhart Show, Gunsmoke,* and *Columbo.* David Lloyd read their *TMTMS* script, and they were hired. The first script that made it to air was a now-classic *M*A*S*H* episode, "The Late Captain Pierce," in which Hawkeye is mistakenly declared dead by the Army. It was that blend of comedy and pathos that immediately distinguished them.

At the time, virtually all sitcom writers were of the Hebrew faith. It almost seemed to be a requirement, if not a cultural and sociological advantage, to be able to capture the angst of the complex characters you were writing about. Glen and Les were Jack Mormons (Mormons who had left the church) from Henderson, Nevada, raised in the Church of Jesus Christ of Latter-Day Saints. For years afterward, Mormons would come to visit the Brothers, looking for their tithe (10 percent of their earnings).

All of the *Taxi* writers worked extremely hard and never disappointed. While they were working on the current week's script, they were also putting together other scripts and editing shows that were already shot for content, as well as casting future episodes of the show. In addition to the Brothers were Barry Kemp, who went on to create *Newhart* and *Coach,* and Ken Estin and Sam Simon, both of whom went on to write and produce on *Cheers* as well. Sam also co-created *The Simpsons* with Jim Brooks.

When it came to *TMTMS*, Jim, Ed., and Stan never thought a script was good enough. They got even more didactic on *Taxi.* Plus, the writers had to deal with the creators' unpredictable schedules. Jim would pick one day to review a script, the Brothers would rewrite it, then Ed. would come in the next day and change it. Also, the four creators started brushing up against one another, and we had to work around their internal friction. Jim had begun his movie career. He'd be gone, come back, and be unhappy.

Most of the notes I got from Jim, Ed., and Stan were given during the run-through. I would explain the scene and production issues. Jim had a way of saying, "Let's do the scene again. Judd, you cross now and say this." A lot of directors would have gotten upset about that, because it stepped over the line into directing territory. I didn't care about any required re-blocking, because that's how Jim rewrote. He could envision scenes in his head.

We were also the first show to create two-part episodes when shows ran too long, rather than cutting out great material. If the Tuesday run-through was hysterical, instead of cutting ten minutes we often wrote another twenty to make it a two-parter. Most of them weren't through-line plots—not conventional two-parters; they were vignettes. We could tack them together and save on production costs. If you missed the first part, you could easily follow the second. I would shoot interstitial "wraparound" scenes of the cabbies reminiscing. The network supported it because the "below the line" budget—non-actors—was reduced. These shows also wound up becoming the most memorable of the series.

In "Memories of Cab 804," John (a character who was written off after the first season) crashes the cab that all the cabbies have great memories of. Elaine recalls meeting a very handsome art dealer and driving him to Connecticut. We asked for a gorgeous guy. Sometimes you get what you wish for. One of Lu's friends was in acting class with Tom Selleck and recommended him. He had been the Marlboro Man in commercials and then started getting acting roles. Tom credited his role on *Taxi* with helping him to land the lead in *Magnum, P.I.*

The chemistry between Tom and Lu was palpable. His character, Mike Belden, starts out in the back of the cab, then in the front seat, then driving the cab. Mike invites Elaine to spend the night with him before he goes to London the next day and can't promise when he will be back. "You're not so perfect—you don't even know when to lie," she tells him. Mike gives her a hundred dollars and tells her it's a down payment on her art gallery, saying, "It's the best cab ride I ever had." Elaine replies, "Oh, this is some tip. What would you have given me if I had stayed the night?" Mike says, "A very sweet memory." And the payoff is that the beautiful and poignant moment is interrupted by Louie, who has been listening on the radio the entire time and announces, "You're better off with the hundred."

Bobby recalls a would-be robber, played by Scoey Mitchell, a sweet, talented comedic actor whom Jim Brooks knew. The robber tries to make off with Bobby's cash box. They hold guns on each other and fall asleep doing it. Bobby eventually takes money from him for cab fare for the entire time the meter was running. Louie has a memory of taking a kid (Chris Barnes) to a fancy private school. The kid tries to hustle Louie out of money, and Louie, true to form, beats the kid out of his tuition money. Tony stops a fare from jumping off a bridge.

Alex picks up a pregnant couple, Ruth and Alan (Regie Baff and Mandy Patinkin, whom we finally got on the show). When the wife goes into labor and realizes that they're not going to make it to the hospital, Alex delivers the baby.

RUTH

Hey, mister. Really, I don't know how to thank you for all this.

ALAN

We don't have a name for him yet. What's your name?

ALEX

Alex.

ALAN

Maybe we'll just get you a bottle of Scotch.

"Fantasy Borough" was another expanded episode. When guest star Hervé Villechaize, Tattoo from the very popular TV show *Fantasy Island,* leaves pictures in Tony's cab, the cabbies all have fantasies of their own. Journalist Eric Sevareid is in the backseat, telling Tony how smart he really is.

TONY

I think it's stupid that half the world is fighting. I mean, it seems to me that if the leaders of these countries want to fight, they should fight and leave us out of it.

ERIC

I think you're going a little too fast for me, Tony.

TONY

Let the leaders of these countries put on the gloves and go a couple of rounds. The match I'd like to see is Carter–Castro.

ERIC

Castro has got the weight on him, you know.

TONY

Yeah, but Jimmy's wiry, and he does a lot of roadwork.

ERIC

What you're suggesting is a civilized alternative to war. Tell me, what would you do, for example, about world hunger?

TONY

Well, like all those fancy White House parties, right? Instead of inviting all those rich people, invite some poor people. I mean, rich people can afford to feed themselves. Right?

ERIC

You seem to have a perspective on world events that somehow eludes the average man.

TONY

You're no slouch yourself.

In that same episode, Latka fantasizes that he is running the garage, with two beautiful blond assistants. Latka emerges from the dispatch booth to chastise now-mechanic Louie, against whom he deploys a military firing squad. Bobby dreams that he is a rock star and Louie is a bum who gives Bobby his last dollar to admit that he knows him at a party. Jim dreams that he is visited by extraterrestrials who "love and understand him" and take him with them. Alex dreams that he falls in love with a beautiful passenger (Priscilla Barnes) and then crashes the cab: "I can't even be trusted behind the wheel of my own fantasy." When he tries to refocus, his romantic fantasy is cut short again—he realizes that the woman is his niece. Louie dreams that he is a wealthy man who lives in a mansion with his wife, Elaine, and the rest of the cabbies are dressed in rags.

Finally, Elaine shares her fantasy. She begins singing "Lullaby of Broadway," dreaming that she is a Broadway star. Pat Birch choreographed all the cabbies joining Elaine in that number, with a finale in which each one walks behind a column and emerges in white tie and tails. I had to learn to shoot with a split-screen so they could transform into formal wear. We relit and converted the garage set into a Broadway stage.

One Tuesday, an episode called "Shut It Down" was reading so well that they decided to make it another two-parter. The striking cabbies elect Elaine shop steward to deal with Louie, who proposes that if they go on one date he will accede to the demands. Elaine contemplates the idea and has conditions:

ELAINE

We meet at the restaurant; we part at the restaurant. I get to bring
a friend, and we sit at separate tables.

LOUIE

Fine. Let me alter that just a tiny bit. It's at night, it's dinner.
I pick you up; I take you home. It's just the two of us. And
sometime during the evening, within the hearing of at least
two other people, you must call me "Stallion."
None of this is negotiable.

ELAINE
Except stallion.

LOUIE
Especially stallion!

They articulate their respective proposals as they walk across the garage, each following closely behind the other, matching step for step, in a collective-bargaining dance.

Unlike the other two-parters, this was a chronological episode, with no interstitial segments. I shot it all in one week, which was unheard of. At the end of the week, I collapsed. I was never more tired after any other show I directed.

We shot *Taxi* on Friday nights (which is now unusual, because most actors want to use the weekend to learn their lines), followed by our famous wrap parties. These attracted lots of celebrities, including the casts of *Happy Days, Laverne & Shirley, Mork & Mindy, Bosom Buddies,* and *Working Stiffs*. Danny became good friends with John Belushi, and he and Danny Aykroyd—only a few years into *Saturday Night Live* and just recently having taken the country by storm with their Blues Brothers musical act—performed at one of the parties. We'd have four or five huge parties a year with playlists we put together. They'd go all night and then some of us would go out to breakfast afterward. We were young and really enjoyed one another. Tony (who was also from New York), Lu, and I went roller-skating and to baseball games together. The cast became the cool kids at the Paramount lot, but we were also the kind ones. We were like a family—which I can say is true about most of the sitcoms I became deeply involved with.

Andy Kaufman was hired by the *Taxi* creators to play Latka, the mechanic, based on one of his characters, Foreign Man, which he had done on *Saturday Night Live*. Andy was a genius. He had a mind that no one had seen before in a comedian—or anyone else, for that matter—and a brave nature to do something for as long as it took until people laughed. I had never seen a comic who didn't care if the audience laughed. He would go out and do a routine and keep doing it. He'd come onstage and start reading from *Gone with the Wind,* and the audience would sit there baffled, out of their minds. And then, all of a sudden, they'd start laughing. Andy offered ideas in his act that first created outrage, then laughter. He was brilliant that way.

Latka, who came from a fictitious Eastern European country, spoke in a made-up language Andy created that included ibi-da, which meant yes or that is so, and yaktabay, which likely meant some anatomical part that you directed someone you didn't like to kiss. In "Latka's Revolting," Lenny Baker, a sweet and funny actor (who passed away too soon at thirty-five), played Baschi, Latka's friend from the old country, who tries to recruit Latka to return and participate in a revolution. Despite all of the cabbies' protests, Latka feels compelled to return and fight. At Latka's going-away party, Louie pretends to chew out Latka one last time, and through the translucent glass in the door we see Louie wishing Latka well and hugging him, moving Latka to tears.

When it's made clear to Latka that there are only eight rebels, including him, going to fight, he tells Baschi to "kiss his yaktabay." Baschi makes one last attempt by having his group sing their national anthem, "Ibbe-Da, Yak Temani, Ibbe-Dorfnish, Ibbe-Da" (written by Stan Daniels), while the cabbies sing "Yankee Doodle," winning over the rebels one by one through passionate patriotic music, the way Victor Laszlo did in *Casablanca.* At the beginning of the episode, Latka is listening to a daily radio broadcast from his country. If you listen carefully, you'll recognize Judd Hirsch's voice as the radio announcer. He asked for his turn to do Sid Caesar gibberish and had a lot of fun doing it.

Andy had agreed to do *Taxi* if a friend of his, Tony Clifton, could be on as well one day. Tony Clifton was actually Andy's alter ego. They were the same person.

In Andy's stand-up act, the Tony character was a really bad lounge singer who opened for Andy. People would hoot and jeer, wanting Andy, and Andy would come on, never acknowledging that they were the same person. There were times that Andy appeared in public with his close friend and performing partner Bob Zmuda, who would dress as Clifton, just to throw the audience off.

After the first few weeks of rehearsal, Andy came to me and said he had day–night reversal, which meant he was up all night and slept all day, and asked if he could come in after lunch. And I said sure, because Latka's scenes weren't instrumental to the plot; they were mainly Judd or Danny setting him up. Andy had a photographic memory, and all his bits would kill, so it was an easy request to agree to.

We finally came to the episode where we hired Tony Clifton to play Louie De Palma's brother. So, to be clear, Andy Kaufman was playing Tony Clifton playing Louie De Palma's brother. The first day of rehearsal was October 2, 1978, the day the Boston Red Sox, who hadn't won the World Series since 1918, faced the New York Yankees in a one-game playoff at Fenway Park to decide the American League East title. Yankee Bucky Dent hit a seventh-inning three-run homer that clinched the title for the Yankees (I apologize for the digression unless you're a baseball fan, and then you'll understand).

Tony Clifton came in, cigarette in hand (Andy never smoked). He was dressed in a frilly shirt and prosthetics that covered everywhere but his hands, which gave him away immediately. He started barking all these commands: "C'mon, let's rehearse." Tony Danza and I were in the prop room, watching the Yankee game, broadcast live from the East Coast. We said, "As soon as the game's over." We watched the end of the game and then went to work. It was quickly clear to all of us that Clifton's performance wasn't going to make it to television. Andy was working so hard at playing Tony that it was difficult for him to play Louie De Palma's brother. We had a run-through, and we decided that we had to fire Tony.

The producers called Andy's manager, George Shapiro, and said we'd decided to let Tony Clifton go. The next day George called and said Andy agreed but on the condition that Tony had to be fired in front of everybody, with a hooker on each knee.

The day of reckoning arrived. Ed. came down to the soundstage to fire Tony. Andy/Tony said, "No," and a big fight ensued, with everyone yelling and screaming. Judd and Tony Danza loved it. Jeff Conaway was pissed off at Andy's self-indulgence with Tony. We pulled the actors over to the side and said, "Just enjoy the theater. You'll never see anything like this again in your life."

Tony kept balking. Judd said, "Okay, I'll play." He went out to the soundstage and screamed at Tony and took him and his entourage offstage. The whole thing was raucous. It was a spectacle. The next week, Andy came in and didn't discuss any of it. Like it never happened. Genius.

It's harder to tell stories about offbeat characters, because they're almost always one-dimensional sidekicks. Both writers and directors have to work harder to find ways to generate dimension. Creatively, Latka was a double-edged sword, because while there were limitations to what could be done with Latka, he could also more easily be transformed into other personas. In "Latka the Playboy," he is upset that no one takes him seriously and that women especially see him only as a cute immigrant. "I do not have too much success with American women. You see, the men from my country are not for some reason attractive to the women in your country. We do not, as a matter of fact, have much luck with the women in my country." Taking matters into his own hands, he goes on vacation and, in a sequestered eight days of reading only *Playboy* magazines—to "alter his lifestyle to fit the fast lane"—and listening to a tape of an FM-radio DJ—to learn to "talk so that when women hear my voice, they will just relax"—he transforms himself into Vic Ferrari, a slick, smooth-talking, obnoxious womanizer. He walks over to the woman (Robin Klein) who rejected him when he was Latka:

VIC

I can take one look at you and tell that you've heard every phony line in the book. So one more isn't going to hurt you, right? She's laughing. But seriously, now, the first few moments of a relationship set the tone for the whole thing, if you know what I mean. So let's be honest. My name is Vic. I'm into Italian cars, Technics stereos, Australian films, and beautiful ladies. If you're interested, let's talk. If not, it's been fun.

KAREN

Vic, huh?

VIC

No. Not Vic huh. Vic Ferrari.

KAREN

Ferrari. That isn't your real name, is it?

VIC

Why don't you tell me after you see how I perform on a tight corner! [slaps himself] Terrible humor, Vic! But I love that smile. Come on. Walk with me. Talk with me.

BOBBY

Are you seeing what I'm seeing?

TONY

It's like Dr. Jekyll and Mr. Heckle!

Despite Latka's newly found confidence and success with women, no one likes Vic, including Vic, who, with Alex's help, reverts to the lovable Latka. Vic was a durable character and returned, along with other characters that became part of Latka's multiple-personality disorder.

In "Mr. Personalities," Latka assumes Alex's persona. When both go to a psychiatrist, Latka's Alex becomes less of an impersonation and morphs into an intense self-reflection and character analysis:

LATKA AS ALEX

Well, Doc, I've been thinking about my life a lot. Where does Alex Reiger go from here? I mean, I don't want to crab. Yeah, let's take a shot. But when you examine my life and a bad marriage: My wife was cheating on me, which was probably my fault, I shoulda caught it sooner. My daughter's grown and we're not as close as I'd like. She does seem grateful, but I think that's primarily for not inheriting my nose. We can forget about how I screwed up things right now. I was thinking just the other night, I got a mediocre job, which I do very well, but it doesn't stimulate me. That's right. I like my friends, but the nature of the relationship seems to be that I'm some kind of authority figure. I listen to their problems and I'm not supposed to have any. I take pride in accepting things the way they are, but I just realized that maybe that's because it's an excuse for not having any ambition. I'm starting to realize that my love for life is unrequited.

As Latka is about to make a monumental breakthrough for Alex, he reverts to his foreign-man self.

Reverend Jim Ignatowski was a revolutionary and seminal character for both television and film—a former addict who was screwed up by his drug use but was still a sweet and generous person. We did a few episodes where he was stoned. We never showed the drug use, but we implied it. We got away with it by portraying him as a "former" addict.

You cannot describe to somebody who's not in the process what that moment is like, when you know that the actor is not only right for the part but is often the only one who can play it. I was there when Christopher Lloyd came in to read for Reverend Jim. We had similar responses on *Cheers,* when Nicky Colasanto came in to play Coach; Dan Hedaya came in to read for Nick Tortelli, Carla's husband; and Woody Harrelson read for Woody Boyd; and on *Will & Grace,* when Sean Hayes read for Jack McFarland. There's an instant spark and you can't imagine anyone else in the role.

The role of Jim was originally written as a guest spot during the first season. The character was to perform the "paper wedding" ceremony between Latka and a call girl (Rita Taggart) so Latka could stay in America. Danny knew Chris from *One Flew Over the Cuckoo's Nest.* On the day of his audition, Chris showed up in sneakers with no laces, tattered jeans, a jeans jacket, and his hair askew. He started reading, and everyone in the room had their "oh my God" moment. Chris's audition had everyone hysterically laughing, and his performance was so memorable that he was brought back for a second-season episode that established him as a regular character. For the entire first week, he came to rehearsal dressed like Reverend Jim. At his first after-party, Chris wore a white shirt and jeans, with his hair slicked down, and it was the first time anyone had seen him that way.

The biggest laughs I ever had as a director were during "Reverend Jim: A Space Odyssey." Jim has to take a driver's-license exam in order to become a cabdriver. The other cabbies take him to the Department of Motor Vehicles and help him cheat on the written exam:

JIM
Eyes . . . ?

ELAINE
No, don't put two.

JIM
Oh, they mean color, don't they?

BOBBY
Mental illness or narcotic addiction?

JIM
Now, that's a tough choice . . .

"What does a yellow light mean?" Jim whispers to his friends from the Sunshine Cab Company, who are standing nearby. Bobby whispers back, "Slow down."

Jim considers this, then responds, "What . . . does . . . a . . . yellow . . . light . . . mean?" The joke is repeated again and again—each time more slowly. The laugh went on for forty-five seconds, one of the longest in the history of television. My first thought was: *"Not cutting it!"*

Many of the *Taxi* episodes were morality plays. It was a vehicle—pun intended—for friendships and loyalty, for doing the right thing and protecting one another. At the same time, it was about normalizing the wacky and the disenfranchised, figuring out what high predicament Louie, Jim, and Latka could get into. In "Jim the Psychic," Jim has visions that come true. He predicts that something horrible will happen to Alex:

JIM
Thursday night at your apartment. Seven P.M. You'll be with a friend—I couldn't make out who. You'll drink a glass of water very quickly. Somebody is going to mistake you for a girl. You'll do the cancan in a green shirt wearing a catcher's mask. And then comes the crazy part. . . . There'll be a knock at the door, you'll go to the door, you open it . . .

The superstitious Louie is drawn in, but the pragmatic Alex refuses to have his life determined by anything other than his own free will. Louie goes to Alex's apartment on Thursday night to protect him. "I'm not gonna tempt fate, Louie, I'm gonna beg fate!" The defiant Alex puts on a green shirt and catcher's mask and dances the cancan. The grandfather clock strikes seven, and nothing happens. Then a knock on the door comes. Louie won't let Alex answer it. "Death is on the other side of the door, Reiger!" When Alex opens the door, it's a young girl (Kiva Dawson) selling sugar cookies. (We couldn't refer to her as a Girl Scout without permission, which we never would have gotten.) Louie starts screaming in horror. So does the girl, who throws the cookies in the air and runs. I won my third Emmy for that episode. The cookies were good too.

I had never met the legendary Ruth Gordon before she appeared in the episode titled "Sugar Mama," for which she picked up an Emmy. Ruth started acting at nineteen and had a stage and film career that continued into her eighties. She was also part of the Algonquin Round Table. My dad knew Ruth and her husband and writing partner, Garson Kanin. It was an honor and privilege to work with one of the grandes dames of the Broadway stage.

In "Sugar Mama," Ruth played an eccentric older woman who befriends Alex after riding in his cab and tries to turn him into a gigolo, which he resists. We cast Aharon Ipalé to play the man who does becomes her gigolo. During rehearsal, I called out, "We need Ruth and Aharon." Ruth laughed uncontrollably before she finally made it onstage. After we shot the scene, I asked Judd, "Why was she laughing so hard?" Judd said, "Ruth thought you said, 'I want Ruth Gordon and a hard-on.'"

At that time, as part of a three-show deal between the John Charles Walters Company and ABC, the *Taxi* creators asked me to direct *The Associates*, a show about a group of fancy Wall Street lawyers, which was a very interesting and promising premise for a sitcom. It was based on a novel by John Jay Osborn, Jr., who had also written *The Paper Chase*. It had great scripts, a great cast, and a beautiful set with a fabulous law library. Martin Short, Alley Mills, and Shelley Smith were three young lawyers who worked for the venerable Wilfrid Hyde-White. It was such an honor to work with him. He was on in years and was having trouble with his lines. The legal papers on his desk were actually his lines in the script, which he would glance at and recite. Tim Thomerson, a very funny comedian, played Danko, the swaggering office-messenger guy.

In *The Associates* pilot, two senior associates, played by John Getz and Joe Regalbuto, are competing for one partner position. Joe's character gets the promotion and John, who would have been a great center, left the show; there was no longer one character to hook into. Sadly, there was no magic. The indescribable ingredient that every show needs to succeed was missing. *The Associates* was nominated for Emmys for both writing and acting, despite the fact that only five of the nine shows shot actually aired.

I also had the best time directing the pilot of *Best of the West* in 1980. It was set in the Old West, with Joel Higgins as Sam Best, who travels west with his wife and young son (Carlene Watkins and Meeno Peluce), becomes the sheriff of a lawless small town, and tries to bring order to the wacky characters. Leonard Frey, who was in the film version of *The Boys in the Band* and both the Broadway production and film version of *Fiddler on the Roof,* played the head bad guy. Chris Lloyd guested as a gunslinger. The show lasted only one season, but two memorable things came out of it. First, co-creator Ed. Weinberger met Carlene on the set and married her. Second, Ted Danson auditioned for the part of the sheriff. While he didn't get that part, his near-term future was about to get very bright.

It was also during this time that I learned I didn't enjoy being a film director. I was approached by producer Aaron Russo, who managed Bette Midler and had produced *The Rose,* about directing a feature. Francis Veber, who also wrote the script for *La Cage aux Folles,* had penned *Partners,* about a straight cop trying to go undercover in the gay community. We had a problem with casting right off. For a piece like this, we needed an overtly masculine character who felt out of place in the gay community. We thought of Clint Eastwood, Charles Bronson, or Steve McQueen. I got Sam Elliott and Peter Riegert. Producer Barry Diller didn't think he could sell the movie with them attached. We ended up with John Hurt as the gay cop and Ryan O'Neal, who would have been great as the gay cop, as the straight cop. Francis wanted it to be apparent that John's character was gay. He wanted to advance the gay-rights movement, which was still taboo as a film subject in 1981.

After this experience, I knew that feature films were not in my wheelhouse. You have to shoot a scene four times from five different angles, and you have to be funny each time. Sometimes you can't get it the fourth time. Between publicity, editing, and rollout, it took two years from the time we started until the time *Partners* was released. That was just too long for me. My head was not in that space.

At this point, I was directing a hit show and winning awards for it. I was really happy, but in the back of my mind I didn't think it was my directing work that earned the awards; it was the acting and the writing. I felt that because I didn't create the show and wasn't producing it, it wasn't *my* show, and my imprimatur would never be associated with the show. I was just a facilitator, the ringmaster, just coordinating, fitting the right three balls into the three holes in the head.

I was trying to stay afloat and influence shows in any way I could while still treading water. I was now almost forty. I had skills, but I still felt less than. I was subjected to a lot of criticism because I wasn't the head honcho. There are nine ways to see a joke, and while all nine can be funny, if your way is different from that of the person who is most powerful, the most powerful person's vision will prevail. I realized that I needed control over the product I was working on as well as my destiny. I was like millions of people who are never completely comfortable working for others. I needed to own the business. It came with the big risk that if the business failed, I'd have no job, but it also came with the immeasurable satisfaction that I was building something and executing my vision.

Part of the growth process, especially if you're entrepreneurial in any way, is to strike out on your own, no matter how good you have it where you are. In the seventies and eighties, Jim Brooks was one of the most important and most talented people in sitcoms. He always treated me professionally and with respect. He had a strong presence and powerful ideas, very often great ones.

The Brothers and I had the same agent, Bob Broder. Broder—who's the only agent I have ever had, and who also became my best friend—was such a tough negotiator that he became known in the industry as Darth Broder. At the end of the third season of *Taxi*, he said, "You guys should think about doing your own show." We liked the idea, so we started talking about it. Around the same time, Jay Sandrich told me, "You'll never know how good you really are until you become your own boss."

Jay's words resonated with me. Glen and Les also knew that their ideas would never be fully realized while they worked for other people. The three of us decided that the fourth season of *Taxi* would be our last. It was time for us to put our own stake into the ground. We had given our talent to a lot of talented people. We didn't know what our creative voices would be or sound like, but we did know we could do a show on our own, because the MTM shows and *Taxi* had given us the training and the experience. We agreed that failure wasn't the worst thing that could happen to us. It was not trying. We knew the ropes, we knew what was required to produce a show, and we had writers and a director. We had to try.

Screwball and Romantic Comedy

FROM WILL THEY OR WON'T THEY TO HEH, HEH, HEH

FRASIER
It's not my fault.

LILITH
If my look was accusatory, it was strictly habit.

In a sitcom, a romantic relationship becomes its own character, and as such, it has to be thought about and developed in the same way. Audiences root for that connection. A typical audience comprises three groups: those who are in love themselves, those who want to be in love, and those who don't know that they want to be in love. That's a lot of people to have to make laugh.

Screwball comedy is a subgenre of romantic comedy that became popular during the Great Depression and thrived until the early 1940s. It satirized the traditional love story and brought together couples who would constantly argue. They were two people you would never think were right for each other, other than the fact they were crazy about each other. In baseball, there's a tricky pitch called the screwball, named because batters find it impossible to predict. That name was right for this kind of comedy, because in a good screwball film it's almost impossible to guess what's coming next. The only thing you can be sure of is that it'll be fast, smart, with the characters cutting at each other in a way that draws the audience in. Sitcom romances, by virtue of all the twists and turns over multiple episodes, have become the modern successor to the 1940s version:

DIANE

Sam, may I have a brief word with you?

SAM

I suppose you could, but I doubt it.

When the Brothers and I were developing *Cheers,* we knew that the core of the show would be the romance between Sam Malone (Ted Danson) and Diane Chambers (Shelley Long). Everything grew out of that connection. From the beginning, there was a smoldering sexual tension between the two that was driven by innuendo:

SAM

Well, a lot of people out there waiting for a wedding; no bride, no groom. Guess it's up to us, huh?

DIANE

My God, Sam, I can't believe my ears. You're serious, aren't you?

SAM

Oh, no, no. I just meant that we should go out there and serve those people some drinks, that's all.

DIANE

Oh, that's what I meant too.

SAM

No, it isn't. What'd you think I was talking about? Come on.

DIANE

Well, for a moment there, I confess, I thought you were
talking about something else.

SAM

And what would your answer be?

DIANE

No, Sam, that's the sort of question that has to be asked
before it can be answered.

SAM

Well, if I heard the answer, maybe it would be easier for me
to ask the question.

DIANE

Very well. The answer is no.

SAM

Well, then, the question was: Have you ever met a man
who gave you the hots more than me?

DIANE

I'd like to change my answer.

SAM

Fine.

DIANE

Then the answer is yes.

SAM

Well, then the question was: Do you want to go to bed with me?

DIANE

I want to change my answer again.

SAM

Well, that's okay, and I'll change my question to: Is there any way
that you would not object to not going to bed with me?

We auditioned actors for the romantic leads of Sam and Diane
for six months. Teddy Danson was still in my head from his *Best of
the West* audition. He was on *Taxi* and had distinguished himself in
both *The Onion Field* and *Body Heat*, where he was sensational as a
prosecutor who danced like Fred Astaire. People had been after
Shelley Long to do pilots for years. We got her to agree to read
for us.

For the final audition, instead of going to the studio offices or the
network's green room, we went to a bar set on Stage 25 at Paramount Studios that was being used for Tom Hanks's sitcom, *Bosom
Buddies*. We catered lunch and invited the executives to see the
final three couples in contention for Sam and Diane: Fred Dryer
and Julia Duffy; William Devane and Lisa Eichhorn; and Teddy and
Shelley. The Brothers wrote a scene that each team performed.
Fred Dryer was a famous football player but didn't have the comic
chops at the time. Billy broke a glass and deftly improvised, incor-
porating it into the scene. He was a little older than what we had
envisioned for the role. Teddy and Shelley were clearly the best
suited for Sam and Diane. They had the kind of chemistry you can't
buy or manufacture. They looked like a couple who longed for each
other, who loved each other so much that it hurt. And they were
funny together. It was all attitude and connection.

Glen, Les, and I made the deal, and then we drew lots to see
who would tell whom that they didn't get the part. I drew Billy. It

was tough telling him, because he was so great. But we made the right choice.

The chemistry was established the moment Diane first walked into the bar and answered the ringing phone:

> DIANE
>
> Are you Sam? Yes, he's here. Someone named Vicky?

> SAM
>
> (He's just come out of his office where he was eating a sandwich and his mouth is full and he can barely speak.)
> No, no, no, no.

> DIANE
>
> She knows you're here. I told her you're here.

> SAM
>
> (He shakes his head.)

> DIANE
>
> Now, look . . . I'm sorry, I was wrong, he had to step out . . .
> Where? Well, I think what happened is he, uh . . . he had to go to mime class. . . . Yes, yes, I'll take a message. . . . You're welcome . . .

> (She looks at Sam to tell him what Vicky said.)

> You're a magnificent pagan beast.

> SAM
>
> Thanks. What's the message?

Sam was downtown, Diane was uptown. Half the audience wanted to sleep with her, and the other half wanted to kill her. And of the second half, half of those wanted to sleep with her too:

DIANE

Do you know what the difference is between you
and a fat-brained ass?

SAM

Nope.

DIANE

The fat-brained ass would!

We nurtured the flirtation and developed the arc of the romance over the first season. We teased the relationship but didn't
act on it. We were drawing the audience in. The characters genuinely liked each other. Diane almost unintentionally tried to improve people she liked, especially Sam. In "Sam's Women," Sam
picks up a beautiful woman named Brandee ("Brandee with two
ee's"):

DIANE

Sam, wait a minute now, I don't mean to criticize. In a way I was
complimenting you. I think you can do better.

SAM

I don't want to do better. You see, Diane, there's certain things in
this life that I really like, and nobody is going to change my mind
about them. I like fun women, hot dogs, game shows. And I don't
care what anybody says about them.

DIANE

Did you read where they found rat parts in hot dogs?

SAM

I like rat parts. It's my favorite part of the hot dog.

Sam has trouble taking Brandee with two ee's home, because suddenly Diane's approval means something to him. She calls him out for never dating intelligent women:

SAM

You know, this week I have gone out with all the women I know, I mean, all the women I really enjoyed, and all of a sudden, all I can think about is how stupid they are. My life isn't fun anymore. It's because of you.

DIANE

Because of me?

SAM

Yeah, you're a snob.

DIANE

A snob?

SAM

That's right.

DIANE

Well, you're a rapidly aging adolescent.

SAM

Well, I would rather be that than a snob.

DIANE

Sam, do yourself a favor, go back to your tootsies and your rat parts. I'd hate to see the bowling alleys close on my account!

SAM

Wait a minute! Are you saying that I'm too dumb to
date smart women?

DIANE

I'm saying that it would be very difficult for you. A really intelligent
woman would see your line of BS a mile away.

SAM

Yeah. Well, you know, I've never met an intelligent woman that I'd
want to date.

DIANE

On behalf of the intelligent women around the world,
may I just say, Whew!

A little while later, cooler heads prevail:

SAM

Hey, look, I am sorry. I said a lot of stupid things I shouldn't have.
I apologize. I was kind of upset.

DIANE

Okay, I'm sorry too. We both got a little carried away,
especially you.

SAM

Well I'll be darned.

DIANE

What?

SAM

I guess I've . . . I've never looked into your eyes.

DIANE
Something wrong with them?

SAM
I don't think I've ever seen eyes that color before. Matter of fact, I
don't think I've ever seen that color before. . . . Yes, I have . . . I
was on a ski weekend up at Stowe. I was coming in late one day,
last person off the slope as the sun had just gone down. And the
sky became this incredible color. I usually don't notice things like
that, and I found myself kind of walking around in the cold hoping
that wouldn't change, wishing that I had somebody there to share
it with me. Afterwards, I tried to convince myself that I'd imagined
that color, that I hadn't really seen it. That nothing on this earth
could be that beautiful. Now I see I was wrong . . .

(Diane is mesmerized.)

SAM
Wouldn't work, huh?

DIANE
Huh?

SAM
An intelligent woman would see right through that.

DIANE
(gradually composing herself)
Oh, oh. In a minute!

Sam's speech about the eyes is very long, but we cut to Diane's
face and she enables you to enjoy the moment. It's not only his
speech, it's her reaction. If that was done in the theater, your eyes
would go to her naturally. On a sitcom, you take the viewer to that

reaction place—the speech is now not long, because of the effect it has on the enraptured.

In an episode called "Pick a Con . . . Any Con," Sam picks up a deck of cards after a tense card game and asks Diane, "Are you feeling lucky tonight?"

DIANE

Whatcha got in mind?

SAM

A game of chance. Simple cut of the cards.

DIANE

What are the stakes?

SAM

If I win, I get to go to bed with you.

DIANE

What if I win?

SAM

You get to go to bed with me.

DIANE

Forget it.

SAM

I understand. You'd rather earn it.

This kind of relationship had been done on the stage and in movies but never before in television. The tease was so important. We knew at episode 7 how strong the relationship was playing.

Diane should have been with fiancé Sumner. Sam and Diane are out of each other's leagues, but there's a great connection between them. She makes fun of him for his lack of smarts, and he makes fun of her for her ever-present smarts. What holds them together is the sexual tension and the bond they can neither control nor resist.

As with *Taxi,* our approach to *Cheers* was to showcase a different character each week, but I thought it was equally important to serve the Sam and Diane relationship in every episode. We thought about how to pace the episodes to let the romance develop, about how to not only create the romantic energy but sustain it. I told the writers to always land on Sam and Diane at the end of an episode, regardless of the actual story.

Because of the *Happy Days* episode where Fonzie literally jumps over a shark tank, the moment a sitcom passes its prime it is said to have "jumped the shark." When you're deviating from the safety of a formulaic relationship, you're navigating shark-infested waters. Even if you do it right, the relationship can slip, and you've jumped the shark. We were creating what has also become sitcom vernacular, "will they or won't they?" television, which was replicated a decade later on *Friends.*

In "Showdown," the last episode of season 1, Sam and Diane's passionate embrace and kiss was a risky scene and wound up as the moment that forever influenced the future of sitcom romance. Diane is about to jet off with Derek, Sam's successful international lawyer brother, whom Sam has always been jealous of:

SAM

And while you're up there floating around, remember the day
I said this: You are the nuttiest, the stupidest, the
phoniest fruitcake I ever met . . .

DIANE

And you, Sam Malone, are the most arrogant, self-centered . . .

SAM

Shut up! Shut your fat mouth!

DIANE

Make me!

SAM

Make you? I'll bounce you off every wall in this office!

DIANE

Try it and you'll be walking funny tomorrow.
Or I should say funnier.

SAM

Y'know, sometimes I really feel like popping you one.
I always wanted to pop you one. Maybe this is
my lucky day? Huh?

DIANE

You disgust me! I hate you!

SAM

Are you as turned on as I am?

DIANE

More!

SAM

Bet me!

(They grab each other and kiss and the screen goes dark.)

SAM

Now I'm gonna nibble on your ear.

DIANE
Sam, don't tell me you're gonna nibble on my ear.
That ruins it.

At the end of the first season, Sam and Diane finally get together. It was a pivotal and highly stressful moment because it would break this beautiful sexual tension. The prevailing wisdom was "Oh my God, you're going to ruin the show!" We said, "If Sam can't get a woman in bed in one year, then what kind of lover is he? What kind of sexy man is he?"

It took us a while to figure out what we were going to do. In situation comedy, the general rule is that you start with the situation and you stick with it. We had a situation that was dynamite. There was a big discussion initially about not getting them together. There were concerns from both NBC and critics over having Sam and Diane in a relationship. We talked about it a lot and reminded the network that we set out to do an evolving relationship, and so it had to evolve. NBC yielded because Brandon Tartikoff and Grant Tinker were allies and supportive of creativity. The plan was to stretch the relationship rubber band over five seasons. We liked that we didn't have to get them back together immediately after their breakup at the end of season 2, but we knew we had to keep figuring out how to advance them. They were still going to dominate the show and have a strong connection. We were extremely careful and as a result never saw the shark, much less jumped it.

The network was concerned that we were tampering with something that worked. During the first season, the titillation between Sam and Diane and the kind of sexy repartee was intense, and people watched the show for that. The standard at the time was that every TV episode had to be complete in itself, so when you watched for the first time you could enjoy it and know where you were. *Cheers* was the first sitcom to do continuing stories and evolving relationships. Every season ended with a cliffhanger, which always involved Sam and Diane. We'd discuss and plot the arc of the season each year. Nobody had done that before; shows didn't have evolving relationships. Boy met girl, they had their obstacles, but then boy and girl fell in love and got married. They never broke up. The *Cheers* dynamic was both complex and dangerous, because it put fan loyalty at risk. It messed with the formula. If we did it right, the audience would become even more invested in the relationship. But it was still a risk. If there was any miscalculation, fans could lose interest and the show would tank.

The last episode of the first season, when Sam and Diane kiss at the end, is one of the best episodes of the series and also one of the best episodes I've ever directed. We had built up the tension between the two of them over the course of the season and brought their relationship to a fevered crescendo—and brought the audience along with it. We hit exactly the right notes.

The ongoing romantic storyline was very unusual. We began toying with the form, relying on the success of the screwball-comedy format, where the audience follows the roller-coaster ride of a couple in love. They got together and split up, multiple times. That tension drove the show for the first five seasons. Once an audience is comfortable on the roller coaster, they enjoy the ride.

A lot of grief and pushback over the couple breaking up during the second season was directed our way, but it subsided halfway through the season when audiences realized they were going to get back together. One handwritten letter with stains on it read, "You have to get them back together; these are real teardrops on the page." The letters were not the only reason we had to get them back together. Had we not, Sam's character and the audience appeal would have been irreparably hurt. We had to protect not only Sam's character but Diane's, because the perception would have been that she was cold and frigid.

There was a similar situation thirteen years later when I directed the Ross–Rachel moment on season 2 of *Friends*. In "The One with the Prom Video," the friends are watching a high school video of

Monica (Courteney Cox) and Rachel (Jennifer Aniston) at Monica's parents' house, getting ready to go to the prom.

That pre-prom video was shot earlier. We put a pimple and mustache on Ross (David Schwimmer) and a pre-nose-job prosthetic proboscis on Jen. We also put Monica in a fat suit. Joey (Matt LeBlanc) and Chandler (Matthew Perry) comment:

JOEY
Some girl ate Monica!

MONICA
Shut up! The camera adds ten pounds.

CHANDLER
So how many cameras are actually on you?

In the video, Monica and Rachel are both excited in their fancy dresses. When it looks like Rachel's prom date has stood her up, the lovestruck Ross is convinced by his father to quickly put on his tuxedo to rescue the damsel in distress. When Rachel's date shows up, a dejected Ross is watching from upstairs, unbeknownst to Rachel, and he doesn't come down. The video is the first time that Rachel has seen what Ross did for her, and she realizes not only how much Ross loved her but for how long. As present-day Ross watches, he is devastated.

The shooting script called for Ross to sit there stunned as Rachel comes over and kisses him. In rehearsal, I staged it so that Rachel walks slowly across the room after seeing the video. The show's creators and co-writers Marta Kauffman and David Crane said, "Isn't it better if it happens quickly?" I said, "No. Ross wouldn't just sit there and watch that moment. It's too humiliating. Ross would be so embarrassed and would try to get out of there as quickly as possible." Ross tries to stop the video, and when the friends won't let him, he makes his way to the apartment door.

I fought for that moment, because it builds the tension. You don't know what she's going to do. As a stunned and emotionally moved Rachel takes the long walk across the apartment, the audience is on tenterhooks, trying to imagine what she'll do when she gets there. When she grabs Ross's face and kisses him on the mouth, the audience responds with intense applause. That marked the beginning of the second-greatest on-again, off-again romance in television history.

You saw the chemistry between Ross and Rachel from the very first scene of episode 1. He has just split up with his wife, who realized she's a lesbian, and is about to get divorced; she comes into the coffee shop in a wedding dress. He wonders whether he will ever find someone else:

ROSS

What if you only get one woman and that's it? Unfortunately, in my case there was only one woman, for her.

JOEY

What are you talkin' about? One woman. That's like saying there's only one flavor of ice cream for you. Let me tell you something, Ross. There's lots of flavors of ice cream out there. There's rocky road, and cookie dough, and bing! cherry vanilla. You could get 'em with jimmies or nuts, or whipped cream. This is the best thing that ever happened to you. Welcome back to the world. Grab a spoon!

ROSS

I honestly don't know if I'm hungry or horny.

CHANDLER

Then stay out of my freezer.

Later, Ross is alone with Rachel:

ROSS

Listen. Do you think—and try not to let my intense vulnerability
become any kind of a factor here—but do you think it would be
okay if I asked you out sometime, maybe?

RACHEL

(with a smile) Yeah, maybe.

ROSS

Okay. Okay, maybe I will. 'Night.

Wanting something physical to correspond to the emotional cli-
max of Ross beginning his new life, I told Schwimmer to grab whatever he was looking at. He picked up an Oreo cookie and split it
with Rachel. Ross still has half the cookie in his hand and pops it in
his mouth to symbolize a great moment. As he leaves the apartment, he tells Monica, "I just grabbed a spoon." After the pilot,
NBC president Don Ohlmeyer sent me a framed picture of the
words "I grabbed a spoon."

Sam and Diane were a decade older than Ross and Rachel. It
was thirties versus twenties. Sam and Diane were also polar oppo-
sites. There was much more innocence to work and play with in the
Ross-and-Rachel dynamic: They were more insecure. Ross and Rachel came from the same Long Island town. They didn't have the
cultural or intelligence gap.

With Sam and Diane, I also began a tradition of having people in
love slap each other out of a mix of intense anger and affection. In
their initial breakup in the last episode of season 2, "I'll Be Seeing
You," as soon as Diane slaps Sam's face, he slaps her back. The ca-
dence of them rapidly slapping each other was funny. Diane esca-
lates by grabbing Sam's nose, which he reciprocates. They both
drop to the floor, as neither of them will let go.

The best sight gags have to be choreographed. The slaps and noses were there. We developed a rationale to get Sam and Diane out in front of the bar, so the audiences, both in studio and at home, could see all the physical business. The positions of their hands were set so that each was holding the other's hand that was holding the other's nose, so they could control the pressure and it didn't hurt too much. For a larger stunt, the actual methodology is developed by a stunt coordinator. Coach didn't fall down the stairs without a stunt coordinator. When Diane flipped Sam onto the pool table, we started out with the director's vision, but then we needed to understand the best and safest way of doing it to get what we wanted from the scene combined with the funniest perspective for the audience. Later on in the series, when Sam dreams about having sex with Rebecca (more on her soon), I turned the couch in the office around, so the audience would see the scene from a different perspective.

We also used subtle physicality when Diane makes her final departure from *Cheers* and goes up the stairs. After Diane leaves the bar, Sam runs after her and hesitates, stopping at the front door. As he walks to the back of the room, Diane hesitates as well. All we see are her legs on the outdoor staircase. She can't see Sam and he can't see her. Her legs turn and she goes back up the stairs and is gone. A heartbreaking moment with no dialogue.

One of the tenets of screwball comedy is the romantic triangle, the third character who frustrates the romance of the protagonists. The best actor to ever provide the third side of the romantic triangle was Ralph Bellamy. He came between Cary Grant and Irene Dunne in *The Awful Truth* and between Cary and Rosalind Russell in *His Girl Friday*. Tall, handsome, and well-meaning, Bellamy's characters were cursed out of the gate because they couldn't compete with the chemistry that was already there, and he'd invariably lose the romance to Cary.

We used that device during the third season of *Cheers*, bringing in Kelsey Grammer as Dr. Frasier Crane, Diane's new paramour and foil for Sam. Initially, Kelsey didn't poll well. The audience hated him, and rightfully so, because they were invested in the Sam–Diane relationship. But the moment the Frasier–Diane relationship ended, the audience fell in love with him.

As soon as Frasier was single, we created a romantic interest for him in the even-more-uptight psychiatrist Dr. Lilith Sternin (Bebe Neuwirth). Glen Charles had seen Bebe perform in a Julius Monk–type revue, *Upstairs at O'Neal's*. Her name had come up earlier as a potential Diane, and Glen brought her up for Lilith. After her first appearance, everyone knew that we had to bring her character back. She was hysterically funny and had amazing chemistry with Kelsey. We were not only lucky to find fresh faces and new talent when we had to, we found people who were brilliant in a different way from what we already had and who could have romantic chemistry with our actors.

Frasier and Lilith's relationship was an exaggeration of Sam and Diane's. They were a one-joke couple, but it got a laugh every time. From the outset, they cut at each other. And they were wildly physically attracted to each other. Lilith wore her hair pulled back in a severe bun. The moment she literally and figuratively let her hair down, she became beautiful and irresistible to Frasier. Their chemistry, wrapped in their intellect, became palpable.

While you feel the Sam and Diane connections in your stomach and in your loins, the Frasier and Lilith relationship is more high class, more intelligent sex. It's a very stylized joke, a dollop of romance, light and frothy. It's atypical because they're two cerebral people who live inside their own heads. As Frasier says, they behave "like rutting pigs," but it's still highbrow. Frasier and Lilith were referencing Marcel Proust, William Butler Yeats, and John Donne. They were playing Noël Coward. We did it a little bit with Diane, but with Frasier and Lilith it was always underplayed:

LILITH

Query: If I had a problem and needed to talk to someone
about it, would it be perpetuating a stereotype to actually
select a bartender?

SAM

Well, that depends.

LILITH

On what?

SAM

On what you just said.

After Bebe became a regular, we developed Frasier and Lilith. *Cheers* was the highest-class drawing-room comedy on television. It was better than anything in the movies. A studio executive said to me, "You can't do Schopenhauer jokes!" But Schopenhauer was getting big laughs.

LILITH

Frasier is not an easy man to live with. He's obsessively compulsive about neatness. The sex is good, but he pouts unless you compliment his performance. Fortunately, his male ego can be satisfied with a simple "Thank you, Conan."

We actually had to downplay Bebe's beauty and talent. Her Lilith had to be severe to be funny. We also had to tone down her skills as a Juilliard-trained dancer. In one episode, where Lilith is trying to seduce Sam to get even with Frasier, she starts dancing on a bed. Bebe was terrific. I had to remind her, "Bebe, you have to dance badly. Lilith has to dance awkwardly." She was breaking character. Once her character was fully developed, Lilith could interact with other characters as well:

LILITH

Well, I'm off. I don't know what the future holds. Whatever happens, I only hope I can realize my full potential, to acquire things the old Lilith never had.

CARLA
Like a body temperature.

LILITH
Very good, Carla. Incidentally, I've taken your little wisecracks for a few years now, you hideous gargoyle, and if you ever open that gateway to hell you call a mouth in my direction again, I'll snap off your extremities like dead branches and feed them to you at gunpoint! . . . God, that felt good!

Another type of romantic pairing is the older couple, the one that has been together forever. They can finish each other's sentences, and each sentence ends with something nasty. They love and can't stand each other at the same time. The best versions have been William Frawley and Vivian Vance as Fred and Ethel Mertz on *I Love Lucy*, and Morey Amsterdam and Rose Marie as Buddy Sorrell and Sally Rogers, Rob Petrie's co-writers, on *The Dick Van Dyke Show*, a couple even though they weren't married. We don't expect them to ever break up.

On *The Millers*, Greg Garcia wrote a great script for Beau Bridges and Margo Martindale as Tom and Carol, a couple who have been together for decades when Tom announces that they're done in front of their son, Nathan (Will Arnett):

NATHAN
Dad, what are you doing?

TOM
Leaving.

CAROL
Tom, stop it. I'm not crawling back to Debbie's house.

TOM

You're not coming with me.

CAROL

Excuse me?

TOM

Forty-three years of marriage. Forty-three years of blah blah blah. And every time I brought up divorce, you convinced me we had to stay together. For the children first. First, they were too young. They needed both their parents. Then they were in college. And that kind of turmoil could disrupt their education. Then after they got married themselves. God forbid we set a bad example, showed them that divorce is an option. Well, apparently it is an option. This one gets divorced after three years just because he wants to be happy? Guess what? I want to be happy!

NATHAN

Come on, Dad, you can't do this. You've been married for forty-three years.

TOM

Let's call it thirty-three, since we haven't had sex in ten.

Two of the most memorable romantic couples in sitcom history are ones you saw only one member of. On *Cheers*, there was Norm's never-seen wife, Vera. Norm would grouse about Vera but really adored her. In "The Peterson Principle," Norm is turned down for a promotion because Vera didn't "mesh" with the other executives' wives. He stands up to his boss and quits. As he speaks to Vera on the phone, he refuses to tell her the truth:

NORM

Listen, honey, no point beating around the bush here: I didn't get the promotion. In fact, I just got so mad at the guy, I just went ahead and quit. Yes, yes, they did. They gave me a reason, hun. What they said was that I'm just not the right man for the job. You just face it, honey, I'm a loser. I don't know why you don't just go and pack up your bags and leave me. Hello? That's very funny. Listen, sweetie, I have something I have to tell you. Even on a terrible day like today, I feel like I'm the luckiest man in the world because I married you. . . .

I don't know. I've had two, three, maybe. I'll talk to you later.

For eleven seasons on *Will & Grace,* Karen (Megan Mullally) was married to the never-seen, obscenely wealthy, and morbidly obese Stanley Walker. The most we ever got to see of Stan was his arm. Anything large or scary becomes larger or scarier in the mind's eye. Karen and Stan met at the Statue of Liberty, "when he was just a huddled mass yearning to eat free." Karen says, "There are one hundred reasons we shouldn't be together, and 7.3 billion reasons we should."

KAREN

One pound of prosciutto, one pound of mortadella, five types of cheese from mild to stinky, a big vat of coleslaw.

JACK

You ordering a deli platter?

KAREN

Having phone sex with Stan.

Audiences also connect with couples who are offbeat and wacky. On *Taxi,* we found a lid for Latka's pot. Carol Kane was brought in to play Simka, Latka's girlfriend and later wife. Carol had been in *Hester Street* and *The Last Detail.* No one knew she had comedy chops. That winsome breathy sound is her real voice. She had a wonderful way of talking and put out a sweet, innocent, and crazy energy. She was *meshugenah* (Yiddish for crazy). We used that crazy as much as we could. She was an amazing foil for Andy, who taught her how to speak his gibberish.

On *3rd Rock from the Sun,* John Lithgow and Jane Curtin were a step above screwball. They were interplanetary. *3rd Rock* was a high-concept story, aliens on earth, something I would normally not take on except for the fact that I really wanted to work with John Lithgow, who was able to successfully adapt to series television after movies. We had initially sought John to play Frasier Crane on *Cheers* (I mention this for no other reason than to piss off Kelsey Grammer, whom I love).

The literally out-of-this-world premise was that aliens come to observe earth and take human form. They are trying to figure out humanity and, not surprisingly, usually get it wrong.

John played Dick Solomon, the leader of the group, flanked by: Tommy (Joseph Gordon-Levitt), a genius in the body of a horny teenager; Sally (Kristen Johnston), a woman for the first time ("pieces of flesh, dangling off of us. Everything that isn't strapped down jiggles around"); and the eccentric Harry (French Stewart), the family burden ("every family has one").

John was totally committed. He jumped into the character with both feet and hands. I directed two pilots and the last episode of the first season. We had a ball.

In the first pilot, Dick falls in love with an earthling and decides to remain on earth. ABC rejected it, claiming that it was too outrageous and not funny enough, that Dick's character was too moon-eyed in love. Tom Werner and Marcy Carsey financed a second pilot and hired Jane Curtin as Dick's new romantic interest, Dr. Mary Albright. After watching the second pilot, ABC passed again. NBC called me and asked about it. I told them to grab it.

It was a hit out of the box. The beauty of Dick Solomon's budding romance is full of mistaken social and cultural mores as he falls for Mary.

In the (second) pilot, "Brains and Eggs," Dick and Mary get off on the wrong foot:

MARY

I must admit, when I first met you, I was attracted to your
flamboyant nature and big head.

DICK

Thanks, because I almost went with the smaller one.

MARY

Even though I am drawn to genius. This is a small office, and you
are behaving like a big hose monkey.

DICK

You're not so bad yourself, woman.

At a faculty party that evening at Dean Sumner's home, Dick attempts to make peace. After Mary applies lipstick, he kisses her on the mouth. She slaps his face, then kisses him back. He tries to reciprocate what he believes is a romantic ritual, so he slaps her. They slap each other again, then she kisses him again. They both swoon. When Dick leaves the home, Mrs. Sumner kisses him goodbye. Believing he now knows new socially appropriate behavior, he slaps her.

If the premise of aliens on earth wasn't wacky enough, in "See Dick Run," Dick is replaced by an alien leader who looks exactly like him. Other than my short stint on *The Patty Duke Show,* I never indulged in the sitcom trope of the double or the evil twin. But here I was with Evil Dick, and the brilliantly funny John stepped out of his already out-of-this-world character. Evil Dick is sent to complete the aliens' mission with "ruthless efficiency":

MARY

Is everything all right?

EVIL DICK

Oh, everything's perfect. For the last six months, I've been a
bumbling fool. As of right now, that's over. I only care about one
thing now, and that's pleasure. Yours and mine.

When she tries to slap him, he blocks her slap and kisses her
hard. She swoons. "You let Daddy drive," he says. I didn't create
slapping, but I definitely embellished it. It became a signature piece
later for Jack and Karen on *Will & Grace*. I never had too many
slaps. I always knew when to stop. It was Punch and Judy; it was
totally unexpected. I'm not sure whether slapping would be acceptable today, as a form of affection or anything else.

In sitcoms, less conventionally attractive couples become beautiful to the audience when they're falling in love. Watching characters who wonder whether they will ever find love and then find
it—it's a through line to the heart. The audience sees the characters
through the affectionate prism of the way they see each other, form-
ing an even more intense connection.

Nerds are not inherently funny; they're just awkward. Good
writing is what elevates them. Most people think that they're unlike
nerd characters and so are free to laugh at them, when they actually
are not all that dissimilar. On *The Big Bang Theory*, Johnny Galecki's
Leonard falls for Penny (Kaley Cuoco), literally the beautiful woman
next door who's out of his league. The nerdy characters yearn for
love and acceptance. They never talk about it, but the audience is
constantly feeling it.

On *Taxi*, "Blind Date" introduced Angela Matusa (Suzanne
Kent), a character based on the real-life story of Ed. Weinberger
hitting on the woman who was the voice of an answering service.
Alex has such great conversations with Angela that he asks her out.
Their actual dinner doesn't go that well:

ALEX

What do you still got your coat on for?

ANGELA

The management requested it. Aren't you having
a good time anymore?

ALEX

I once went out with a girl who pulled a knife on me, robbed me,
and threw me out of a car on the New Jersey Turnpike. I have to
think about that now as a medium date.

Alex tries to reconcile with Elaine how "the hour I had with her
on the phone was one of the greatest conversations I've ever had. A
witty, bright, sensitive girl who came to the door disappeared." He
confronts Angela, telling her he wants to get to know her better:

ANGELA

You want me to open up? Would that make you happy? Make you
feel like you did your good deed for the day? Okay, but then you
better plan on sticking around, because I'm not standing here
alone with my insides on the floor while you walk out feeling you
did the poor fat girl some big favor by helping her get in touch
with her feelings. You want to be a hero, then be prepared to stick
around for the rest of the war, okay?

ALEX

Maybe I will, but can we start slower, like when we went to high
school? Then we'll work up to your insides on the floor.

The episode was so well received that we did "The Lighter Side
of Angela Matusa," where Angela, having lost one hundred pounds,
returns to date Alex. "One particular man I wanted to attract who is
nice to me. He treated me like a person even when I wasn't feeling
like one." When Alex explains that he doesn't feel the same way, she
angrily says, "If I can lose a hundred pounds for you, maybe I can
lose a hundred fifty for somebody with a better nose."

Louie De Palma's character was so rotten that when he got to sleep with a beautiful woman who'd had too much to drink, Elaine said to him, "It's so sad that she mixed drugs and alcohol and spent the night with you . . . when most people only die." We were careful about moments of redemption and humanizing the character of Louie, but when we were able to, it was both funny and poignant. In "Louie and the Nice Girl," the second-season opener, Louie is bragging to Alex and the other cabbies about his wild sex life with his new girlfriend, recurring character Zena Sherman (Danny's real-life partner, Rhea Perlman), punctuating his innuendo with "heh, heh, heh."

But the sweet Zena asks Alex's advice, because Louie has so far refused to touch her sexually:

ZENA

We've been seeing each other for five weeks, and being normal, healthy adults, it's natural we'd have some physical involvement. So why haven't we? I mean, you know Louie—why won't he touch me?

ALEX

You mean he hasn't touched you?

ZENA

I can't even get him to hold my hand!

(Louie seeks Alex's guidance, telling him that Zena was his first.)

ALEX

She's not your first. Everybody knows that when you were driving a cab and tourists wanted to find out where the women were, you didn't tell them, you took them, and whenever possible, you joined them.

LOUIE

Hold on. I don't want you to get the wrong idea. I've had my share
of women and then some, and I've always left them happy. I can't
tell you how many told me, Louie, this is crazy.
I should pay you! . . .

ALEX

Zena is not your first girl. She's your first nice girl!

LOUIE

Yeah, and I can't handle it. I was brought up believing that there
was nice girls and girls you had fun with, and there was no
mixing of the two. I like Zena, I really do, but I can't
even bring myself to kiss her.

ALEX

Well, there's only one thing you can do, Louie. Break up with this
lovely warm person who obviously feels a great deal for you and
spend the rest of your life floating through meaningless affairs
with cheap strangers. You'll have to pay to satisfy your disgusting
physical lust

LOUIE

Great advice!

(Louie goes to Zena's apartment.)

ZENA

You think I'm too good for you.

LOUIE

Nah, you crazy? It's just that you're too good, period. I'm used to
another kind of woman. . . .

ZENA
You know, all those nights when you left me at my doorstep, I'd go
into my bedroom and cry.

LOUIE
Take me to the place you cry.

Zena goes into the bedroom. Louie closes the door and holds it so Zena can't come out. As they are about to break up, Zena asks for one last kiss. The kiss renders Louie's entire body stiff as a board. I had Rhea bend Danny across the top of the couch and kiss him. The scene ends with Zena smiling evilly and saying, "Heh, heh, heh."

That episode was not just important to Louie and Zena. It was important to me as well. To be considered for an Emmy Award as a director, you have to submit an episode of any show from that season. A director can submit only one, where an actor can submit up to three for consideration. We submitted "Louie and the Nice Girl" for Emmy Award consideration. I thought I had a good chance, since *Taxi* had won Outstanding Comedy Series the prior season. In Jim Brooks's acceptance speech, he both thanked me and said that it was too bad I wasn't nominated.

This time, I was nominated, and the four shows I was up against were all *M*A*S*H* episodes. Even though two of those shows were directed by series stars Alan Alda and Harry Morgan, I was optimistic that the vote might be split. I don't remember what I said when I won the Emmy for Best Director. The next day, I walked onto the stage for rehearsal and was met by everyone, cast and crew, cheering for me. That award was my first and will always hold a place in my heart. It was a huge moment of affirmation. I was ecstatic. I still get that way. I'm tried and true and am an inveterate director. When they call your name, it's a sweet feeling. Heh, heh, heh.

My parents, Abe and
Ruth Burrows, with the
recently born me.

As a toddler, I was
already directing
carriage traffic.

At age four in
California, with Mom
in the background.

Part of the
Children's
Chorus at the
Metropolitan Opera.
I'm second from the
top left, in the
cowboy shirt.

My first head shot.

In the
Children's
Chorus of
Carmen.
I'm in the second
row with my head
resting on my hands,
perfecting my best
urchin look.

With Dad, outside the opera theater, where I performed in *La Bohème,* 1952.

Dad, me, and Laurie, Camp Walt Whitman, 1957.

Mom and me at Oberlin graduation, 1962.

My first car, a 1962 Chevy Impala convertible. A gift from my dad, who only bought me the front half.

At the Yale School of Drama, 1965. My first foray into acting, in a play by Plautus.

Submitted for your approval: Working with *Twilight Zone* creator Rod Serling, as he confronts me about my ponytail.

JAMES EDWARD BURROWS
41 Morton St.
New York, N.Y.   March 14, 1974

Dear Mary,

It's certainly been a long time and a lot of
water under the entertainment bridge. Lots
has happened to me since those fledgling days.
I bounced around stage managing for a while,
in fact I remember seeing you in L.A. when you
came to see Hugh O'Brien in CACTUS FLOWER. Then
I took a shot at directing in New York and liked
it so much that I have been doing it ever since.
As you may or may not know I ran the OFF BROADWAY
THEATRE in San Diego for two successful years
and my plan was to follow that with a try at
television.

A year ago I ran into Dave Davis. I got to
know him when I was Dialogue Director for the
Burl Ives TV series. He told me to come over
and visit on your set. I was about to do that
when my father, while directing a show in New
York, fell in the pit. So I went back to help
out. We finally got him out of the pit and I
spent the past year directing extensively for
stock and dinner theaters. In fact I have three
shows currently playing in and around Boston,
so one night you might want to drive up there.
I'll pay for the gas.

But I think it is time for me to attempt to
make a move, take a giant step, change keys,
or to put it delicately, get my ass in gear.
and involve myself in television. So I thought
I would go right to the top, to the best, and
ask if there is any opening, small or smaller,
that I can fill. I think my training in theater
will be valuable to me in TV. However, right
now nothing can be as valuable as being where
the action is and as far as I'm concerned the
action is where you are.

Thank you for being a good listener and a great
lady, and for bringing all of us such joy on
the television.

                    As ever,

41 Morton St.
New York, N.Y. 10014

The letter I wrote to
Mary Tyler Moore
(pre–Wite-Out) that
changed my life.

My first directing credit on
television, on *The Mary Tyler
Moore Show,* 1974.

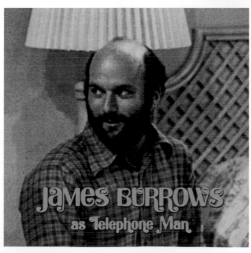

Directing and guest-starring on
my first episode of *Phyllis,* as the
Telephone Man.

I also played a repairman who pissed off the star of *The Bob Newhart Show.*

I adored Suzanne Pleshette from the first time I directed her on *The Bob Newhart Show* and in a few shows years later. Suzie had the greatest combination of the foulest mouth and the sweetest character.

My first TV movie, *More Than Friends,* with Rob Reiner and Penny Marshall.

The *Taxi* cast paying respect to me in the "Fantasy Borough" episode, where each of the drivers' fantasies are revealed.

The legendary Ruth Gordon won an Emmy for her guest-starring role on *Taxi*.

Glen Charles, me, and Les Charles, at the beginning of our eleven years behind the *Cheers* bar.

Having a great time on set with Teddy Danson and Shelley Long.

The *Cheers* cast on the attack. No actual directors were harmed during the making of this show.

My now-iconic and comfortable director shoes, which I wore only on shoot nights for years, until they were beyond repair. It was a combination of uniform and superstition to wear them, until I met my wife.

Rehearsing for the *Cheers* finale with my kids on hand.

With Kirstie Alley on the *Cheers* set. She was making sure I got my nap time.

Our *Cheers* guest stars ranged from television legends, famous politicians, actors, and singers, to Boston royalty: Johnny Carson.

Left to right: Speaker of
the House Tip O'Neill,
me, and
George Wendt.

Harry Connick Jr.

John Cleese.

At the *Cheers* final show party, watching the series finale with 84.4 million other people.

Brandon Tartikoff and Garry Trudeau at the *Cheers* bar for the last show. Hanging behind them is an Al Hirschfeld portrait of the Charles Brothers and me that the cast gave us as a final gift.

With my mentor and friend, Jay Sandrich, and his wife, Linda. I cast all my friends as extras.

Future director Maggie Burrows on the *Cheers* set. It was our first script conference.

Teddy Danson and me in a tearful goodbye as *Cheers* closed up shop.

Sharing a moment with Kelsey Grammer at the Emmy Awards after we both won for *Frasier*.

Future *Friends* stars together on the corporate jet for one last anonymous hurrah in Las Vegas.

Matty LeBlanc, me, my wife, Debbie, and daughter Paris at Wembley Stadium in England for a Bruce Springsteen concert.

Back at Central Perk at the HBO Max *Friends* reunion in 2021.

A *Friends* sandwich, with Matty LeBlanc and David Schwimmer.

With the incomparable Jennifer Aniston.

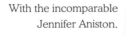

An All-Star Tribute to James Burrows aired on NBC in 2016. It was a joyful and emotional evening for me as friends and casts from many of the sitcoms I worked on shared some of their favorite stories.

Taxi's Danny DeVito, James L. Brooks, Judd Hirsch, Carol Kane, Tony Danza, Marilu Henner, me, Christopher Lloyd, and Rhea Perlman.

Cheers's John Ratzenberger, Rhea Perlman, George Wendt, Shelley Long, and Ted Danson, interviewed by Jane Lynch.

Friends's Lisa Kudrow, David Schwimmer, Courteney Cox, Matt LeBlanc, and Jennifer Aniston, interviewed by Andy Cohen.

Frasier's Jane Leeves, David Hyde Pierce, and Peri Gilpin.

Will & Grace's Sean Hayes, Megan Mullally, and Eric McCormack.

The Big Bang Theory's Kaley Cuoco, Simon Helberg, Johnny Galecki, and Jim Parsons.

Mike & Molly's Nyambi Nyambi, Katy Mixon, Reno Wilson, Melissa McCarthy, and Billy Gardell, interviewed by Jane Lynch.

Sitting on Norman Lear's lap with the *Will & Grace* team, reunited in 2016 to shoot a video supporting Hillary Clinton's presidential run. The chemistry was so great that we got the band back together for three more seasons. Top row, L–R: David Kohan, Eric McCormack, Sean Hayes, and Max Mutchnick; bottom row, L–R: Debra Messing, Norman, me, Megan Mullally, and Shelley Morrison.

Nothing up my sleeves: Giving direction on the first finale of *Will & Grace*.

Celebrating a win for Outstanding Comedy Series at the 2000 Emmys with the *Will & Grace* team. Megan and Sean won for Outstanding Supporting Actress and Actor, respectively.

Cheers, Part I

From its inception, *Cheers* was an endeavor between good friends to create a show about good friends. Our agent, Bob Broder, negotiated a development deal for the Brothers and me with Paramount Pictures. It was one of the first true financial partnerships between a studio and creators. We got a small office on the Paramount lot, and we started talking about what kind of show we wanted to do.

We all loved *Fawlty Towers,* a British show set at an English hotel. Monty Python co-founder John Cleese got the idea for the show after he and the Pythons stayed at a hotel on the English Riviera. Co-created with Connie Booth, John starred as Basil Fawlty, the glib and frustrated hotel manager, who dealt with a variety of demanding guests and eccentric staff.

We loved the outrageousness of it. I was not that big a fan of Monty Python, but I adored *Fawlty Towers*, because that character was so brazen. This was not sketch comedy. There were no dead parrots or Ministers of Silly Walks. Here, John was committed to one character and was a center for other characters.

I have always been a big fan of British humor. It's much more sophisticated, intellectual, and unexpected than most of American humor. There's an amazing blend of edginess and silliness. You don't know where they're going with it. You can say the worst curse words in the world and they sound refined. I went to see *Beyond the Fringe* on Broadway in 1962 with Dudley Moore, Peter Cook, Jonathan Miller, and Alan Bennett. (Side story: When I got to the box office with my tickets, the agent said my seats had been changed. I asked why, but they enigmatically wouldn't tell me. We'd been moved to the second row. Right before the show began, I looked back to see who had our tickets—it was President John F. Kennedy and First Lady Jackie Kennedy.) I watched the show and roared. I had never seen anything like this. I was so in love with these guys, who were Monty Python before Monty Python, maybe a tad more intellectual. They were way ahead of their time. At Yale Drama, when I had to do a required scene in acting class, I did one of their monologues: "I could have been a judge, but I never had the Latin." I got roars.

When it came to agreeing on an idea for the show, the Brothers and I knew that most everybody loved bars, especially sports bars. The Brothers had grown up in Las Vegas, and one of our earliest ideas was to set the bar in Barstow, California, because we thought about its proximity to Las Vegas and how the guests on the show would stop over in Barstow en route to or from Vegas. The main action would take place in the hotel bar. The structure was similar to that of *Fawlty Towers* in that the stories would walk into the bar.

Once we settled on a sports bar, we ruled out New York City as a setting, not only because it had been overdone but, more important, because it had multiple teams for the same sport. We considered Boston, Philadelphia, and Detroit, where local fans *really* love their sports and everyone roots for the same team. We decided on Boston because there was an accent and because it was such a distinctive town—working-class and cosmopolitan at the same time.

We spent two months going to bars to study the atmosphere. Glen called me one night at one A.M. my time, which was four A.M. in Boston, and said, "I found our place." It was the Bull and Finch, a bar located below street level. We used it as a model. The downstairs aspect gave us a lot of creative opportunity. We used the image of feet on the staircase a lot during the run.

Setting the show in a bar was controversial. We got a lot of letters from the Midwest, where temperance was the prime tenet of local towns. The network had some reservations because, until that time, everybody thought of a bar as a depressing place where helpless people went to drown their sorrows. We did everything we could to counteract that perception and the attendant trepidation and make Cheers look like a British pub where people from all strata of society came and had a good time together. Our goal was to make it a place that was welcome and safe, where people could feel comfortable and be excited to go to every Thursday night.

We tried to speak to the issue of alcoholism. There was a deliberate effort on our part to emphasize responsibility and safety on your way home. The pilot was the only episode where Norm gets so drunk that Coach has to take him home. Sam was a recovering alcoholic, somebody who didn't touch it anymore but was dealing with his demons every day.

In "Endless Slumper," Sam lends his lucky bottle cap to a fellow pitcher, Rick (Christopher McDonald), who's in a slump. Rick's slump ends, and when Sam asks for the cap back, Rick says he lost it in Kansas City. Sam explains its significance to Diane: "It's the cap off the last bottle of beer I ever drank, last anything I ever drank. I remember holding on to that bottle cap during some pretty rough nights. I'd wake up in the morning and I had its imprint in my palm.

I mean, it was flat because I was squeezing it so hard. When I was tempted to have a drink, sometimes I'd look at the bottle cap and it would stop me."

Sam is terrified that the loss of the cap will cause him to backslide into drinking again. In a tense and poignant moment, Sam, alone at the bar with a nervous and supportive Diane, takes the cap off another bottle of beer, pours himself a tall glass, and stares at it for what seems like an eternity. Tempted to drink from it, he finally skillfully slides the glass around the corner of the bar and decides to make the just-removed cap his new lucky bottle cap.

The only time Sam falls off the wagon is when Diane leaves him at the end of the second season and he goes on a bender. It's the only time he crashes and burns. When we found the opportunity to do something with a character that was unexpected, we did it. Sam is reacting to the love of his life running off with an artist. We thought that Diane leaving Sam would be too overwhelming for him because their connection was so deep. We felt Sam was very vulnerable at that point and would have a setback and the audience would understand that raw emotion and connect with it.

When it came to designing the set for *Cheers,* strong attention was paid to detail. More than anything else, we wanted class and warmth. We hired Richard Sylbert, an Academy Award–winning art director, to make the set look as beautiful and inviting as possible, since the characters were drinking what many in America still considered "devil's brew." Richard was very dignified, often decked out in a safari jacket while smoking a pipe. He had never worked on a television production before. He asked for a salary of five hundred dollars for every show produced, which was unheard of. I told Paramount, "Pay him, even if you have to take it out of our share."

His gorgeous design included a square bar, an office, and a pool room. It was twice the size of the original Bull and Finch. Richard devised a walkway behind Norm's seat leading to the bathrooms and pool table with a front piece on wheels, a quadrangle. We would roll it out of the way to get to Sam's office, and the restrooms would disappear. It was both beautiful and functional. On the *Cheers* set, there was linoleum on the floor to simulate tile. I had the faux tile laid from under the bar all the way to the audience, so they could feel like they were in the bar.

When it came to shooting, we liked the look of film. We were doing a bar, and we wanted it to look as pretty as possible. Film has a softness to it that videotape doesn't offer. It showcased the beauty of the all-wood bar and the warm colors. It was clearly not a dive. *Cheers* was filmed in five-minute-long segments with four cameras recording various angles simultaneously. Above the stage, sixty-four lights illuminated practically every area of the set. You couldn't have light stands on the floor for a multi-camera shoot. We had clean, high-quality close-ups. I put the camera everywhere to see what the set would look like. One shot from the camera run-through is in the pilot, from the pool room into the bar when Coach comes out of the bathroom. I looked at every camera angle—I like maximizing whatever set I'm on. We used the pool room, Sam's office, and the staircase to Melville's, the fancy restaurant upstairs, which you rarely saw.

We trained the cast early on to "ABR/ABF": Always Be Reacting/Always Be Funny; to always assume they were being watched. In theater, when one actor is speaking, another actor can take a beat. Here, there was a camera on everyone all the time. If we found a great reaction shot, we used it.

After the fourth episode, Les said, "Everything's too bright." I made a conscious effort to tone it down to make it moodier. There was no way I could shoot the bar to make it smaller or more intimate. It was a very appealing upscale neighborhood place. You could take a date there and they would be impressed.

The original Bull and Finch patrons hated us. We ruined their watering hole by making it famous and a place you had to visit when in Boston. Eddie Doyle was the bartender. Finally, he said, "Screw it, we're doing great business." Tom Kershaw owned the Hampshire House, the restaurant above. We had never asked him if we could use it for the exteriors. Tom was a Harvard MBA and owned the entire building. When we finally asked, he said, "Yes, on one condition—that you pay me a dollar a year." He knew what the merchandising revenue would be if the show was a hit. He changed the name of the Bull and Finch to Cheers, and he sold shirts. He was careful to put "Boston" under the Cheers logo, so as not to run afoul of Paramount's copyright. The bar is still open under the Cheers name.

We realized that we needed one other critical element, a couple at the center of it all, so we tried for a Spencer Tracy–Katharine Hepburn dynamic. The earliest incarnation had Sam Harrison, a former linebacker for the Boston Patriots, as a bartender in Boston, with a female boss. The idea was that this ladies' man has to work for a woman. We thought we could get a lot of comedy out of that scenario and from the ensuing tension. The Brothers never wrote that version of the script. Instead, they developed a funnier, more poignant relationship.

When we pitched *Cheers* to the network, we described it as "a light-beer commercial," because back then there were all those Miller Lite commercials with "Marvelous Marv" Throneberry, Bubba Smith, Bob Uecker, and Mickey Spillane. The network loved it. Broder made the first of two significant deals in my career, with then–NBC president Fred Silverman and Michael Zinberg, who had produced *The Bob Newhart Show* and taught me a lot about cameras and was now NBC's vice president of production and development. They bought the show based on our collective pedigrees. Broder's deal was a two-for-one. Like a free-throw shot in basketball, we were given two shots to score once. We would get to shoot two pilots and they would have to put one on the air. We never got to any second ideas. The first one worked.

Fred then left for CBS and was succeeded by Grant Tinker, which couldn't have been better for us because of his mentorship and his philosophy about supporting creativity and innovation. The other unsung hero of *Cheers* was Brandon Tartikoff. He was the youngest entertainment president of a major network when he took over the NBC reins in 1980 at thirty.

NBC was dead last behind its network competitors when Brandon got the job. In a three-way network race for audience, the joke was that NBC was number four. Even Johnny Carson, whose *Tonight Show* generated a third of NBC's revenue, was reportedly in talks to move to ABC. Brandon's work was cut out for him.

Back then you couldn't get the weekly show-ratings results online, so Brandon would call me every Friday morning with the Thursday-evening numbers. When we had less than a 20 percent share of the audience, he would always follow the news with, "Don't worry." He sent us a note: "Would you want to live in a world where *Cheers* only gets a 19 share?"

Brandon was smart, funny, and one of the sweetest people I've ever known. He had a "television brain." He came up with the idea "MTV police," which evolved into *Miami Vice*. He was one of the few people in the business who understood the writers, who they were, and what they were trying to do. When he gave a note, we didn't react like it came from "another network guy." We responded with the respect accorded to someone who knew what he was doing.

We became close and fast friends. We both loved sports. We went to baseball games and Super Bowls. We were both newly married and had young children. Our kids played together.

Brandon later became president of NBC and went on to run Paramount. He was a "television whore," in the best possible way. He grew up watching and loving it. He appeared on *Cheers, Night Court, Saved by the Bell,* and *Saturday Night Live*. Like the studio moguls of the 1930s and '40s, who were as famous as their actors, he was one of the first network executives of the modern era that people recognized on sight. We lost him to Hodgkin's disease way too young, at forty-eight. I still miss him.

Grant Tinker's philosophy was: "Respect the audience. Don't look at them as alien beings." He told his people, "You're young. You're well educated. You love this medium. Why don't you start doing programming that would make you race home across the freeways at night to get to your television sets because you had to see it? Start thinking about the audience as you. What do you want to see?"

Glen, Les, and I sat in our small office for a while and hashed out ideas, characters, and structure. During rewrites of any show I'd been on before, there was always someone taking shorthand, collecting all the various comments, but the Brothers didn't need anyone else. They were able to remember everything that was said and then revise the script. They had it all in their heads. They were gifted at doing a very long buildup, and it all paid off with a quick punch line. Five years apart in age, they spoke very softly and had an almost twin-like language in which they communicated with each other. Over time, I cracked the code and learned what they were saying and how to communicate in that language. Definitely more important in my life than learning Latin.

Also, if you're in a writers' room, you must have a great memory for movies, theater, television, books, and other social and cultural references that you can draw on. In that environment you're pitching suggestions like "Why can't we do this scene from *Citizen Kane* only twist it a little bit." The variation on the theme is what great writing, particularly sitcom writing, is all about. Taking it and making it your own. Glen and Les have a remarkable facility for remembering lines.

They could even play with each other creatively, if not kindly. In an interview, they were each asked about the most sentimental moment in their careers. Les poignantly recalled a letter he'd received from a woman whose child was hospitalized with a serious illness, from which she recovered. During a life-threatening twelve hours, she was at wits' end with worry. An episode of *Cheers* got her through the roughest moments of her life. Without missing a beat, Glen turned to his brother and said, "Now I can tell you. I wrote that let-ter." (He didn't.)

The Brothers went off to write the script. Two months later they sent me the first draft. I read it and couldn't believe it. I told them, "You brought radio back to television!" It was smart and literate. We knew that if the story felt real and real characters were introduced, the jokes would come. The thinking was that when people got to know the characters, they would be inherently funny later on. If a joke presented itself, they went there. There was also a big differ-ence between the twenty-six minutes of time allotted then versus the twenty-two minutes of modern sitcoms. Those extra minutes of real estate were huge in terms of allowing story and jokes to breathe.

Unlike *Taxi,* which had a dark look, *Cheers* was intentionally bright and welcoming. Also unlike *Taxi,* the characters wanted to be there. *Cheers* was initially not a very physical show. People came in and sat down and talked. The lead was incredibly charming, and complementing him were characters not seen on television before: the intellectual blonde; the crusty waitress; the good-hearted and dull-witted coach; the mailman who thought he knew everything; and the guy everyone knew—Norm.

Despite his incredible skills as an actor, Teddy Danson didn't have to act at being a good person. He was and still is the sweetest guy in the world. He was a rock-solid anchor. Because Teddy didn't look like a football player, Sam Harrison became former Boston Red Sox relief pitcher Sam "Mayday" Malone, based on Bill Lee, nick-named "The Spaceman," who played for the Sox and then the Expos. Instead of dressing up Teddy in a baseball uniform and pho-tographing him to simulate his ballplaying years, we used a picture of the similarly tall and lanky Jim Lonborg, the first Sox pitcher to win the Cy Young Award, who also later pitched for Milwaukee and Philly.

Sam Malone was "the best short reliever to ever play the game," who once "struck out Cash, Kaline, and Freehan with the tying run on second," and who lost his career and fortune due to alcoholism and wound up with one last investment, a local bar. The Brothers came back to me with Diane Chambers as an erudite graduate student, which was just genius.

Teddy Danson was not a jock. Teddy was a farceur from Carnegie Mellon. But he was a good-enough actor to learn how to look like a ballplayer. He improved a lot over the first couple of shows. I took him to his first baseball game. The St. Louis Cardinals were playing the Los Angeles Dodgers. I knew the engineer for the Cardinals' TV and radio broadcasting from when we both worked in San Diego, and my theater bought advertising with the Padres. He arranged for us to meet the famous sports announcer Jack Buck (whose wife, Carole, was in the original company of *How to Succeed in Business*).

The storyline of the pilot, "Give Me a Ring Sometime," has Diane on her way to get married in Barbados. She comes into the bar with her fiancé for a quick drink. He tells her to wait for him while he goes to visit his ex-wife and retrieve his grandmother's antique gold wedding ring from her. Diane waits. She meets Sam. You can see right away they're meant for each other. There are a couple of permutations of the fiancé coming back, including not being able to get the ring from the ex-wife. He finally comes back and says he's going back with the ex-wife. Diane is left alone, and Sam hires her.

We also introduced Carla, Coach, Norm, and Cliff. We had sent Teddy and Nicky to bartending school so that their skills would look realistic on camera. There weren't a lot of fancy drinks made at the bar, just beer and liquor poured from spouted bottles, and lots of lemons, limes, and onions being sliced. Teddy and Nicky created their own pieces of business themselves.

Shelley was a good-looking comedienne. She played that pretentiousness so well—a little strident but never over the line. She could do a joke or comment or smirk on the boorish behavior of the guys. Diane was always trying to educate them, including and especially Sam. That was her goal. She never belittled anyone for lack of smarts. When they didn't understand something, she explained it to them. She got them to dress up in tuxedos and took them to the opera. That tableau was so funny—each time I panned the camera, somebody was sleeping.

When Shelley got pregnant, we thought about introducing that into the storyline, possibly with someone else as the father, which would have made Sam more protective and paternal. If Sam was the father, we would have married them off quickly, because that was appropriate at the time. We decided not to do anything about it, so I shot Shelley standing behind the bar or holding a tray or a towel to conceal her belly.

There are archetypal characters that become staples in sitcom casts. You have the sweet, dull-witted character who supports the center, ranging from Ted Baxter and Reverend Jim to Coach and Woody. The character who is different from everyone else—the alien—gets the same response as the center. The alien is also a way to tell a story. In the *Taxi* pilot, John is in the cab with Alex as he explains the backstory of the characters. In *Cheers*, Diane is the alien, often above the other characters. Her lofty attitude fosters interactions and revelations. That's called "laying pipe." You have to tell the story without looking like you're telling the story. You're not supposed to see the strings. I marvel at that skill writers possess. When I was writing, you not only saw the strings, you saw the entire ball of twine. I wasn't able to disguise the story or the plot.

The skill set also requires the ability to craft a tease. You want to keep the audience watching, so you deliberately hold something out that the audience expects but isn't sure of. Larry David is great at that. On *Curb Your Enthusiasm,* he so meticulously constructs and develops the story that when he wraps up, you think, "That's why he did it." The wonderful nature of the show is how the seemingly disparate plots realign and coalesce at the end.

Twenty-five years after a baseball rolled through Boston Red Sox first baseman Bill Buckner's legs in the bottom of the tenth of game 6 of the 1986 World Series at Shea Stadium and Buckner was unfairly blamed for the Bosox losing the series, Larry created a *Curb* episode in which Larry makes a game-costing error during a softball game in Central Park. He later runs into a consoling Buckner at an autograph show. As the two walk up Park Avenue, they run into fans who still blame Bill. The episode ends with Larry outside a New York apartment building on fire. A mother is holding her baby out a window, with firefighters down below holding a jumping sheet, ready to catch the baby. The mother lets go of her baby, who lands in the sheet and bounces back into the air. In what can only happen in Larry's *Curb* world, a passing by Buckner dives and catches the baby. It was as poignant as it was funny.

When it came to casting, we got very lucky. After the arduous task of finding Sam and Diane was completed, we looked to round out the ensemble. The Brothers had a coach in high school named Ernie Pantusso. That became Coach's name. Coach was based on several baseball figures: Yogi Berra, Sparky Anderson, Don Zimmer, people who are very charming and funny without meaning to be. There's something about baseball that breeds this philosophical and eccentric approach to life.

We saw a number of actors for the role of Coach, including Sid Caesar. Sid thought he already had the part when he came in to audition. We decided he wasn't right for Coach. His persona was too much for the show. We were concerned that his famous presence would make the rest of the cast look too unknown. Genius that he was, the balance would have been out of whack. Also, we thought Sid would always require a large part written for him. *Cheers* was never going to serve any one character; the stories were going to drive how big each part was.

We had seen Nicholas Colasanto in *Raging Bull* and *Fat City*. Like Ed Asner, Gavin MacLeod, and Ted Knight, he played mostly tough-guy parts and had never done comedy before. He was also a director. Nicky had a bad heart and was already sick when we hired him, but he never told us how serious his condition was. Nicky's audition blew us away. He could play dull-witted, funny, sweet, and innately wise at the same time.

COACH
(answering phone)
Hello, Cheers. Yeah, just a sec. Is there an Ernie Pantusso here?

SAM
That's you, Coach.

COACH
Speaking!

Coach was the father figure on the show, listening to everyone's problems, but Nicky played him like a twelve-year-old. Coach held the record of being hit in the head by more pitches than anyone in the major leagues. He acted as if the blood had trouble getting to his brain. He was a sage who nurtured Sam from double-A ball in Pawtucket through the major leagues, and now Sam takes care of him. In "Sam's Women," a former patron, Leo (Donnelly Rhodes), comes into Cheers, desperate to get advice from Gus, the deceased former owner and bartender. "You got troubles? You take them to Gus, he straightens them out just like that!"

LEO
Gus is gone. Nobody can replace Gus. Gus had all the answers!

CARLA
All but one.

LEO
What am I gonna do without Gus?

COACH
Leo, will you stop it? And ever since you came through that door, it's been Gus this and Gus that. And I'm fed up with it. I'm taking you on, Leo. You and all your problems. Now, come on, sit down!

LEO

I don't know . . .

COACH

Sit! Lay the problems on the bar.

LEO

Last semester, my son comes home from college with his new
fiancée, who's black.

COACH

I've been thinking about that, and it's a tough one.

LEO

But there's more.

COACH

It's a problem of communication. Here's what you do when you
get home. You sit the kids down and you say to your boy—what's
your boy's name?

LEO

Ron.

COACH

Right. Ron. What's Ron's fiancée's name?

LEO

Rick.

COACH

Rick. You say, Rick—Ron? Rick and Ron?

NORM
Suck it up, Coachie!

COACH
Well, Leo, if you're that unhappy about it, just throw them out and tell them you never want to see them again.

LEO
I can't do that. I love the kid. Oh, I see what you're saying. If I can't accept the kid the way he is, I'll lose him.

COACH
Boy, that's good.

LEO
But when you put it that way, what choice do I have? Thanks, Coach. You know, you're not Gus, but you're not bad.

COACH
Leo, even Gus isn't Gus anymore.

LEO
Thanks, Coach.

NORM
You really took him.

COACH
Took him? I had him for breakfast!

Nicky would often have trouble remembering his lines, so he would tape pieces of dialogue all over the bar. Sam once asked Coach, "What do you think about this?" Nicky responded, "You're sitting on my lines." Nicky kept a picture of Native American chief

Geronimo in his dressing room. After he passed, we put it on the upstage wall in the bar, to keep his memory alive. In the closing scene of the finale, before walking offstage, Sam adjusts the picture in one last homage to Coach.

I've always been careful about breaking the fourth wall. We would never do it in a show where we were telling a story. You don't want to destroy your credibility by acknowledging that there's an audience. It compromises the quality. I like to keep the proscenium out of respect for the audience and keep them in front of the curtain.

Having said that, *Cheers* was the first sitcom to create multi-episode story arcs, which are now a staple. It required a lot more effort and devices to catch up viewers who had missed the prior episode, including breaking the fourth wall. Coach's less-than-smart character was perfect to get any audience member caught up:

COACH

Hi, my name is Ernie Pantusso. I'm supposed to tell you what happened last week on *Cheers*. Well, I'm good at explaining things, because I used to be a baseball coach. Here, let me illustrate. Now, you may remember me from my playing days in the minors; I still hold the league record for the most times hit by a pitch. That's as good as a hit. Anyway. Where was I? Last week on *Cheers*, this fella Semenko came into the bar. He's a very famous artist. While he was here, this Semenko fella saw Diane and he got an idea. He decided to paint her picture. He thought there was something special about her puss. Diane loved the idea, 'cause she'd heard of this fella and thought he was good. As you all know, Diane's very smart. Well, the trouble is, when Sam met this artist, Semenko, he hated him. He told him he couldn't paint Diane's picture and he told him to get outta the place. Semenko started to go and Sam left the room. Diane pretended to go along, but then Diane went behind Sam's back. Hey, wait a minute. This is starting to look like a diagram for our old double steal. As soon as the pitcher goes into his windup, the runner on first breaks for second and the runner on second breaks for third, or if second and third are occupied, the runner on second breaks for third and the man on third goes home. The batter hits the ball to the opposite field, which means the fielder's play is at home plate. Wait a minute. I'm sorry. This isn't a double steal at all. These are directions to my daughter's house. No, I'm wrong again. She moved. Or did she? Anyway, Diane was going behind Sam's back. . . .

The smartest, most insightful thing Coach ever said was in "Peterson Crusoe," where Norm drops everything and announces that he's going off to live in Bora Bora. When Diane says, "You know, it took a great deal of courage for Norman to do what he did. I admire and envy him. He has heeded Thoreau, who admonished us that, quote, 'Life is frittered away by detail. Simplify, simplify.'" Coach says, "Why didn't he just say one 'simplify'?"

Dave Davis was the first person to recommend an audience run-through on a pilot, and I've done it on every show since. Three days before we actually shoot, I run the show in front of a "test" audience, to get a sense of where they're going to laugh, whether they like these people, do we have story problems, et cetera. It's a relatively informal process, so much so that the cast still reads from their scripts. They don't necessarily have to be "off-book."

Running a show in front of an audience before there's anything at stake, even before there's film in the camera, gives insights you would never get otherwise, and those insights are often crucial to the development of a show. Outside services solicit people to be part of studio audiences. Cast and crew members bring in family and friends. You preferably want non-industry people, because industry folks tend to sit on their hands and do not applaud or laugh as much as wide-eyed civilians.

When we were rehearsing the *Cheers* pilot, the audience provided was composed entirely of Seabees (United States Naval Construction Battalions) from Camp Pendleton in San Diego. We were sweating bullets, because there was a lot of sophisticated comedy in the script and we weren't sure how this audience would react. Fortunately, the *Cheers* run-through turned out to be an almost religious experience.

George Wendt entered for the first time and said, "Afternoon, everybody!" And, of course, everybody yelled back, "Norm!" Then Teddy said, "What do you know?" And George said, "Not enough." It was really a straight line in the script, but it got this huge laugh from the audience. I turned to my two partners and said, "Wow, they're laughing not only at this joke but they're laughing at this character, the person saying it." Right then I had a sense that we had something special.

SAM

Closing time.

NORM

Hard to believe seventeen hours can slip by that easily.

In our imagination, Norm Peterson's version of *veni, vidi, vici* was "I came, I drank, I stayed." He was loyal to the bar first and his wife, Vera, second. Everyone had their own Norm. The Brothers knew a man who was a regular at a bar they worked at in Las Vegas. He'd come in every day, sit in the same spot, and order "just one beer." Then he'd order "just one more." He'd still be there at closing time.

George Wendt played an exterminator on a *Taxi* episode, so we already knew him. He was already committed to a Gary David Goldberg show, *Making the Grade*, which fortunately, at least for us, only lasted six episodes, freeing George up to become Norm. We had originally named the character George, but you don't want an actor with the same first name as the character they're playing. When I directed Ted Knight playing Ted Baxter on *TMTMS*, it was very frustrating to give direction and notes, so I asked that the character name be changed. There was a real Norm Peterson who was a friend of Les's from college. I waived that rule later when it came to Woody Harrelson/Woody Boyd.

Normally, the bar regular will walk to the closest seat near the door, but we already had Diane sitting in that spot in the pilot. I couldn't seat Norm next to Diane. Diane was absorbing the Cheers characters, and we wanted her commenting, not sitting in the middle like she was part of the conversation.

When Norm came through the front door, he walked across to the bar and sat on the right side, next to Cliff. While I have been credited with coming up with people shouting "Norm!" as George walked into the bar, it was actually Nicky Colasanto's idea. We wound up with ten of the greatest seconds of sitcom history each week, every time Norm walked in and made a joke. The Norm'isms— the interchange when Norm walks into the bar in each episode— became harder and harder to write, because the audience expected so much. Norm would lumber in, and his battle cry of "Afternoon, everybody!" would be followed by the entire bar yelling out a welcoming and unifying "Norm!" When asked by Sam, Diane, Coach, or Woody how he was and what he wanted, he always had a funny rejoinder:

SAM

What's up, Norm?

NORM

My nipples; it's freezing out there!

SAM

What are you up to, Norm?

NORM

My ideal weight if I were eleven feet tall.

WOODY

Hey, Mr. Peterson. Jack Frost nipping at your nose?

NORM

Yeah. Now let's get Joe Beer nipping at my liver, huh?

WOODY

What's going on, Mr. Peterson?

NORM

Let's talk about what's going in Mr. Peterson.

SAM

Hey, what's happening, Norm?

NORM

It's a dog-eat-dog world, Sammy, and I'm wearing
Milk Bone underwear!

George was so funny walking. He could grab the handle on the bar and turn himself around into the seat. We even had a scene where Norm and Cliff get to Cheers and find two other guys sitting in their seats. They look as if they might have heart attacks. The space-time continuum was suddenly out of whack.

Sometimes when we were shooting the bar, the camera caught George's shoulder while focusing on Teddy. I'd whisper in his ear, "Georgie, right cheek," and he would put his weight on his right butt cheek so we could get the shot. The left-cheek instruction worked as well.

On *M*A*S*H*, Larry Gelbart's philosophy was "Take your characters and put them in the last place they want to be." We had a similar philosophy: Make the writers' lives really easy by making the characters' lives really hard. Giving these people real-world problems, breaking their lives apart, gave us a lot of stories to develop. Every character wanted something or had some kind of problem, except for Norm, who was wonderful and essential in a different way, because he was the anchor for the group. Because Norm was relatively happy and well-adjusted, everything was fine.

For the role of Carla, the surly bar waitress, we already knew about and were considering Rhea Perlman, since she had played Zena, Louie's girlfriend, in *Taxi*. But the network wouldn't hire her without a reading. She nailed the audition and channeled some of Louie into Carla, the acerbic waitress:

NORM
Hi, Carla. How're the kids?

CARLA
Two of them are ugly; one's obnoxious; and one's just stupid.
He's my favorite.

Carla was a hotheaded Italian waitress, neighborhood Boston born and raised. She had a rough life and a chip on her shoulder. We wanted a stark contrast between Carla and Diane, an erudite, uptown, overeducated woman. Carla was a survivor, a realist, and was very fertile. "I can't let any man touch me, talk to me, or see me, or I'll be shooting out kids like a Pez dispenser."

John Ratzenberger came in to read for the part of Norm. According to Ratz, he was looking for a chair to sit down on and I said, "You're not here to chat." He had been writing and directing in England for ten years. This was his first Hollywood audition. The audition didn't go well, but as he was leaving, he turned to us and asked, "Do you have a blowhard?" We asked, "What are you talking about?"

Recalling that as now "the five greatest words in my life," he said, "In New England, where I'm from, every bar has a horse's ass know-it-all, someone who pretends to have the knowledge of all mankind between his ears and is not shy about sharing it." Ratz became the sixth wheel, Cliff Clavin, whom we named after our ob-gyn (my wife's, actually). We wanted Cliff to wear some kind of uniform to imply authority, so we made him a mailman. We also thought that as someone who delivered magazines, he would know all the headlines but not much more:

> CLIFF
> I tried to serve on a jury, but they disqualified me.

> NORM
> Yeah?

> CLIFF
> I can't understand it. They went for my theory.

> NORM
> What theory is that?

> CLIFF
> The one about bringing back the guillotine.

> NORM
> They turned you down?

> CLIFF
> I guess the old inmates are running the asylum.

> NORM
> Cliff, there's a guy back here who thinks you
> know nothing about photosynthesis.

CLIFF

Where is he? I'll straighten him out!

Cliff saw himself as the wing nut that held Western Civilization together. He had no self-perception of his own ineptitude. When someone said he had a big mouth, he said, "You know, it's a genetic quirk in the Clavin family that we all have two extra teeth. You see, that's the only way that we can prove that we are the rightful heirs to the Russian throne."

He was also an expert on politics: "If you go back in history and take every president, you'll find that the numerical value of each letter in the last name was equally divisible into the year in which they were elected. By my calculations, our next president has to be named Yalinek McWawa."

When Sam needs legal advice, Cliff says, "Sammy, according to the landmark case of Pennoyer versus Neff, jurisprudence is the latter part of diction." Pennoyer is a real legal case. The rest is made up.

Cliff was a perfect foil for Carla's insults:

CLIFF

What a pathetic display. I'm ashamed God made me a man.

CARLA

I don't think the guy's doing a lot of bragging about it either.

A "know-it-all," he ended up doing all but one episode without knowing anything about anything. That was Ratz's creation. He originally had a deal for seven shows. When he got the eighth script and saw he wasn't in it, he came to say goodbye and thank you. I looked at him and said, "We'll find a place for you." We thought, "This guy is too good." We found both a classic character and life-long friend.

Cheers had a group of "barflies" to bring energy and atmosphere, as well as accents, to the show. To lend authenticity, we needed

guys with Boston accents, to compensate for most of the cast not
having one. The barflies included Jack (Jack Knight) and Tom (Tom
Babson), who spent half his time in Cheers studying for the bar
exam; after a few unsuccessful attempts, he finally passed.

Al (Al Rosen) was background and atmosphere, until an episode
where we gave him one word of dialogue. In "Fortune and Men's
Weight," in response to Carla asking, "Who is the biggest bigwig of
them all?" expecting the answer to be God, he yelled out, "Sinatra!"
and became a cult figure. Al was a character actor who was also a
stunt man for the Three Stooges.

Rhea's father, Philip Perlman, a retired factory manager, also
started out as an extra but became a regular. He looked like a barfly.
He was eighty-five at the time and Rhea wanted him to get out of
the house, so we made him one of the supernumeraries. When Al
Rosen passed away, we gave his dialogue to Phil. Rhea's sister,
Heide Perlman, had been a writer–producer for a few years before
she went to work for Tracey Ullman. *Cheers* became the full em-
ployment act for the talented Perlmans. When Rhea's husband,
Danny DeVito, came around, I'd yell, "Here's Mr. Perlman!"

We brought in Fred Dryer, who was in the final audition to play
Sam, for four episodes. He played Dave Richards, one of Sam's
friends and former teammates, now the sportscaster of "I on Sports":

DAVE

Well, well. What do we have here? Hi, I'm Dave Richards,
an old teammate of Sam's.

DIANE

Diane Chambers. Sam's new waitress.

DAVE

Sam have his brand on you yet?

DIANE

Hardly.

DAVE

Well, you're in for a lucky day. Not only am I incredibly good-looking, I'm incredibly rich and incredibly nice.

SAM

And incredibly married.

DIANE

Well, I am sorry to hear that.

DAVE

You are?

DIANE

Yes. I was hoping to reject you solely based on your personality.

Fred Dryer was a defensive end for the Los Angeles Rams. He was a real-life Sam Harrison, the wide receiver for the Patriots we first envisioned as the lead character. I said to Teddy, "Watch Freddy's every movement. That's who Sam Malone is. He's a peacock. He's always spreading his feathers. Watch how he grabs his groin." Teddy didn't have the grip around the persona of the athlete yet. Working with Fred helped him a lot. I told the NBC executives to put Fred in a drama. Not long after that, he became the star of the NBC Saturday-night hit *Hunter*.

We came up with an ex-husband for Carla. Dan Hedaya, with his hunched, swarthy Mediterranean looks, including amazing eyebrows, played Nick Tortelli, whom Carla referred to as "scum with ear hair." Nick believed he could hypnotize any woman, including Diane. We paired Nick with a tall, blond, and ditzy new wife, played by the tall and blond Jeannie Kasem, the real-life wife of disc jockey Casey Kasem (yes, she really talked like that).

Everybody on *Cheers* had done theater, which allowed us to play with the other actors and also play for an audience. Occasionally we got film actors, and we worked to get them on the level of the cast member they'd be playing off. If you underplay on a sitcom, you're dead.

We were in search of a theme song for the opening of the show. I had a good friend named John Angelo whose wife, Judy Hart, was a songwriter. I asked if she could send me a couple of songs. She sent me one called "People Like Us," from the musical *Preppies*, which she was working on. We loved it. It totally embodied the spirit of what we wanted to do. Then she couldn't give it to us because the show went to Broadway. I said, "What else you got?" She sent two more songs, one of which was "Where Everybody Knows Your Name," which was even better:

> *Making your way in the world today*
> *Takes everything you've got*
> *Taking a break from all your worries*
> *Sure would help a lot*
> *Wouldn't you like to get away?*
> *All those nights when you've got no lights*
> *The check is in the mail*
> *And your little angel*
> *Hung the cat up by its tail*
> *And your third fiancé didn't show*
> *Sometimes you want to go*
> *Where everybody knows your name*
> *And they're always glad you came*
> *You want to be where you can see*
> *Our troubles are all the same*
> *You want to be where everybody knows your name*
> *Roll out of bed, Mr. Coffee's dead*
> *The morning's looking bright*
> *And your shrink ran off to Europe*
> *And didn't even write*
> *And your husband wants to be a girl*

Be glad there's one place in the world
Where everybody knows your name
And they're always glad you came
You want to go where people know
People are all the same
You want to go where everybody knows your name

It knocked our socks off immediately. It was the epitome of what our show was about. Today, theme songs on shows are virtually non-existent: Because episodes run for twenty-one and a half minutes, there's no time. But *Cheers* was in the era where TV theme songs became chart-toppers. The song was a megahit, reaching number five on the pop charts. It was positioned to go to number one—then Michael Jackson's *Thriller* album came out. Between "Billie Jean" and "Beat It," our theme song was knocked out of the top ten. We definitely made the right choice.

For a theme song to be a hit, the show has to be a hit first. And a great theme song must have a hook—the melodic phrasing and exact lyrics that get you into the song. *Cheers* had that melodious line "Where everybody knows your name." Lots of hit shows, like *The Bob Newhart Show*, don't have a memorable theme song. They don't have the hook. *TMTMS* had that hook "Turn the world on with her smile."

If the show doesn't live up to the music, it won't last. The Joey Scarbury theme song for *The Greatest American Hero*, "Believe It or Not," became a huge hit but didn't perpetuate the success of the show. Likewise, neither did Johnny Sebastian's hit theme for *Welcome Back, Kotter*, which likely got only a few people into the show.

Whether you have a great opening song or not, if you can get to a point where a great cast meets a great script, you're halfway home. The rest is about the network putting a show in the right spot. That extra push comes from a great lead-in and from little competition. People will tune in to watch stars that they know, but for a show without established stars, there is a nurturing period. Otherwise, a great show could and still does get prematurely canceled.

Cheers debuted on September 30, 1982, at nine P.M. We started out with very low ratings. During the Thanksgiving week it ranked seventy-seventh out of seventy-seven shows, definitely a turkey. It would be a great understatement to say that we had a lot of room for improvement. Nobody watched the show when it first aired. There was no reason for the public to watch the show. No stars.

We had a thirteen-week guarantee from NBC, with seven scripts ready to go. The live studio audiences reacted to Sam and Diane immediately. We realized that the show was going to be as much about these two people falling in love as it would be about the bar. As they started taking off, the Brothers started rewriting. One script was rewritten even before it got to a table read. They were that focused and driven. Their work ethic was off the charts.

The vibe on the set was one of collaboration. I could say anything about the writing and the Brothers could say anything about the directing, without worrying that we would offend one another. We all knew that the more collaborative we were, the better the show would be. During the run-through of each week's show, we talked about what worked and what didn't. We'd include the actors in the conversation. While there was no specific chain of command, I was privy to it all.

Not many people were watching NBC at that time. But the network and the press loved us, including Bill Carter, then at the *Baltimore Sun,* and still a good friend. Anyone who says that they don't read reviews is lying, especially in television. During those years of only three networks and no cable, reviews helped us build a following and sent viewers our way who weren't watching television, or if they were, they weren't part of NBC's audience. Our first fan letter came from Norman Lear: "The work is brilliant, and that part of me which is forever a member of the audience is deeply grateful for the pleasure you bring." We knew we were doing something right. We also had support from Gary Nardino, who was the head of television production at Paramount.

Warren Littlefield, then–NBC vice president, said, "NBC was

the network of *Diff'rent Strokes* and *Hello, Larry*. We had no DNA for sophisticated comedy." NBC had just launched *Cheers* and *Hill Street Blues*, which *were* sophisticated adult comedy and drama. And while they were the foundational building blocks for what NBC would become, neither started out that way. Both were dead last in the ratings.

As Warren and Brandon Tartikoff were discussing whether to renew *Cheers*, Grant Tinker asked, "Well, do you have anything better?" When they said no, he said, "I think you answered your question." So *Cheers* was picked back up. Without Grant, Brandon, and Warren, *Cheers* might not have made it on the air past a couple of episodes. Those three loved television, and while concerned about ratings, they were also concerned with doing innovative work, as opposed to imitative work.

During our first summer, when we were in repeats, *Cheers* got all the way up to ninth place. Everybody had already seen the current season of *Simon & Simon* and *Magnum, P.I.*, two CBS hits that were rerunning opposite us, but nobody had seen *Cheers*. Dramas don't repeat well—it's not that big a surprise the second time Magnum figures out who the murderer is. The audience was willing to give us a chance when these other shows were in reruns. Slowly, through word of mouth, people tuned in. We started to get a following. And the Emmys were a big boost as well. We picked up nine awards during the first two seasons.

It was in 1984, during our third season, that we became a bona fide hit. NBC's legendary Thursday-night prime-time lineup was launched; initially consisting of *The Cosby Show, Family Ties, Cheers, Night Court,* and *Hill Street Blues,* the network branded it "The Best Night of Television on Television." Despite the rise and fall of other shows in the lineup, *Cheers* became NBC's anchor for the rest of its run, especially for the advertisers' most coveted demographic, eighteen-to-forty-nine-year-old viewers. *Cheers* created and then owned the nine P.M. real estate that has been the anchor for Thursday-night television since. The fact that we didn't start out as a hit and the audience gradually embraced us and stuck with us made the success even sweeter.

In the 1970s, the big comedy night was Saturday. In the 1980s, the venue changed to Thursdays, mainly because movie studios would advertise their Friday releases on Thursday evening television, and sitcoms were more popular and therefore got more bang for the advertisers' buck than any other type of show at the time.

The Brothers and I formed a partnership that created and produced television shows, beginning with *Cheers*. When we were discussing what to name our new partnership, we considered Hat Trick Productions, Funny Incorporated, and Two Former Mormons and a Reform Jew Entertainment, which was already taken. We finally settled on Charles Burrows Charles. When we were presented with a mountain of contracts memorializing our agreement, I told the Brothers, "I'm okay with a handshake." We shook hands and to this day have never signed a contract.

You can't get any nicer in Hollywood than when two guys give you a "created by" credit that you neither deserve nor ask for. The Brothers were my heroes and my teachers. I was in awe over how they pulled off all the work they had to do. They had a lot of respect for the audience and wrote that way. Their character-driven comedy meant that jokes fit characters like tailored suits and weren't interchangeable. The Brothers taught me how to tell a story in ways I didn't know before, how to go a page without a gag so when it does come, it's unexpected. Together, we knew to go for the heart, to make the audience care, and to make them laugh.

The Brothers brought intellect and upscale humor into the television business for the first time in a while. We did Updike, Kant, and Marx jokes and made H. L. Mencken references; we used the word "pomme de terre" a lot. The network kept asking, "How is the audience going to know?" And we said, "We don't care." Diane said a lot of things that audiences didn't understand completely or sometimes not at all, but they certainly got the intent, and the fact that no one else in the bar got what she said made it okay.

If you're going to direct all or most of the shows in a sitcom, you should also try to become a producer, in order to protect your artistic vision and the integrity of the show. A producer's responsibility is everything from reviewing the initial script to making sure the episode gets on the air. You have to worry about story arcs and who to hire for which jobs, including overseeing daily and weekly budgets and set design.

I've been executive producer on eleven shows I've worked on: *Cheers, Will & Grace, Back to You, Mike & Molly, The Class, Gary Unmarried, Man with a Plan, Partners, Crowded, Superior Donuts,* and *The Millers.* If I didn't direct as much on a show, I wouldn't have taken the producer title. In television, generally the show is run by the writer–producer. The director–producer title is much rarer.

Cheers was driven by great characters and great dialogue. I brought them in, sat them down, and they talked. This was the first time in my career that I wasn't getting any agita from a producer, because I was the producer.

From the very opening of *Cheers,* the light and funny tone is set, with a teenager (John P. Navin, Jr.) walking into the bar and trying to get a drink out of Sam:

BOY
How about a beer, chief?

SAM
How about an ID?

BOY
An ID? That's very flattering. Wait till I tell the missus.

SAM
(looks at the boy's ID)
Ah, military ID. First Sergeant Walter Keller, born 1944. That makes you thirty-eight. Must have fought in Vietnam.

BOY

Oh, yeah.

SAM

What was it like?

BOY

Gross.

SAM

Yeah, that's what they say: "War is gross." I'm sorry, soldier.

BOY

This is the thanks we get.

Instead of just throwing the kid out, Sam is gracious. It immediately shows the audience that he's a decent man and a worthy center. Everyone likes Sam, in part because he's got flaws and vulnerabilities. He's a recovering alcoholic. He's also a very compassionate person. The character and his point of view are crucial to the success of the show, because the audience sees this bar and all its wacky patrons through Sam's benevolence. The windows of the show are his eyes, his soul, and his passion for his bar and the people in it.

We could underplay the jokes because they were so good. *Cheers* looked effortless, because of the way it was played. Other than a few tough moments, like Sam and Diane arguing, it was always an understated show, which means we wanted the audience to figure it out. Like radio, where comedians competed with each other with just their voices, the subtlety was crucial to the show. We'd undersell the joke so you'd have to meet us halfway.

That was attributable to Teddy Danson, whose best skill was that he could throw away a joke as part of another action, like pouring a beer. That's the way a bar actually is. People have conversations. They don't scream or yell unless there's a problem.

Throwing away jokes is a particular style of comedy. The jokes become more like subtle comments. Henny Youngman didn't toss off comedy (Woman: Too late for the garbage? Garbage Man: No, ma'am, jump right in). Chris Rock screams his comedy and you're already on board. Dave Chappelle underplays his pieces; he waits for you to get on board. Steven Wright and Woody Allen never hit anything hard. That subtlety is as important now as it ever was, given the rise of comedy podcasts and new generations of audiences getting their laughs from people they are only listening to.

The best laughs I've ever directed were on people's backs. A joke is often funnier if it's said over someone's shoulder as they're leaving a room or under their breath. Not hitting it hard makes it funnier. On *Mike & Molly*, I directed jokes to be told to the hanging coats. That style works best in an ensemble. Kelsey as Frasier threw away jokes. Roseanne Barr threw jokes away; most of her show was underplaying. If you have a hard-hitting center, like John Lithgow, jokes are shot into outer space.

It helps if your center can do that, because the subsidiary characters can't. Rhea couldn't ever throw away a joke, because her jokes were too vitriolic. We thought of Carla as Groucho Marx, a sniper poised to insult. Her comedy was "sharking." Whenever she appeared behind a character, I'd tell Rhea, "Shark in there." I had her deliberately chew up her targets. Rhea would coordinate her business where she was serving, deliver a scathing line, and then disappear. Ratz couldn't throw away lines, because Cliff was a blowhard, loud by nature.

We first saw Harry Anderson, for whom we wrote the part of Harry the Hat, when he appeared on *Saturday Night Live*. He'd previously made his living doing floating three-card-monte games on the streets. He was lucky to be alive, as the card sharks were always getting threatened. We thought he would be a great character to have in the bar. He was constantly trying to con Sam out of money. In one show, Harry helps Diane cover the pool table in the back room and then tries to walk out of the bar without paying, telling Sam he paid Diane. When Sam calls back to Diane, she yells, "It's covered."

In between *Cheers* seasons, I was able to do pilots and show off my wares to the larger community. I got a call from Reinhold Weege, a great writer who worked on *Barney Miller,* asking if I thought Harry could be the lead of a show. Harry was certainly likable and funny enough, so I supported him. *Night Court,* which starred Harry, was one of the first pilots that I shot. He and John Larroquette were terrific. So was Selma Diamond, who had been one of Sid Caesar's writers. In the opening, Judge Harry is introduced by court bailiff Bull Shannon (Richard Moll), who wrote his name on each hand so he wouldn't forget. When Harry enters the courtroom, everyone stands. When Harry sits down, the room sits down. Harry jumps up again and the room jumps up, to Harry's "Gotcha!" I loved coming in and seeing how I could put my imprimatur, my "stink," on a show. I was in pig heaven. I felt I was exactly where I was supposed to be.

During the early years of *Cheers,* we weren't interested in famous guest stars. The show was going to succeed because people tuned in for the regular cast, not because a star was on one episode. That said, *Cheers* eventually did become a showcase for actors because of the visibility. We tried to be generous. We knew that for some actors it was a once-in-a-lifetime chance. A lot of people went on to stardom after small turns on the show, including Julia Duffy; Markie Post; Sherilyn Fenn; Deborah Shelton, who was Miss Virginia; and Anita Morris and Karen Akers, who were both on Broadway in *Nine.* The first customer in the second episode was Keenen Ivory Wayans, and in that same episode Donna McKechnie played Sam's ex-wife. I got to work with Nancy Marchand again in a later season, when she played Frasier's mother. When Frasier was listening (yes, I know what I did), she appeared to like his choice of girlfriend Diane, and as soon as he was out of earshot, she threatened to kill her.

Steve Kolzak, whom we stole away from NBC Entertainment, was our first casting director. He was Harvard-educated and had a great eye for talent. Sadly, he was one of the first victims of AIDS. Steve's mother was secretary for then–Speaker of the House Tip O'Neill. Tip saw the show and asked if he could sit at the bar next to Norm:

CARLA

Hey, you know, you look a little like Tip O'Neill.

TIP

A lot of people say that. I'm really a better-looking fella than he is.

SAM

Oh my God, you are Tip O'Neill. How do you do?
Oh, I'm Sam Malone.

TIP

You used to throw for the Sox.

SAM

Yeah, that's right. What are you doing here at Cheers?

TIP

Well, I'm walking down the street. A lady stopped me, started to tell me about her philosophy of life and philosophy of government. And so I ducked in and thought I'd have a quick one.

SAM

Well, what can I get you here?

(Diane comes into the bar and sees Tip again.)

DIANE

There you are. Mr. Speaker, forgive me for being so relentless, but
I really want to talk to you.

SAM

Diane, step into the office.

DIANE

I'll be right back.

SAM

No, she won't.

NORM

(returning from the bathroom)
One more quick one, Coach, and then I really gotta run.

CLIFF

Hey, Norm, what were you saying last week about that
do-nothing Congress down there in D.C.?

NORM

They're a bunch of clowns.

CLIFF

You think so, huh?

NORM

You can take the average guy off the street and
he can do a better job.

CLIFF

Nah.

NORM
(gesturing to Tip)
Sure. This bozo right here could probably be a better
congressman than them.

TIP
You know, I may run for office someday.

NORM
You're out of work too, huh?

TIP
No, I'm the Speaker of the House of Representatives.

NORM
Don't be ridiculous. That would make you Tip O'Neill and me . . .
a horse's butt.

TIP
You said it, not me.

Not long after, we got Dick Cavett to play himself. When Diane
sees Dick, she starts harassing him with her poetry:

DIANE
The sky was gossamer—

SAM
Diane. Somebody wants you at another table.

DIANE
Who?

SAM

Everybody at this one. I'm sorry about that, Mr. Cavett, she gets a
little overexcited sometimes.

CAVETT

That's all right. Happens all the time.

SAM

I'm Sam Malone. I'm the owner of the bar here. You want
anything, you just call me, all right?

CAVETT

Wait—Sam Malone. You used to play baseball.

SAM

Yeah. You remember me?

CAVETT

I saw you pitch once in Yankee Stadium.

SAM

Is that right? Did I have a good night?

CAVETT

I hope so. You had a lousy day. I remember you hit three batters
and gave up back-to-back homers. You remember that game?

SAM

I had a drinking problem back in those days. There are a few
things I don't remember, like 1974, 1975 . . .

CAVETT

'75—the year you won the pennant.

SAM

We did? Well, hey, how about that!

We did go for one iconic name during the first season. While we eventually cast British actress Glynis Johns as Diane's mother in "Someone Single, Someone Blue," she wasn't our first choice. We tried to get Lucille Ball. We reached out to her, and she agreed to meet with us. The Brothers and I went to her house in Beverly Hills and sat in the living room with Lucy and her second husband, Gary Morton, whom she married after she and Desi Arnaz divorced. We pitched her on the idea. Gary chimed in with something. Lucy cut him off and said, "Gary, remember where you were." As we left her house, we were trying to decide if Lucy meant "Remember where you were in that story you were telling" or "Remember where you were before you married me." Lucy turned us down.

We had better luck with John Cleese, who had become a fan and actually asked to be on the show. In "Simon Says," he plays a famous marriage counselor and former Oxford classmate of Frasier's who comes to Cheers. Diane, now engaged to Sam, immediately wants a session with him to see if their impending marriage will work:

DIANE

I think it's safe to say that Simon Finch-Royce saved hundreds— nay, thousands of marriages. It's even rumored that he had a hand in saving Chuck and Di.

CARLA

Speaking of which, why don't you up chuck and die.

Frasier offers to pay for the session as a wedding gift: "I was considering the gravy boat, but I think our relationship transcends mere crockery." After a gruelingly long session with the couple, Simon tells them, "Not only should you two not get married, you should never see each other again." We had some trouble writing the episode, until John stepped in and saw something we didn't: "You're working too hard for me and my character," he said. Once we realized that, we were able to keep our adulation from becoming an impediment, and we finished the script.

The Frasier Crane character was added in the third season of *Cheers*. Diane goes off with the artist Semenko (Chris Lloyd). I thought Chris played that role a little too big, especially since none of the rest of the cast did, but it worked. Then again, in any role after Reverend Jim, Chris played it smaller. Season 3 opens with Diane, unable to handle her breakup with Sam, in what Carla refers to as "the loony bin," and a brokenhearted Sam on a bender. Enter Herr Doktor, Frasier Crane. We created Frasier for the third episode of the third season as a plot device. To get Diane back to the bar, her doctor tells her that she must return and confront her demons. The reveal of Frasier was a surprise that shocked everyone. A total Charles Brothers brilliant moment. Diane and Frasier overlapped for three seasons. The original version of Frasier Crane was a pompous ass. The character's last name was originally Nye. Kelsey thought the last name didn't fit him, and, at Kelsey's suggestion, it was changed to Crane.

Kelsey had been doing *Sunday in the Park with George* with Mandy Patinkin. Mandy had recommended Kelsey to Paramount's New York casting director. We started to see people, and we got a tape from New York with four actors. Up came Kelsey's face, and we all started laughing when we saw his audition. We hired Kelsey for four episodes. He drove out from New York and for a time was living in his car on the Paramount lot.

Early on, it became clear to us that Kelsey was perfect for the part. The precision with which he could deliver his lines was like the creative blending of a surgeon and a concert pianist. After the first episode, we said, "You're going to stay with us for the year." According to Kelsey, we never called him to tell him that he got the part. He went back to the hotel room we'd got him at the Holiday

Inn on Vine and Hollywood Boulevard, and on the table in the room was a green box he didn't recognize. Inside was a bottle of Dom Perignon, and on a little card it said, "Welcome to Cheers." I still think that was better than a phone call. We had no idea that he would end up playing Frasier not only for the duration of *Cheers* but for another eleven seasons on the spin-off *Frasier*. Kelsey won an Emmy for playing the character on *Frasier* and was nominated for playing him on *Cheers* and *Wings*. Kelsey's four-episode gig wound up lasting two decades, the greatest tribute to his ability. Kelsey has a stentorian voice, an incredible stage presence, is extremely smart and skilled, and can play a pompous ass who's also sympathetic better than anyone I know. One of my favorite *Cheers* episodes is "The Heart Is a Lonely Snipehunter." The guys take Frasier to hunt for the fictitious snipe. The duped Frasier isn't really duped and tells Diane how he will exact his revenge, but he's exhilarated over becoming one of the gang. We couldn't have been happier for both Frasier and Kelsey.

Writing for Frasier Crane required not just an ear for pomposity but a talent for witty, rapid-fire dialogue. The Brothers brought in Peter Casey and David Lee, who had been writing for *The Jeffersons* and had impressed them with a *Cheers* spec script. It was rare in sitcoms for established writers on one show to submit spec scripts and for writers of a certain type of comedy to change writing styles.

When we lost Nicky Colasanto at the end of the third season, we made a conscious decision not to replace Coach but to bring in someone younger, to go for a different feel. The NBC Thursday-night lineup at the time was *Cosby, Family Ties, Cheers, Night Court,* and *Hill Street Blues*. Michael J. Fox was the breakout star of *Family Ties*.

We decided to go with a "rube," a naïve bartender. We had auditioned an actor that we liked. But on the final day of auditions, Woody Harrelson, a kid from Lebanon, Ohio, came in. He was big and bulky, nothing like what had been written. Woody was an understudy in *Biloxi Blues* on Broadway, and he also had a small part

in the Goldie Hawn film *Wildcats*. That was the entirety of his acting credits—but he was about to become part of the regular cast of
Cheers.

Woody was reading for Woody Boyd. People thought we'd
changed the character's name to suit the actor. We didn't. It was a
real "meant-to-be" kind of role. After impressing casting director
Lori Openden, Woody was brought in to meet the Brothers and me.
His nose was running, and he pulled out a tissue. Just as he walked
in the door to meet us, he blew his nose loudly. It was so well-timed
I knew he had what we needed. He was not only funny, he had a
presence. We hired him and he started work the next day.

> WOODY
> Boy, this bachelor party should be keen.

> SAM
> Keen? I don't know about Indiana, but around here when
> guys get together to send another guy off to his doom,
> things can get a little raunchy.

> WOODY
> You guys ever dress up farm animals in women's clothing?

> SAM
> No.

> WOODY
> Then I'm one up on you.

We set up the storyline that Woody and Coach were pen pals.
They didn't exchange letters—they exchanged actual pens. Nicky
and Woody were great in different ways. Woody played the innocent
perfectly. Woody not only replaced Coach, he infused the show
with a much-needed youthful energy, which is necessary for any

cast that has worked together for a while. As a director, you have to make sure the cast is having fun rehearsing and, just as important, when they're not rehearsing. Woody had an immediate rapport with the rest of the cast. We were thankful.

When Woody walked around the bar, I asked him if he could jump over it instead. Fortunately, he was able to, and it became a seminal moment for both character and show. He was adorable doing it, and it pissed off everyone else, especially Teddy. During rehearsal, Teddy tried to jump over the bar. It was not a good moment for either Ted or the bar.

When you cast somebody new and unknown, it's like peeling layers of an onion. If you're successful with one layer, you go to the next one. If an actor measures up, it makes everyone's life easier and interesting. If they can't, maybe they're not right for the salad. With unknown actors, you never quite know what you're going to get. There's the sense that when audiences laugh or are moved, they feel like they've discovered something, that they've turned unknowns into icons. We didn't know what we had with Woody. We learned what he would become. He could play comedy and drama. Oliver Stone cast him in *Natural Born Killers*. We had no idea that he could be that demonic in one film while also being so compassionate in *Three Billboards Outside Ebbing, Missouri*.

Woody brought foosball, water guns, and spitballs to the set, turning the middle-aged cast into fun monsters chasing one another around. The requisite adrenaline was there, in large part because of the influx of his vitality. That cast was unrestrained.

One day I came in for rehearsal, and the only person there was Shelley. The guys had decided to take a "ditch day." Ratz had just bought a forty-two-foot Grand Banks, and they sailed to Catalina. George called in "sea sick" and claimed "pier pressure." Normally, I would have been pissed. But the point of a ditch day is not to tell anyone. I loved that I helped create a close company. If the work would have suffered, they never would have done it. Generally, as long as the star falls into line, everyone else will as well.

On *Cheers* we didn't socialize outside the workplace the way we did on *Taxi*, because, unlike during *Taxi*, we were older and most of us were married with small children. We had our fun on the set, which is how we liked it. We were a jazz band and could riff with one another. If we had a nugget of gold, I wouldn't over-rehearse it. I'd relax on it and let them hit it on show night. We didn't overthink things. I didn't want to drill the cast, unless there was a complicated physical scene, a sensitive dramatic scene, or a guest star. And with a guest star on a hit show, the pressure was more on the guest, who was often intimidated by walking into such a close-knit ensemble.

There were a lot of parties on *Cheers*. We had our wrap parties onstage, because we had our own bar. Our Emmy parties were at an outside venue, downtown, and were used to celebrate or assuage. We drank a lot, even more when we won. And we did win a lot of Emmys. We also had a first-night party every year at Chasen's, where we always served chicken pot pie. We'd watch the season opener, after which everyone would toast the show. The best toast, hands down, was from Jerry Belson, whom we had gotten to work with us as a punch-up guy on scripts. As everyone went around the room toasting, Jerry got up and said, "I've worked on a lot of shows," and then sat down. The place went crazy. I've stolen it and used that toast at least ten times since. Thanks, Jerry.

There was a time where it was de rigueur for every show to do a Thanksgiving episode. The upside was that everyone identified with it. The downside was that it's such a warm and cherished holiday. You have to be careful how you make fun of it, but you also have to come up with a new way of doing it that is both funny and memorable.

First, a backstory is created to justify the characters being together for the holiday, the same way you crafted the original backstory that had them at *Cheers*. In "Thanksgiving Orphans," Cliff's mother is feeding the homeless, and Cliff isn't interested in doing that this year. Norm's wife, Vera, is visiting her family, and Norm definitely does not want to go. Woody decides not to travel to Indiana to his family. Sam's girlfriend at the time has her sister in town, and they don't want to spend the holiday with Sam's friends. Carla's kids are with her ex-husband, Nick, and his new wife, Loretta. Diane has been invited to a party by one of her professors but discovers that he intends for his graduate students to work as servers at the party. Last but not least, Frasier is just plain lonely. So everyone joins together for dinner at Carla's new home.

You keep adding to that. A screwup with the turkey leads to dinner being so late that all the side dishes get cold. A little food is thrown and suddenly everyone is ready for a food fight, when Diane, dressed in traditional pilgrim garb (which of course only Diane would have), walks in on them from the kitchen, where she's just been checking on the turkey. You have turkey, mashed potatoes, yams, and pilgrims. Now you have to find some business. In this situation you have the luxury and responsibility of characters doing things they wouldn't normally do.

The Brothers always had the idea of a food fight. They subscribed to the time-honored axiom that there's nothing better than throwing mashed potatoes at someone you love. The food-fight scene is amazing solely for the fact that Teddy got cranberry sauce smack-dab on Shelley's white pilgrim outfit. Hoping to get Sam back, Diane throws a pie at him but instead hits Vera, who has showed up to surprise Norm. This was Vera's only appearance on the series (her voice was heard a number of times), and she was played by George's real-life wife, Bernadette Birkett. In keeping with never showing her, Vera's face was covered in pie.

I shot that scene twice. We couldn't back up to any earlier lines and the cast literally couldn't move, because they were slipping on the food. They also had to take a break to shower. We donated all the food we didn't use to a local food bank. Ultimately, we gave up on trying to top ourselves at Thanksgiving. We stand by our food fight.

We had one interesting crossover, where the bar was used on another show. Three doctors from *St. Elsewhere*—Westphall (Ed

Flanders), Craig (William Daniels), and Auschlander (Norman Lloyd)—come to Cheers. Carla waits on them, Cliff annoys them, and Norm apologizes to Dr. Auschlander for all the trouble he caused when he was his accountant. Conversely, there was an episode of *St. Elsewhere* where the PA system announces a meeting with "Doctors Charles, Burrows, and Charles."

Cheers, like *Will & Grace* sixteen years later, became not only a hit sitcom but a cultural phenomenon. Any association with the series generated not only instant and grand exposure but also immediate credibility, because of the affection and respect the audience had for the characters. Later guest stars included Red Sox third baseman Wade Boggs, who was eventually traded to the Yankees, former Little Rascal George "Spanky" McFarland, and singer Bill Medley, who never lost that lovin' feeling. The bar was part of a 1983 Super Bowl special, which had 80 million viewers. Bob Costas hosted a segment with the gang during the 1986 World Series between the Boston Red Sox and the New York Mets.

We were careful about maintaining the image of a Boston bar and respectful of all things Bostonian and from Massachusetts. I shot teasers outside with Michael and Ethel Kennedy. You'd have to put air quotes around the guest stars for them, because with all respect, except for some Bostonians, no one would tune in to watch them. Senator and presidential hopeful Gary Hart asked to appear in "Strange Bedfellows" two years before the scandal broke that forced him to drop out of the election. His people knew the impact a brief cameo would have. In "Bar Wars VI: This Time It's for Real," Norm and Cliff mistake Senator John Kerry—twelve years before he ran for president—for the local news anchor and ask for his autograph. When he explains that he's actually their senator, they pass on the autograph. In the open of "Sam Time Next Year," Sam and Norm run into Governor Mike Dukakis, who was the Democratic presidential candidate three years earlier.

To study what we were doing, I had young directors and actors sit in on the show, including Tommy Kail, who went on to direct *In the Heights* and *Hamilton*; future *Murphy Brown* and *Mad About You* director Barnet Kellman; Tom Moore, who directed *'night, Mother* and the original Broadway production of *Grease*; and *The Wonder Years* star Fred Savage, most of whom were weaned on one-camera shows. We had become our own incubator. I was happy to pay forward what MTM had done for me. One of the most iconic people who came in to watch me direct was *Pink Panther* and *Breakfast at Tiffany's* director and *Peter Gunn* co-creator Blake Edwards. His wife, Julie Andrews, was thinking about doing a sitcom. I was in awe of him, and I think he was in awe of us because he had no idea what we were doing.

After the first five years, we were running like a well-oiled machine. I was really happy. We had something that we created and were nurturing. The feedback was fantastic. We were raising our own child. Acclaimed author Kurt Vonnegut told an interviewer at the time, "I would rather have written an episode of *Cheers* than anything I've written."

We thought nothing could derail us. Nothing, that is, except Shelley telling us that she wanted to leave the show. Each of the principal cast had been signed to five-year deals, and Shelley told us she wasn't going to re-up. The Brothers and I were immediately pissed—not at Shelley so much, but because this finely tuned machine was now missing an integral piece. This was the Sam and Diane show. Shelley knew she was going to give up a lot of money. That's how strongly she believed in her movie career. She wasn't wrong. She had success in *Irreconcilable Differences* with Ryan O'Neal and *Outrageous Fortune* with Bette Midler.

We had to figure out quickly what we were going to do.

Cheers, Part II

SAM

That was easy. Wait. Let's try some more compromises here. I want to sleep with
you twenty-five times, but you don't want to sleep with me at all. Am I right?

REBECCA
Right.

SAM

Okay, so what's half of twenty-five?

REBECCA
Your IQ.

The ending of Sam and Diane was big news. Once they got
back together in season 5, people told us how stupid we were for
breaking them up in the first place at the end of season 2. We didn't
care. We wanted to prove that we could do the show without Shelley, because we wanted to show how good the ensemble was. After
she was gone, we knew we had to dig.

That said, we were concerned that our plan for the final breakup
would leak out before we had a replacement for Diane. To protect
our franchise (and possibly our lives), we shot two endings to the
season 5 finale, one version with Sam and Diane staying together.
The live audience saw them get married. For the version we shot
with Shelley and Ted that ended up on the air, we had no audience

at all. Shelley took so long to get ready for the second version that I missed the Paul Simon concert I had tickets to. (Well, seeing Paul was important to me.)

When it came to replacing Diane, we knew we didn't want to create another waitress character. The comparison alone could hurt us. It wasn't fair to any actress or to the show to follow the unique chemistry of Sam and Diane. Luckily, we still had the idea from early on that we had never implemented: Sam working for a woman. Our original conception was a Suzanne Pleshette type, a tough, beautiful woman.

The Brothers started writing. They created Rebecca Howe, a no-nonsense corporate executive who is assigned to manage the bar after the heartbroken Sam sells it and travels around the world to try to forget Diane. The casting process ensued. The first words out of casting director Jeff Greenberg's mouth were "Kirstie Alley."

Kirstie was doing *Star Trek II: The Wrath of Khan.* I saw her star in *Cat on a Hot Tin Roof* at the Mark Taper Forum, and she was extraordinary. She held that room. We needed someone who knew what they could do onstage. We were, however, concerned about whether she could do comedy. The Brothers went to visit the set of the movie *Summer School* and asked director Carl Reiner whether Kirstie could do comedy. Carl said, "You got your girl!"

Dynasty was very popular at the time, and we were also looking for a Joan Collins type. Kirstie brought that glamour to the table. I wish I could tell you that we didn't go "Booah" when she came in to meet us, the way the stunned Sam does when he first meets Rebecca, overwhelmed by her beauty. But "Booah" did come out of Glen Charles's mouth, which made me laugh so hard.

Kirstie had the voice, looks, and presence we wanted, but we thought that we were subject to the old rule of "When you're house-hunting, never buy the first house you see." We continued searching. We couldn't do an open casting call, because the show was too prominent and too visible. The media storm would have been awful. We couldn't take Sam and Diane away from America without a real plan going forward. We met with Sharon Stone, Kim Cattrall, Marg Helgenberger, Madolyn Smith, and a few others. Nobody could beat Kirstie.

Kirstie showed up for the first reading as Rebecca dressed as Diane, in a blond wig and a skirt. It was hysterical. While she made a grand entrance, her first run-through was abysmal. It was our fault. We had written Rebecca as a martinet. She wouldn't give Sam Malone the time of day. She was mean. It wasn't working. When we got back to the office, Teddy and Rhea came in and we discussed what had happened. Teddy said, "I just want to hug her." I kept thinking about that. The Brothers and I knew there was something in what Teddy said.

After the few scenes in the run-through, Rebecca was still not funny. Then we got to a scene where she goes into her office, Sam's old office. For some reason she couldn't get the door open. She started wrestling with the doorknob, and we cracked up. It dawned on us that we had to make her a modern-day woman who thinks she's empowered but sometimes can't emotionally get through the day. The moment we found her frailty and vulnerability, we had it. All of a sudden she became hysterically funny—a woman who looks strong, tough, and mean but is a cheese soufflé on the inside. Bingo! She nailed it. We were very fortunate.

After five years of on again, off again, nose grabbing, hair pulling, and passionate reconciliations, the audience knew that when Sam told Diane, "Have a good life," it was really over. We assumed that if Shelley had stayed past her five-year run, Sam and Diane would have gotten married. We would have had storylines related to the wedding and then children. In the first episode of the sixth season, Woody recaps: "Miss Chambers went off to write her book, and that didn't work out. Last we heard, she was out in Hollywood trying to write for TV." We had our final parting shot, wishing Diane the worst possible fate we could imagine.

There was a lot of pressure being the new kid in school, especially when replacing one of the most popular characters on television at the time. Kirstie pulled it off. We now had an intense dynamic between Sam and a woman who would never have sex with him. The writers were always watching the actors to see what they could weave into the characters. Kirstie showed us a trick she'd learned from her uncle when she was ten, where she could put a lit cigarette in her mouth and bring it back out with her tongue. We couldn't wait to use it in "My Fair Clavin."

On set, Kirstie quickly became one of the gang. Shelley was not fun in the over-the-top sense. By contrast, some of the cast members were scared of Kirstie's manic, crazy energy. At the 1991 Emmys, I won for Best Directing for *Cheers* and Kirstie won for Outstanding Lead Actress in a Comedy Series. Her acceptance speech still stands out in Emmy lore, because after she thanked the creators and the cast, she thanked her husband, Parker Stevenson, "the man who has given me the big one for the last eight years." I got to go up again to accept the award for Best Comedy Series. "We were good, but now we're venerable," I said. I thanked Glen and Les, "every writer we've ever had, because that's what makes the show great," and the cast. "You see some of them here. One of them walked off with a big one."

As we moved forward, we knew we didn't want to do the show just around Rebecca and Sam in a romance. While they were attracted to each other, there was no deep emotional connection. They weren't having sex, but there was sexual tension between them. In the same way Sam was a skirt chaser, Rebecca was equally shallow, attracted to only wealthy, powerful men. But the show was no longer centered on Sam and a love interest. We made it about the rest of the bar, allowing the terrific ensemble to take center stage. We had created layered characters that we could mine for stories. It was great to have so many bullets in the creative gun.

Cheers went on for another six years, as popular as ever. If Kirstie wasn't as good as she was, people would have said that *Cheers* walked out the door with Diane. When you have a cast with depth and range, you can write anything and have each character react to the same line or thought. The best thing about the *Cheers* ensemble was that you didn't have to go far to find a funny attitude for anyone. Since the Sam and Diane dynamic was no longer driving the show, we developed George, Ratz, Rhea, Woody, Kelsey, and Bebe's characters, as well as those of the men who would date Rebecca and throw her over. We got funny out of Tom Skerritt, who could play light comedy, as Rebecca's boss, Evan Drake, and then from Roger Rees as billionaire Robin Colcord. Norm finally gave up being an accountant and took up house painting, which, unlike accounting, he was actually quite good at. It also turned out that he had a unique gift for interior design, even pretending to be gay to get work.

Admiral William J. Crowe, the chairman of the Joint Chiefs of Staff, appeared in "Hot Rocks." He was a fan and asked if he could be on. He was the perfect guest. He wasn't running for anything. He wasn't famous enough that advance notice would get more people to watch, and he could get a different reaction from each character:

SAM

Hey, everybody, guess who I brought back with me?

WOODY

Sam, how'd you do it? The doorman at the Ritz Carlton!

CLIFF

Good lord! That's Admiral William J. Crowe, Jr., chairman of the Joint Chiefs of Staff himself.

WOODY

Wait a minute. The chairman of the Joint Chiefs of Staff is a doorman at the Ritz Carlton? No wonder they charge you so much over there.

SAM

Woody, this really is the chairman of the Joint Chiefs of Staff. He
was at the same dinner I was.

CROWE

The Navy can't afford to pay the salary of a doorman.

SAM

He recognized me from my ballplaying days.

CROWE

Nobody gives up towering home runs like Sam Malone.
I wish our missiles flew as high and as far.

CLIFF

Admiral William J. Crowe, Jr. Voted admiral, 1974. 1983:
commander, U.S. Pacific Command. 1985: appointed eleventh
chairman of the Joint Chiefs of Staff. Wife: Shirley.

CROWE

I'm impressed, young man. How come you know so
much about me?

CLIFF

Simple, sir. I'm an American.

CROWE

Us guys in uniform have to stick together . . .

FRASIER

Hello there, sir. I'm Dr. Frasier Crane.

CROWE

Hello, Doctor.

FRASIER

This is my number. I have treated Napoleon, Teddy Roosevelt, and I know I can help you.

CROWE

Doctor, I really am the chairman of the Joint Chiefs of Staff.

FRASIER

Aye, aye, Admiral!

CROWE

But I'll keep your card. I know a lot of people at the Pentagon who could use your services.

Cliff then regaled the admiral with his concept for a submarine with wheels—and I got to see the aide who carried the briefcase that contained the nuclear codes.

A number of strong additions as recurring cast members drove storylines. Frances Sternhagen played Cliff's mother. Joel Polis and Robert Desiderio played Gary, owner of Cheers's rival bar, Gary's Olde Towne Tavern; and Keene Curtis played John Allen Hill, the pompous owner of the upstairs Melville's, who became Sam's nemesis. In comedy, a nemesis is an instigator. It's not just his journey but how he impacts the other characters that makes it interesting.

In sitcoms, not a lot happens emotionally for people. If you're doing eleven years, you can't have major changes; otherwise you'll be done in eleven episodes. Characters move a quarter of a centimeter every episode, with tight boundaries. Too many changes are a concern. With each episode, we had to pretend that people were tuning in for the first time. John Allen, as Sam's nemesis, offered a plot point. It's about advancing the other characters.

Glen Charles was a big hockey fan, so we created a romance between Carla and Guy "Eddie" LeBec (Jay Thomas), a French Canadian goalie with the Boston Bruins, who stops at Cheers for a drink. Carla falls in love immediately, and Eddie invites her to watch him play:

CARLA

Eddie stopped forty shots! I haven't seen a guy have a night like that since Harmon Killebrew hit those three moon-shot homers off of you, Sam.

SAM

Yes, I was certainly lucky to be there to see that, wasn't I?

Even as their affair put a temporary jinx on the Bruins' winning streak, Carla got pregnant with twins by Eddie, to coincide with Rhea's real-life pregnancy. Despite multiple superstitions, in "Little Carla, Happy at Last," we married them off.

Jay was a stand-up comedian and a disc jockey and was still on Power 106 radio in Los Angeles while he was on *Cheers*. When a caller asked him what it was like to be on *Cheers,* his glib and nasty response was "It's brutal. I have to kiss Rhea Perlman."

That was it. He insulted Rhea, which meant he insulted all of us. He crossed the family. Jay was fired unceremoniously. Since he was no longer on the show, Eddie also had to go. In our world, you don't wind up sleeping with the fishes; you die a violent yet comedic death. After he's cut from the Bruins, Eddie takes a job with a traveling ice show as a penguin. In "Death Takes a Holiday on Ice," Eddie gets killed by a slow-moving Zamboni machine, saving the life of a fellow penguin, Gordy Brown (*Wings*'s Thomas Haden Church, in his first television role).

At Eddie's funeral, to add insult to Ice Capades fatality, and to make sure no one thought that Eddie had any redeeming qualities, we created a backstory that Eddie was a bigamist and had a second wife in Canada. Annie De Salvo played the second grieving widow, who bore more than a passing resemblance to Carla. The funeral broke out into a bar fight, with everyone in the melee, except for Norm, who remained in his seat, drinking a beer.

The Brothers were with the show full-time for five seasons. They gradually stepped back from producing but were always there at the beginning of each season to plot out the storylines, character arcs, and individual episodes. Most sitcoms have seven to eight writers a year; we had ten. Over the course of the show, we had dozens of writers, as churning out material for a weekly show is grueling and burnout happens really fast. It's normal for writers to run out of ideas for one sitcom and move on to another, where the new platform stimulates their creative juices. It's a great training ground for management as well. You can tell by a writer's demeanor, the type of suggestions they make, and how they get along with the team whether they can eventually become a producer and run the show.

Writers Ken Levine and David Isaacs were with us for three years, followed by Sam Simon and Ken Estin. We had David Angell; Peter Casey and David Lee; Cheri and Bill Steinkellner; Phoef Sutton; and Dan Staley and Rob Long. Tom Anderson and Dan O'Shannon, partners from Cleveland, were nicknamed "the Bologna Brothers" (in the days before each set had a fancy chef, we ordered in for lunch. Every day they'd order bologna sandwiches with mayo). We had immaculate writing from David Lloyd, who was with us most of the time. David's one regret in life was that he didn't live during the time of the Algonquin Round Table.

Wings also grew out of *Cheers*. Angell, Casey, and Lee came to the Brothers and me for support and backing. We helped them develop the show about Joe and Brian Hackett (Tim Daly and Steven Weber), two pilot brothers who run a one-plane airline out of a small commuter airport on Nantucket Island. Crystal Bernard's Helen, their childhood friend who runs the lunch counter and is a cellist, was an interesting character. Tony Shalhoub's cabdriver Antonio didn't come on until later in the show's development. The airport-terminal set had lockers on the second floor, which we ended up using for the pilot, the same way we maximized all the space in Cheers.

Leading up to the pilot, Steve was playing the leading man, which felt too close to Tim's straitlaced brother. I brought back his irreverence and had him sit on bookcases and on bars, drawing immediate distinctions. We needed to differentiate between the brothers: Joe, the buttoned-down, responsible one, and Brian, just the opposite. I directed only the pilot of *Wings,* which had a successful eight-year run. I worked with Steve again on the short-lived *Cursed* (later renamed *The Weber Show*), a name that was sadly more prophetic than helpful.

The quality of the *Cheers* episodes never declined. I tried to always be there to inspire and support the writers. There was tremendous pressure on the writing teams. This was the big league: If a joke didn't work, it wasn't the cast's fault, it was the writers'. Also, everyone knew that a writing job on *Cheers* could catapult them into a long and successful television career. One of the final gifts we gave out were silver Tiffany key chains with the inscription "It was the best of times, it was the best of times."

Getting to direct Johnny Carson, whom I adored, was a total *Cheers* highlight. Johnny began hosting *The Tonight Show* in 1962, and for thirty years America grew to trust him the same way they trusted Walter Cronkite to deliver the news. We met the guest stars when he met them. On the air—he was Johnny. Between the *Today* show and late night, NBC made a fortune, and they mined it.

On "Heeeeere's Cliffy!" Cliff submits a joke to *The Tonight Show.* The guys alter the rejection letter to make it seem that Carson accepted his joke. Cliff takes Norm and his mother to Burbank, and they are seated in the studio audience. Norm bribes the cue-card guy to slip the joke into Johnny's monologue. Johnny reads the joke and starts making fun of it, and Cliff jumps out of his seat and starts arguing with Johnny.

Johnny was a fan of *Cheers* and agreed to make an appearance. He was very sweet—and all business during the taping. He had a show to do that night. We got our scenes in just a few takes and got him out of there. He was very reserved on set. I saw him perform in Las Vegas. He was hysterical, much broader and saltier.

After directing 237 of 270 episodes, I finally felt comfortable with the cast and the team and loosened the reins. My impetus for being there at that point was that I loved the cast, crew, writers, and the bar. Actually, a bout of walking pneumonia derailed my ability to direct "Christmas Cheers," and Tommy Lofaro finished the show. It was the first episode of *Cheers* that I didn't completely direct and only the second time in my career that I shared directing credit with someone.

The *Cheers* cold opens/teasers are as good as any you'll ever see on a sitcom. I am still so proud of those. The network offered us a teaser or a tag, which is a teaser at the end of the show. We chose a teaser. Networks like teasers because, if you don't go to a commercial before a show starts, you'll keep the audience from the previous show. If you start with content, it's tougher to change the channel. We did a teaser before the theme and then a commercial. Once we teased, they stayed.

Hand gestures became a thing. In "Friends, Romans, and Accountants," a guy in a tuxedo walks in and starts tapping on the bar and counting, using his hand to gesture.

SAM

Diane, do me a favor. Pour Mischa there a really quick beer.

DIANE

Sam, what is he doing with his hand?

SAM

He's the cymbals player for the symphony in the middle of a concert. He's counting out a long rest so he'll know exactly when to get back.

Diane counts out his change: "One twenty-five out of twenty—that's one fifty, one seventy-five, two, three, four, five, ten, and twenty." Mischa loses his count and angrily runs out of the bar. "Musicians are very temperamental," Diane says.

I pitched an idea where someone is tapping his fingers on the bar and what that leads to. It starts with Norm unwittingly tapping his pencil on the bar as he reads something. That is followed by someone two seats down tapping a deck of cards in the same rhythm. Someone else begins to tap on the face of his watch, and a woman moves her high heel against her other ankle to the same beat. Woody and Carla's tapping galvanizes the bar. Guys from the pool room come out and start tapping their cue sticks on the floor. The chef and waiter from Melville's come down the stairs clapping their hands. The entire bar is somehow tapping and clapping as Woody sings Queen's "We Will Rock You."

After doing more than two hundred episodes, I decided to take a couple of weeks off a year. While we let other people direct, we kept it within the family. We were that protective of the show and of one another. Given the closeness we'd developed, it would have been a very tough set for a new person to break into, especially as a director. Tommy Lofaro, my assistant director, helmed five episodes. Ratz directed four, including the one where Cliff has squeaky shoes. He also directed "What Is . . . Cliff Clavin," the episode where *Jeopardy!* comes to Boston and Cliff becomes a contestant. The categories are Civil Servants, Stamps from Around the World, Mothers and Sons, Beer, Bar Trivia, and Celibacy—Cliff's dream board. Cliff gets almost every question right but bets everything and blows it on the Final Jeopardy! question, which he answers incorrectly. He still claims that he won, a standard device in comedy and more recently in politics.

Alex Trebek comes to Cheers and unexpectedly runs into Cliff:

ALEX

Cliff. Hey, listen, I'm very sorry about what happened to you on
our program this afternoon.

CLIFF

So you admit that you were out of line by telling me I was wrong?

ALEX

Well, I wouldn't go quite that far. The fact is that a case could be
made for your point of view. I think the problem for us was in the
way we phrased our answer—it allowed for more than one
possible question.

CLIFF

So you got my forty-four thousand bucks?

ALEX

No. No, I don't.

CLIFF

Oh, well, then you're probably going to have me back as a
returning contestant then, right?

ALEX

No, we're not going to do that either. I know this isn't what you
want to hear, but believe me, we're as upset about what happened
as you are. You know, it's a funny thing. You spend years hosting a
show and you get into the habit of thinking there's just one correct
question for every answer. But life doesn't always work out that
way. The world is much more complex, and you discover that there
are many different ways of looking at the universe.

CLIFF

Yes. Well, what are you gonna do?

ALEX

I think I'm going to quit my job as host of *Jeopardy!*
Maybe spend a little time in Tibet.

CLIFF

Aw, no, Alex. Sit down here. I mean, you don't
know what you're saying.

ALEX

How can I go on hosting the program if I'm filled
with all these doubts?

CLIFF

Think about what *Jeopardy!* means to America. It's more than just
a game show. I mean, it's as much a part of the national fabric as
the postal uniform that I wear with pride every single day.

ALEX

So you think I should stay as the host of *Jeopardy!*?

CLIFF

Absolutely.

ALEX

And you won't bear me any ill will if I do?

CLIFF

Bite your tongue!

ALEX

All right. It's settled. I'm going to stay on as the host of *Jeopardy!*

CLIFF

You hear that, everybody? I saved *Jeopardy!* I gotta go call Ma.
She'll get a kick out of this!

NORM

That's all right. You're a regular guy coming in here to make Cliff
feel better. That's great.

ALEX

I just came in here for a beer, but I saw Cliff and I figured I'd
better say something. So I made up that story about quitting.
He scares me.

NORM

You too?

Producer Tim Berry, who also worked with me on *Chicago Sons,
George & Leo,* and *Union Square* and later worked with Teddy on
Becker, directed three episodes; Tom Moore and Rick Beren each
directed two. George directed one, as did Michael Zinberg. After
mentoring me at MTM and helping to greenlight *Cheers,* Michael
and I had come full circle.

We went all-out farce when Woody and Kelly (Jackie Swanson)
got married. (People still sing the silly "Kelly Song," which Woody
wrote himself.) We shot "An Old-Fashioned Wedding" in one night.
We did the first half of the hour-long show on the *Cheers* stage and
the second half on another stage, which was set up as a regal
kitchen. We gave each member of the audience popcorn and then
escorted them to the next stage. We had two swinging doors in the
kitchen, which is much funnier than one swinging door. Another
one of my rules: If you can only have one door, it has to be a swing-

ing door, and it has to be in a kitchen. We also had a dumbwaiter, dogs, a staircase, an unseen backyard, one drunk minister and one dead one.

The beauty of farce is that you can do a lot of silly things, misunderstandings, and physical comedy. People like to see other people fall down, especially people who are authority figures and people they don't like. It makes them feel that those people are just like us and gives them a sense of justice. If it's well-rehearsed and perfectly executed, farce is hysterically funny. *Noises Off* was hilarious on Broadway. Lucille Ball did farce all the time; that was in her wheelhouse. There were a lot of farcical pieces on *Frasier* as well.

I planned out extra time to rehearse the cast for the wedding episode. If you can't rehearse a farce, it won't be good. It requires precision timing. The shoot was tricky. We had too much material to cover to shoot every scene twice. David Lloyd wrote a 1940s-style script. The *Cheers* ensemble is in the kitchen, delivering the liquor. The previously unconsummated yet eager Woody and Kelly have sex the morning of the wedding. Sam is trying to keep them away from each other and from her father (Richard Doyle), who says to Woody, "I don't think I've ever hidden the fact that I dislike you intensely. I know that this may sound like fatherly advice, but it's a threat." Jackie could play the innocence to match Woody's. Richard was out of the South Coast Repertory company and did all the plays in Long Beach. They were both perfectly cast.

Rebecca's bickering with the arrogant Chef Maurice (Daniel Gerroll) causes him to walk out and take his staff with him. Sam assembles the barflies to step in and assist. The script called for ferocious dogs to be one more disruption at Woody's wedding. I said, "No. Ferocious dogs are meaner when you only hear their barking." Dogs named Attila and Hitler who bark loudly off camera are much scarier. Each time Woody appears in the kitchen, Sam throws him out the side door, where the vicious dogs are. Each time Woody winds up outside, he's chased by the dogs and comes back in with more of his tuxedo in tatters. Then the minister dies.

SAM
Are you sure he's dead? Frasier, you sure?

FRASIER
I trained as a physician. Believe me, he's dead. You don't
make that mistake twice.

They put the minister in the dumbwaiter. Cliff is taking flash
pictures, blinding everyone. Uncle Roger (Milo O'Shea) is also a
minister but won't marry the couple without being "somewhat
sloshed," so they get him drunk. To stall, Lilith is sent out to sing to
entertain the guests. The gorgeous Cousin Monika from Germany
(Colleen Morris) throws herself at Sam:

MONIKA
I'm Cousin Monika.

SAM
I'm Uncle Sam.

(She kisses Sam and then leaves to be with her husband.)

SAM
You believe that—she's married!

REBECCA
She didn't seem to be a fanatic about it.

(The seductive Monika gives Sam her stockings and then returns
later and offers Sam her garters.)

MONIKA
As long as you have my stockings, I thought you might need
something to hold them up.

SAM

This is wrong. Listen, this is my buddy's wedding today; I can't
spoil it. Besides, I have certain moral standards that
I just refuse to compromise.

MONIKA

Right after the wedding, my poor husband has to fly to Dusseldorf.

SAM

Okay, but I'm buying breakfast.

(They are still dealing with the deceased minister.)

NORM

I hate to be the one to break this to you, but the body seems to
have fallen off the dumbwaiter.

(Sam puts Carla in the dumbwaiter to retrieve the body and keeps
releasing the rope, causing Carla to free-fall to the basement. Carla
comes up and tries to kill Sam.)

SAM

Okay, now, if we can get the body in the wine cellar and Frasier to
fix Uncle Roger and Rebecca to fix the cake and Lilith to entertain
the guests and Cliffy to fix Woody's pants, then we'll be all set.

The closest I have ever come to a controversial show was on
Cheers, when we tried to do an episode where one of the women
Sam slept with has contracted AIDS. Sam gets tested and awaits
the results. In a poignant moment in his office alone, he prays to
God and says, "If I'm okay, I'll never touch another woman." It was
a great premise, but once the word "AIDS" was used in rehearsal,
we all felt that it was too controversial for the time. We changed the
premise to a paternity test. In "Swear to God," Sam vows that if he's

not the father he won't have sex for three months, which, not surprisingly, becomes extremely difficult to keep.

Reaching one hundred episodes was a major benchmark for a sitcom (or any other show). At that point, television stations would start bidding on shows for syndication. There are no longer syndication deals per se. The last shows that scored big in syndication were *The Big Bang Theory* and *Modern Family.* Shows are now streamed online. It's a lot cheaper to stream than previous syndication deals, and streaming deals are made even before the show first airs, based on the cachet and quality of who is involved. Having said that, with lots of streaming spaces to fill, I still get small residual checks from shows that I did that were not that successful, which means they are airing somewhere.

John McLaughlin, host of the Sunday morning political talk show *The McLaughlin Group,* hosted our two hundredth episode. Glen and Les suggested his name as we didn't want the typical or expected entertainment or talk-show host. He was strictly a political guy. The funniest person he had ever worked for was Richard Nixon.

When John walks into the bar, Woody incorrectly recognizes him from television: "You keep the Gorgeous Ladies of Wrestling from tearing each other apart." The cast and creators were onstage in front of a capacity crowd at the Paramount Theater, the screening room on the studio lot. We had so many more clips and interactions that we had to cut for the version that aired. John was terrific as host and was a surprise choice for the audience.

We started running out of ideas after two hundred twenty-five episodes. More than a decade after Cheers served its first customer, Teddy told us that he would not be back for a twelfth season. The Brothers and I had planned on only a couple more seasons anyway. We never tried to talk him out of it. It was different from when Shelley left. We knew the bar was the star, but it was Sam Malone's bar, and it was time to close it.

In one of the last episodes, "It's Lonely on the Top," we had what is now an iconic moment in television history. When Carla is promoted to bartender, she mixes a drink called "I Know My Redeemer Liveth" ("One drink and you won't recognize your best friend"). When the group comes in the next day hungover and with little or no recollection of what happened the night before, Carla confesses to Sam that she slept with one of them but can't remember who. When Carla finds out she slept with Paul (Paul Willson), she is despondent over having a dark secret that she'll have to live with for the rest of her life. Sam consoles her by sharing his darkest secret—that he wears a toupee! Sam's hairpiece was one of the most well-guarded secrets in Hollywood. We approached Teddy about coming clean before the episode was even written. He was totally on board. It was a huge reveal and showed the level of Sam's friendship, as well as his vulnerability.

To end the series, we decided to go out on top. The Brothers felt that since they wrote the first episode, they should write the last one as well. Unlike *M*A*S*H,* which concluded with the end of the Korean War, we didn't have a logical stopping point. We wanted to have some closure for Sam and deal with what happens when a young man realizes that some of his pleasures are deserting him or aren't healthy for him anymore. Because of what was going on at the time on the sexual front, people were being more disciplined about sex. The sexual revolution was running out of steam. Sam couldn't drink anymore and couldn't carouse as much. He had to find a way to move into a more mature part of his life.

The Brothers wrote a great script. From the first reading to what was on the air, a lot of changes were made and a lot of nuances added. Since it was the final show, we also had the real-life emotion of the actors playing with us, so the poignancy was built in. It was really sad but also really wonderful.

For the finale, we wanted to wrap things up as best we could. We knew we wanted to get Diane back in the bar, and we knew we wanted all the characters to have a poignant moment. NBC milked the crap out of it. They not only gave us ninety minutes to fill, they actually did a preshow special with Bob Costas talking about what was about to come and how wonderful it was going to be. We had nothing to do with that. They tried to turn the finale into the Super Bowl. The resemblance didn't end there: *Cheers* had been the highest-priced show in television a few times, with thirty-second commercials going for as much as $300,000. Commercials in the final episode shattered the record for a television series, fetching a staggering $650,000 for thirty seconds, a figure associated only with Super Bowls. As a result, the Brothers and I became the most successful bar owners in history. We couldn't have been happier about all that attention and pageantry. Even President Bill Clinton said that he wanted to appear in the final episode. We wrote an entire segment involving Bill coming into the bar. Shortly before we were about to start filming, Hillary's father passed away, and Bill had to back out. We took it as an incredible compliment that he even asked and appreciated the acknowledgment of how influential the show was. But at that point, even an appearance by POTUS would not have drawn attention from the impact of the *Cheers* finale. If you're leaving, there's no better way to go out than on top. Everyone we knew was part of the celebration.

On May 20, 1993, the last episode of *Cheers* aired. We took over the Bull and Finch and had a massive tribute to the series. The cast and producers were all there. Live feeds went out to all the stations, with interviews and hype.

We had finished filming the show two weeks before that and were in Boston just to have a good time. Each year after the sixth season, we'd go back to Boston for a week to shoot exteriors, and we were always treated like a national championship team. This time we were met with a motorcade and police escorts. I remember George saying, "Now I know what it's like to be a rock star." Over the years, we had dinners with Governors Mike Dukakis and Bill Weld, and Mayor Ray Flynn. It was still glorious but also sad, because the show was ending.

We knew that this was the final goodbye. For years after that, the

Brothers and I resisted reunion shows, and after twenty-five years it was just too long, anyway. As confirmed by the *Will & Grace* reboot, which worked, you can do a reboot where you remember the characters, the way they were when they were successful. The *Cheers* folks aged gracefully but not as well as the *Will & Grace* troupe. There's this whole thing about reconnecting with your first boyfriend or girlfriend thirty years later. You might be inquisitive and interested, but you'll always have in your head what they looked and sounded like at eighteen, and you kind of want to preserve that youthful memory. We wanted to preserve what we had.

For the finale, we had artist Ross Bleckner, who had become a friend, *Doonesbury* creator Garry Trudeau, and Brandon Tartikoff, who was one of the main reasons we had the bar, as patrons. Our wives were there as well. Everybody who was associated with the show at one time or another was sitting at that bar, including every network executive and Paramount person, writers, and producers. We used to put people in the back of the bar, where I knew you would see them because of the traditional shots I had in the show. We actually auctioned off the opportunity to sit in the bar and gave the proceeds to charity. I always put these people in a spot where they could be seen and didn't have to react. Always upstage, but never next to Kelsey or Ratz.

The entire Thursday-night programming was dedicated to *Cheers*. *The Tonight Show* hosted live from the bar. Then–NBC president Warren Littlefield put on an apron and tended bar, serving for Boston sports legends, including Red Sox pitcher Roger Clemens. It was an amazing and emotional event and is still the second-highest-watched finale in television history, with 84.4 million viewers, second only to 1983's *M*A*S*H* finale, which had 105.9 million.

"One for the Road" revolves around the return of Diane after being away for six years. We reached out to Shelley, and fortunately she was excited about joining us one last time. After Sam and Diane's plans to make each other believe that they are now happily married to other people fall apart, they realize that maybe it's fate that they should rekindle their relationship. After announcing their engagement—to the disapproval of their friends—they conclude that it probably won't work. They're not right for each other after all. We knew that. That's what made them great. We had a different version of "happily ever after" in our heads.

When we shot the final scene of the last show, where they're all sitting around smoking cigars, it was everything I could do to keep from crying. The last patron to leave the bar is, appropriately, of course, Norm. There's one final customer, who comes along after the bar is closed, and Sam doesn't let him in. We cast our agent, Bob Broder, for the part. He was the perfect guy to do it, and poetic since he was the guy who got us the bar in the first place.

We ended the show as we opened it. Sam was married to his bar. Cheers was the real love of his life. He loved people, and owning Cheers allowed him to create this beautiful community of friends who were his family.

Cheers was a turning point in my career. I was a producer, and I was nurturing something I had co-created. This came from my loins, my soul. This was our *Three Men and a Baby*. We worked very hard and were lucky enough to come up with the right idea at the right time and work with a group of brilliant and unknown actors and hitch our wagon to their stars and watch them rise.

Frasier

DAPHNE
What's so hard about telling Roz you were wrong?

FRASIER
You see, it's not the same as Dad being wrong or you being wrong. I have a
degree from Harvard. Whenever I'm wrong, the world makes a little less sense!

I had had an amazing fifteen-year run with *Taxi* and *Cheers*.
While I had learned a tremendous amount directing *Taxi*, with
Cheers I also gained an understanding of what it meant to "own" a
show. It was *our* show. The Brothers and I loved going to work every
day with the cast and crew, all of whom we hired and worked with
for years. It was energizing to be part of a creative process, nurturing actors and writers and adding my own creativity to the mix. This
desire to be part of a collaboration in the name of comedy has continued for nearly thirty years—and counting.

After a few more projects together, the creative and versatile
Brothers left show business to pursue other creative interests. Running a show is arduous. It takes a lot out of you, especially if you're

involved in the weekly writing. We had never thought about being the next MTM. We loved what we were doing, enjoyed working together, and were very satisfied with our partnership on *Cheers.* Twelve years is a great run for any collaboration. I was on the ground for all eleven seasons of *Cheers,* and they always had their hands and hearts in the process, up to and including the finale.

After *Cheers,* I had a deal with NBC where we were partners on pilots. Don Ohlmeyer agreed to send me all their scripts, but I wasn't precluded from looking at other networks' scripts. I was able to direct pilots for other networks, as long as I continued to do shows for NBC. *Friends, Will & Grace, Caroline in the City,* and *NewsRadio* were all under that deal.

During the last season of *Cheers,* David Angell, Peter Casey, and David Lee came to the Brothers and me and said they wanted to do a show with Kelsey as Frasier. We had no doubt that Kelsey could carry a show on his own. They went off and wrote the pilot, in which the Frasier character, who was a barfly and supporting character on *Cheers,* was transformed into a lead character. As *Cheers* was closing shop, the new team reaped the benefit of retaining many of the crew, as well as the soundstage and time slot. The Brothers and Kelsey wanted me to direct as an added protection of the character and show. I was in. Glen and Les had created the character, and Kelsey and I had nurtured it for nine years. We were all determined to make the transition as smooth, creative, and successful as possible.

David Angell, God rest his soul, was a wonderful man. He was always teased about how he could write so funny and still be the dullest person in the room. David and his wife, Lynn, had been in Cape Cod and were flying back to Los Angeles for the Emmys (as executive producer of *Frasier,* he had been nominated for Best Comedy Series) when their plane, Flight 11, was taken over by terrorists during the 9/11 attacks and crashed into the North Tower of the World Trade Center. We had a memorial ceremony for him at

Paramount. Steve Weber, who worked closely with David on *Wings*, said, "I can only imagine the last moments, when David and Lynn looked into each other's eyes and held one another, knowing what was going to happen."

Cheers ended in May of 1993 and *Frasier* debuted in September. Kelsey's twenty years as this evolving and enduring character was a credit to the combination of great writing and the quality of the actor who played him. The series opened with Frasier sharing his story with his radio audience:

"Six months ago, I was living in Boston. My wife had left me, which was very painful. Then she came back to me, which was excruciating. On top of that, my practice had grown stagnant, and my social life consisted of hanging around a bar night after night. I was clinging to a life that wasn't working anymore, and I knew I had to do something . . . anything. So, I ended the marriage once and for all, packed up my things, and moved back here to my hometown of Seattle."

From the first insightful and introspective paragraph, which had the truth in jest of Frasier and Lilith, Kelsey was a new version of Sam Malone. So much more complicated, smarter, more erudite, and with all the characteristics of a psychiatrist—great at solving their patients' issues and equally terrible at solving their own. Although Frasier evolved, there was still the vestige of the original character, always insecure and angry but with the foundation of warmth and decency. He's listening.

Frasier could no longer be as hysterical or exorcised as he was on *Cheers*. No more hit-and-run comedy. He was now the spine of the show and had to be the sounding board. Frasier not only had to maintain his comedy, but as the new center, he had to react to each of the ensemble's comedy. That required more equanimity than on *Cheers*.

One of the defining characteristics of Frasier is that he loved fully, wholly, deeply. He fell hard. Frasier has always been George

Bailey from *It's a Wonderful Life*. When it was his turn to do what he wanted to do, it took a backseat to someone else's needs. But also like George, Frasier is "the richest man in town" because of that love that he in turn gets from family and friends.

While directing each episode, I had a special shorthand with Kelsey on set. He would yell, "Let's kick the pig," meaning let's move it along, or he would break into song with his version of "The Good Life." Like with Judd Hirsch and Teddy Danson, I could say, "Kels, give me a forty-four." It was code for nothing. I was telling him, "Do whatever you want, I'm watching you. If you do anything I think is off, I'll let you know. I have your back."

To continue the story of Dr. Frasier Crane as he moved from Boston to Seattle to become a radio-talk-show psychiatrist, we needed to create new characters around him, including a homecare worker, producer, brother, and father.

When Jane Leeves was cast as Frasier's father Martin's home-care worker, Daphne Moon, I wanted her to be eccentric from the outset. While rehearsing the pilot, I said, "Do something strange when Frasier opens the door." I had her put her hand inside her dress to adjust her bra. No exposition, just physical comedy. When Frasier opens the door, she looks embarrassed and he looks nonplussed. During the interview scene, I told her to empty as many things from her large handbag as possible before getting to her résumé. Frasier and Martin (John Mahoney) watch as she removes a whisk broom, a Nerf heart, and a bottle of nuts.

We had originally cast Lisa Kudrow as Roz Doyle, the radio producer at KACL. We replaced her with Peri Gilpin, because as great an actor as Lisa would be in *Friends* and in everything she's done since, the Roz role didn't fit her. Lisa had a more wispy, ethereal style, which wasn't working. Roz's most important role in the pilot was to credibly deliver the Lupe Velez speech, which was the key to the pilot and to Frasier developing a relationship with Martin. Roz is making Frasier aware that things aren't going to happen the way you think they're going to happen:

Title Card
LUPE VELEZ

Frasier is rushing back after taking a break. Cut to inside the KACL radio studio; Roz is in her booth. Frasier enters hurriedly, slams the door, and sits down.

FRASIER

They have *got* to move the bathroom closer to the studio! [puts his headphones on] We'll be right back after these messages.

(rips off his headphones)

Can't I put that on tape?

ROZ

What's eating you?

FRASIER

Oh, I'm sorry. It's just this thing with my father and this . . . this person he wants to hire. I thought I'd started my life with a clean slate and a picture of what it was going to be like, and then, I don't know . . .

ROZ

Ever heard of Lupe Velez?

FRASIER

Who?

ROZ

Lupe Velez—the movie star in the thirties? Well, her career hit the skids, so she decided she'd make one final stab at immortality. She figured if she couldn't be remembered for her movies, she'd be remembered for the way she died. And all Lupe wanted was to be remembered. So . . . she plans this lavish suicide—flowers, candles, silk sheets, white satin gown, full hair and makeup, the works. She takes the overdose of pills, lays on the bed, and imagines how beautiful she's going to look on the front page of tomorrow's newspaper. Unfortunately, the pills don't sit well with the enchilada combo plate she sadly chose as her last meal. She stumbles to the bathroom, trips, and goes headfirst into the toilet . . . and *that's* how they found her.

FRASIER

Is there a reason you're telling me this story?

ROZ

Yes. Even though things may not happen like we plan, they can work out anyway. [moves toward her booth]

FRASIER

Remind me again how it worked for Lupe, last seen with her head in the toilet.

ROZ

All she wanted was to be remembered. Will *you* ever forget that story?

(Roz returns to her booth and signals to him. He puts his headphones on; everything from now onward is on the air.)

FRASIER

We're back. Roz, who's our next caller?

ROZ

We have Martin on line one. He's having a problem with his son.

FRASIER

Hello, Martin. This is Dr. Frasier Crane; I'm listening.

MARTIN

I'm a first-time caller.

FRASIER

(Pause as Frasier realizes that the caller is his father.)
Welcome to the show. How can I help you?

MARTIN

I've just moved in with my son and, er, it ain't working. There's a
lot of tension between us.

FRASIER

I can imagine. Why do you think that's so?

MARTIN

I guess I didn't see he had a whole new life planned for himself,
and I kinda got in the way.

FRASIER

Well, these things are a two-way street. Perhaps your son wasn't
sensitive enough to see how your life was changing.

MARTIN

You got that right! I've been telling him ever since I got there!

FRASIER

I'm sure he appreciated your candor.

MARTIN

Well . . . maybe sometimes I oughta just learn how
to keep my trap shut.

FRASIER

That's good advice for us all. Anything else?

MARTIN

Yeah. I'm worried my son doesn't know that I really appreciate what he's done for me.

FRASIER

Why don't you tell him?

MARTIN

Well, you know how it is with fathers and sons, it . . . I'd have trouble saying that stuff.

FRASIER

Well, if it helps, I suspect your son already knows how you feel. Is that all?

MARTIN

Yeah, I guess that's it. Thank you, Dr. Crane.

FRASIER

My pleasure, Martin.

MARTIN

D'you hear what I said? I said *thank you*!

FRASIER

Yes, I heard . . .

ROZ

Dr. Crane, we have Claire on line four. She's having a problem getting over a relationship.

FRASIER
Hello, Claire. I'm listening.

CLAIRE
I'm a . . . well, I'm a *mess*! Eight months ago my boyfriend and I broke up, and I just can't get over it. The pain isn't going away . . . it's almost like I'm in mourning or something. . . .

FRASIER
Claire, you *are* in mourning. But you're not mourning the loss of your boyfriend. You're mourning the loss of what you thought your life was going to be. Let it go. Things don't always work out how you planned—that's not necessarily bad. Things have a way of working out anyway. Have you ever heard of . . . Lupe Velez?

(He gives Roz a glance.)

Peri was a great Roz and delivered the speech powerfully. As Frasier's radio producer, she was a strong and tough foil. I had worked with Peri before, on both *Cheers* and *Flesh 'n' Blood*. Her character was named after Angell, Casey, and Lee's real-life producer, Roz Doyle, who was from England and who passed away in 1991. Almost prophetically, when Peri auditioned for *Wings*, Roz had helped her with her hair and makeup choices. To add to the karma, when Peri was offered a choice of jackets to wear in the first publicity shots for *Frasier*, she picked the one that belonged to Roz Doyle.

Peri worked very hard for her role. One day I saw her standing off in a corner by herself saying her lines out loud. I knew she had the role nailed down, and I yelled, "Stop rehearsing!" She was also a little intimidated in the beginning about working with Kelsey. To which I also yelled, "Take the stage! He needs someone to play with!" And from that moment on, once given permission, the two of them were great together.

You can't bend an actor into a role, especially when they're not suited for it. The instinct has to be there. You don't ever want to take someone who's okay and make them good. You want to take someone good and make them great. They have to be able to keep up; otherwise, they'll be replaced or the part gets shortened. Everyone has to leave it all on the field.

A typical *Frasier* story would have Frasier falling on his face, with his pomposity getting in the way of his life, while always being sweet at heart. Balancing his ability to do so much good helping people against his arrogance is the key to the enjoyment of the character. The audience is being given permission to laugh when someone else is struggling.

Frasier Crane was a complicated character played with such ease. There was so much more ammunition in his artistic and creative guns for us to develop. Kels can move an eyebrow and make you laugh. Frasier could always come back from any faux pas or screwup. Kelsey played Frasier with a little Jack Benny weaved in— as straight man to everyone else in the ensemble, who would make fun of him, the same way Jack's ensemble made fun of him. Both could play off any eccentric character in the troupe. Kelsey even did a special for NBC saluting Jack Benny and pointing out their respective characters' and casts' similarities.

The key to Kelsey's final maturation into Frasier was creating the Niles Crane character to play the old Frasier-like character from *Cheers*. Niles became Frasier, and Kelsey became Sam Malone. Angell, Casey, and Lee wrote up, just as the Charles Brothers did on *Cheers*. They didn't care what the audience expected—they elevated the comedy with upscale jokes, humor, and farce, and the audience met them more than halfway.

Casting director Jeff Greenberg was the one who said, "I have the guy to play the brother." David Hyde Pierce was on a show called *The Powers That Be,* and he became Niles, Frasier's younger brother, also a psychiatrist. What more do you have to say about someone who can play a scene with Kelsey Grammer and get his own huge laughs? David had a skill for doing a subtle joke and playing with it.

The conventional wisdom was for Frasier to have a blue-collar, not very evolved "mouth breather" brother and for the comedy to come from the clash between them. Martin Crane, their father, wound up becoming the contrast. Niles was to the outside of Frasier in terms of punctiliousness and overintellectualized self and was a ball carrier of emotion. I set up contrast right away to make sure the clean lines were there between the characters.

Frasier and Niles were brothers who clearly loved each other. Despite that, or because of that, Frasier thought Niles was a fool and Niles thought Frasier was a pompous ass. They bickered like a married couple and had the subsidiary relationship with their blue-collar father, who provided grounding for their highbrow attitude. That formula worked consistently for eleven seasons because of incredibly well-written scripts and a gifted cast that acted within that construct.

By crafting Niles to be similar to the incarnation of Frasier in the early seasons of *Cheers,* we preserved many of the idiosyncrasies that originally endeared Frasier to the audience. Initially, there was no second scene for Niles in the pilot, but I had the writers create a new scene to fully establish the character. At their new favorite coffee shop, Café Nervosa, the brothers get to spar and banter:

Title Card
THE BROTHER

Frasier is at Café Nervosa. Niles Crane, his younger brother, is standing next to him, recounting a story.

NILES

So I said to the gardener, "Yoshi, I do not want a Zen garden in my backyard. If I want to rake gravel every ten minutes to maintain my inner harmony, I'll move to Yokohama." Well, this offends him, so he starts pulling up Maris's prized camellias by the handful.

Well, I couldn't stand for that, so I marched right into the morning
room and locked the door until he cooled down.

(Frasier has been nodding his head, but he has
obviously not been listening.)

NILES
Tell me you would have handled it differently, Frasier.

FRASIER
Oh, I'm sorry, Niles, I didn't realize you'd stopped talking.

NILES
You haven't heard a word I said.

FRASIER
Niles, you're a psychiatrist—you know what it's like hearing people
prattle on about their endless lives.

NILES
Touché. And on that subject, I heard your show today.

FRASIER
And?

NILES
You know what I think about pop psychiatry.

FRASIER
I know what you think about everything. When was the
last time you had an unexpressed thought?

NILES
I'm having one now.

I told David, "Before you sit down, take out your handkerchief and wipe the seat." It turned out to be a character-defining trait. As the fastidious and neurotic Niles meticulously wipes down the chair, Frasier watches incredulously. David added a nice touch by offering the handkerchief to Frasier. "No thank you" was Frasier's polite yet curt reply. It was an insight into how obsessive and ridiculous the character could become. Niles spent five minutes wiping down that chair and the next eleven years wiping down everything else. The chemistry between Kelsey and David was a great joy to watch and gave us plenty of creative opportunities.

Other than my suggestions as director, the Brothers and I felt no need to add any other input into the *Frasier* pilot and/or subsequent scripts. We knew how good David, Peter, and David were. They used words like "Lalique," "eclectic," and "atelier." As on *Cheers,* they didn't care if the audience understood each nuance. They didn't lose the character. As Frasier moved to the lead, Niles became the old Frasier. They cast a father (who was actually only ten years older than Kelsey) and added the characters of Roz and Daphne and ran with it.

John Mahoney got to play Martin Crane because of a *Cheers* episode about a man hired to write jingles for the bar. We hired Ronny Graham for the part. He was as eccentric as he was talented. We had the dress rehearsal, broke for dinner, and Ronny drove off the lot and never came back.

We were trying to figure who to cast for Ronny's part. I had seen John Mahoney on Broadway in *The House of Blue Leaves,* so I knew he played the piano. We hired him. He came out and we shot a few scenes, then I said, "John, now you have to play the piano." John said, "I don't play the piano."

We had actually killed Frasier's father off in the ninth season of *Cheers.* Frasier walked in with a stuffed owl and said his father was a famous professor and the owl was his prized possession. He asked Sam if he wanted to keep it in the bar. Sam said, "Hell, no." Frasier told him, "Toss it." That was the end of his sentiment about his dad.

The continuity aspect was fixed on *Frasier* in an episode when Sam visited Frasier and said, "You told me your dad was dead," and Frasier replied, "I lied."

Martin Crane's character complemented and provided creative contrast to Frasier's. He was an ex–police detective, a blue-collar guy who sat on a beloved old Barcalounger recliner covered in duct-tape patches where the fabric had ripped. Marty was a great working-class foil to his highbrow sons. When Niles refers to a restaurant's menu as "to die for," Marty replies, "Your country and your family are to die for. Food is to eat." That's where Frasier came from. That was his childhood. That's why you could sympathize and understand him. As pompous as he was, he came from decent, hard-working stock, which is also why he was so comfortable at the bar on *Cheers*.

John Mahoney got very sick and died way too young from complications related to throat cancer in 2018. Most people don't know that he was from England. He trained with and was a resident member of the Steppenwolf Theatre Company in Chicago and worked onstage before breaking into film and television. In 1998, it was his idea for me to direct Steppenwolf's *The Man Who Came to Dinner*, the George S. Kaufman play, with him as Sheridan Whiteside, the radio star who is "friend to the great and near great." Whiteside is arrogant and self-absorbed, but he protects the kids in the family from their parents and takes care of his secretary.

I blocked the show in a day and a half, and then I started running it. The funniest bits came after blocking. We played with what didn't work and added new business. The cast was initially nervous about my style. Mahoney reassured them. "Trust him," he said.

Mahoney was terrific as the cantankerous Whiteside. Steppenwolf has a Founder's Night performance for press before a show opens. In the scene where three convict characters are brought in to see Whiteside, I had Gary Sinise, Terry Kinney, and Jeff Perry—the three Steppenwolf founders—play the convicts and surprise

Mahoney. He had to turn upstage for two minutes because he was laughing so hard.

Peri, David, Mahoney, and Jane all had to play in the same color as Kels, one of heightened reality. During the first year, we also had Dan Butler as Bob "Bulldog" Briscoe, the station sports guy, who was loud and over the top and taunted Frasier. He spoke a language that Frasier didn't understand.

Just as Frasier didn't comprehend sports, he similarly had no clue about anything mechanical. And that's where the comedy came from. In "Seat of Power," Marty pushes Frasier to fix his own broken toilet. Niles disagrees:

FRASIER

You know, Niles, I'd actually like to fix the toilet
just to prove Dad wrong.

NILES

Frasier, when a man is born with superior genes, the last challenge
he should face involving a toilet is learning how to use one.

FRASIER

Yes, but we've conquered the intellectual world. But in the world
of nuts and bolts, we are at the mercy of tradesmen.

(Their attempts at home repair result in the toilet overflowing.)

NILES

The plumber has been called, the wine is properly chilled,
suddenly my world makes sense again.

FRASIER

We've had a tough day, tangled with a little pipe
and porcelain. Now it's Montrachet time.

NILES

Oh, when you think about it, our only mistake today
was trying to fix that toilet ourselves.

FRASIER

Yes, we tampered with the natural order of things.

NILES

But now order has been restored. By hiring a plumber, that
plumber can now afford, say, a Dolly Parton album. His part in it
can finance a national tour, which will, of course, come to Seattle,
allowing some local promoter to make enough money to send his
cross-dressing teenage son to us for 150-dollar-an-hour therapy.

FRASIER

To the circle of life!

The plumbers turn out to be the Kriezel Brothers, Danny and
Billy (John C. McGinley and Mike Starr), Danny who bullied Niles
and Billy who was Frasier's nemesis in junior high school. Frasier
talks Niles out of stuffing Danny's head into the toilet to get revenge
on him, but while he calms Niles down, he can't resist doing the
same thing to Billy.

The one set of characters you will never have a problem with,
will never have to kill off or recast, are the ones that actually don't
exist but still make valuable contributions. The characters you never
see provide great foils and allow reactions for their onscreen and
real-life counterparts; while non-corporeal, they still achieve legendary status. Characters left to the imagination let the audience
work with their mind's eye, and often the vision is better than anything or anyone that can be cast.

With offscreen personas, sometimes you hear just a voice, other
times nothing at all: Carlton the Doorman on *Rhoda;* Vera, Norm's

long-suffering and virtually never-seen wife; Sam Malone's more successful brother, Derek, whose face was obscured by all the people surrounding him. Dr. Niles Crane was married to the waif-like heiress Maris:

NILES

Let's get some lights on. (claps)

FRASIER

Good Lord, what the hell is that?

NILES

Maris had it made after she lost power in a storm. Battery-operated; works on a clapper so you can find it in the dark. Only problem was, the poor thing, try as she might, could never clap hard enough to activate it.

I also delivered my second television baby in cab 804. In "Flour Child," after Frasier's Mercedes breaks down, he, Niles, and Martin get into taxicab 804—an homage to *Taxi*—and the pregnant driver (Charlayne Woodard) goes into labor. Martin delivers the baby, which prompts Niles to question whether he and Maris would be good parents. He tests himself by carrying around a bag of flour, pretending that it's a baby. Niles's potential paternal skill is tested as the bag is dropped, poked, and burned.

As in *Taxi* and *Cheers,* episode ideas often came from real-life experiences. "Adventures in Paradise" was inspired by writer/producer Chris Lloyd. On vacation on a small island in the Caribbean, Chris ran into his old boss, Paul Junger Witt, and his wife, Susan Harris, who were literally next door. Frasier whisks his new girlfriend, Madeline (JoBeth Williams), to Bora Bora, but the idyllic vacation is ruined when he goes out on the balcony and sees that Lilith is literally next door.

It ruins Frasier's time with Madeline. He has so much unfinished business with Lilith, and he is a little jealous of her new boyfriend, Brian (James Morrison). He pretends to have raucous sex in his room to make Lilith jealous. I told Kels to grab the frame of the bed and attack it fiercely. Jumping around like a monkey, he let loose his rage and frustration. I gave Kels license to explore the outer edges of his character. Watching Frasier go from his most dignified intellectual to his most insecure and total freak-out got huge laughs from the audience.

Frasier always carried a world of emotion and pathos with him, even with a laugh. Kelsey, in his heart, lives on the borderline of comedy and pathos. There are also many moments where it comes bleeding through in his performances. Earlier in the same episode, on his first date with Madeline at a fancy French restaurant, Frasier winds up mediating between the irate owner and his young daughter, who has just told him she is pregnant after sleeping with the busboy. "You're angry because you think that the bond between father and daughter is broken. That is a temporary emotion. That bond cannot be broken." After the scene was over, Kelsey cried. I responded (hypocritically, since I'm usually the first to cry at emotional moments) with "There he goes!"

Ideas can come from the most disparate places. I had seen *Schindler's List* that year and, like most people, was so moved. I remembered how director Steven Spielberg staged the scenes on the balcony with Ralph Fiennes and Liam Neeson. In "The Candidate," Frasier endorses a congressional candidate, Phil Patterson (Boyd Gaines), and he's all in. He really believes in this guy. At a certain point they have a conversation where Phil confides that he was abducted by aliens. I staged the scene on Frasier's balcony, with him looking up at the sky as he hears the disquieting revelation. You're on Frasier's back as you watch it stiffen. He expresses horror without using his face and then slowly turns. Less is more. Frasier then has to deliver a commercial message, struggling to endorse "a visionary who cares about the little people." I saw Steven at the Directors Guild Awards, where I had just won as Best Director for the *Frasier* pilot, "The Good Son." When he congratulated me, I said, "You're next." No surprise, he won the DGA award the same year, as well as the Oscar.

One of the most fun things I got to do on *Frasier* was direct episodes that included former *Cheers* cast members. In "The Show Where Sam Shows Up," we deliberately kept his appearance a secret from the audience. When Teddy came out, the audience went crazy:

ROZ
So this is the Sam Malone you've always talked about, the one who has no respect for women and treats them like dirt. You need anyone to show you around Seattle?

SAM
Well, you know, tell you the truth, I'm all right with the city, but I get real lost in my hotel room.

FRASIER
Oh boy, just look at the two of you face-to-face. I imagine wild animals all over the Northwest lifting their heads, alerted to the scent!

Téa Leoni was great as Sam's fiancée, Sheila. Sam and Sheila met at a support group for sex addicts. It turns out that Frasier had an affair with Sheila prior to Sam's visit, not knowing that she was Sam's betrothed. Frasier struggles frantically to keep his friend from finding out.

"The Show Where Diane Comes Back" was a play within a show within a lot of baggage. Diane comes to Seattle to work on a play based on her own life. The play is Diane's version of Cheers, with Diane as the center of that universe. John Carroll Lynch plays

Franklin, the character based on Frasier. Frasier tries to get closure by explaining to Diane how hurt he was by being left at the altar. He winds up consoling her.

It was closure for us as well. It was the first time, other than the *Cheers* finale, that we had worked with Shelley since she left the show. The raw nerve of her departure all those years earlier was assuaged by the fact that we'd had six more seasons. Shelley was never the easiest to work with. She didn't enjoy *Cheers* as much as everyone else did, but she was terrific, and we wouldn't be having the conversation if Shelley had not been Diane.

In "The Innkeepers," Frasier and Niles have bought Seattle's oldest restaurant, and it is opening night. As in "Thanksgiving Orphans" and "An Old-Fashioned Wedding," we got to play with everything that goes wrong, from live eels to a snooty kitchen staff. Both Frasier and Niles go through the wrong swinging doors and knock someone unconscious or break someone's nose. I may have had more fun with swinging doors than Noël Coward.

Again, this type of farce required a lot of rehearsal because the timing needed to be perfect. When the entire kitchen staff quits, Niles, Roz, and Daphne pitch in. Daphne is slamming live eels on the table to kill them. Roz's hair gets blown out into a huge mess by putting too much lighter fluid in the cherries jubilee dessert she lights up ("Big blue flash . . . cherries everywhere"), which is followed by the sprinkler system going off. Niles yells, "I hope you're satisfied! You've thinned my brown sauce!" Bulldog says, "The sprinklers are so great! My date's dress is clinging to her like Saran Wrap!"

As Frasier tries to mollify the quickly exiting patrons, he calls for the parking attendant to get one of the cars. A car crashes through the wall, like cymbals ending the music of the farce, with the elderly attendant sticking his head out the car window to announce, "Number twenty-three is ready."

To add insult to injury, Marty answers the telephone. "Table for two? Smoke-damaged or not smoke-damaged?" Frasier turns to Niles and says, "We could tell people he died in the explosion."

Sometimes an inanimate object, even one piece of furniture, becomes a character. It reinforces a character, an idea, a mood. On *Frasier,* I put the duct tape on Marty's chair in the pilot. To me, the duct tape was a metaphor that worked on a few levels: You don't throw away something that's functional and sentimental. Also, that old recliner was the only piece that didn't fit in with Frasier's sophisticated furnishings and eclectic, elegant African art décor. That was Marty Crane, the person who didn't fit in, and that was what the show was about: Frasier giving in, to his father and to the world around him. Losing his rigidity was how the character grew and changed. Frasier constantly complained about the chair but wouldn't get rid of it.

Martin's chair was always a contentious topic. In "Give Him the Chair," Frasier attempts to get rid of it. Martin hates the replacement. Frasier tracks the old chair down to the set of a high school show, and after a student suddenly takes ill, Frasier is blackmailed into replacing him for the opening night's performance in order to recover the chair.

In "Look Before You Leap," Frasier implodes on live television when he can't remember the lyrics to "Buttons and Bows," the song Bob Hope made famous in *The Paleface.* Kels has a great singing voice. It's a fun challenge to direct someone with good pipes to sing badly. We had to find the right song and then shot it three times to get to that exquisite level of bad.

The story was based on a real-life incident that happened to the great Leslie Uggams. Leslie was asked to sing "June Is Bustin' Out All Over," a song not in her repertoire, at a live concert at the National Mall in Washington, D.C., on the Capitol lawn. She had the cue cards lined up the night before. It was raining all night, and that morning, "The guy holding the cue cards slips and falls and the cards go in the other direction. I had to keep going, and whatever came out I said it. I made up my own language. The cue-card guy was still laying there. I was going through a line of people. I was trying to scat like Ella Fitzgerald. Every once in a while, you heard me say, 'June is bustin' out all over.' I walked off the stage and no one said a word. Not the producers, not the audience, not my husband. I thought that was the end of it, until months later a friend called and said, 'Do you know you're in every gay bar in America?' I asked, 'Doing what?' 'That song.' Thank you, YouTube!"

Frasier was an instant hit for all the right reasons. The audience knew the character, the acting and writing were brilliant, the Thursday-night lineup the show was included in was great. We were preceded by *Mad About You, Wings,* and *Seinfeld.* At that point NBC was the king of sitcoms. *Frasier* won Emmy Awards five years in a row.

I had thought about becoming the resident director for *Frasier,* but ultimately the show was not my baby, and it would have been another eleven years of doing very similar albeit amazing material. Plus, David Lee was a great director. That said, a *Frasier* reboot has been announced, which will reunite Kelsey, David, Peri, and Jane. I look forward to seeing how that develops with this great and talented group.

Friends

Fine! Judge all you want, but: Married a lesbian, left a man
at the altar, fell in love with a gay ice dancer, threw a girl's
wooden leg in a fire, LIVE IN A BOX!

MONICA GELLER, TO ALL HER FRIENDS

I am constantly amazed, but not surprised, by how seductive *Friends* is, how the world fell in love with it and how it keeps getting rediscovered by each successive generation that watches it. The story of a group of twentysomethings who help each other get through an important and confusing time in their lives, early adulthood—where everything they know is changing and none of the old rules work, and the one thing they know is that they can count on one another—is an enduring theme, with the six remarkable people playing characters who have endeared themselves to multiple generations of viewers.

There is a certain eternal glow to the show that is amazing to watch and is part of why it is not only evergreen in America but successful all over the world. As Jennifer Aniston said, "*Friends* planted a flag that touches people's hearts in a way that nothing else can. It premiered at a time where there was no Internet and no cellphones. People had conversations with one another. While we were so far away then from where we are now, young people are still tapping into the connection between six people who don't have all the answers but are helping each other figure it out."

David Crane and Marta Kauffman had just come off a hit with HBO's *Dream On*. I received their pilot script, which they co-wrote, called "Six of One," which became the basis for *Friends Like Us* and then *Friends*. It was late in the 1994 pilot season, and I had already committed to directing four other projects. I had a good sense about *Friends* and knew two things immediately: One, I didn't have time to direct it, and two, I had to direct it. It became the last pilot shot that year.

As opposed to one center or no center in a show, sometimes everyone becomes a center. David and Marta introduced their twentysomething characters and then they introduced jokes. I fell in love with these six kids on the page immediately. Other than Chandler, who's glib, bringing the witty repartee, everyone is doing character jokes. The funny comes directly from the characters.

Also unique was the fact that 95 percent of the original pilot script made it to air. In multi-camera sitcoms, you fix problems and address issues during the table read. That said, our pilot table read for *Friends* went as well as any reading could have gone. I had only one note for David and Marta: Joey and Chandler were too similar. In Joey's original incarnation, he was too smart. They "dumbed" him down a bit so the two characters wouldn't play in each other's wheelhouse.

The scripts were fabulous. Like *Cheers*, it was a really funny and evolving show, especially because of the Ross and Rachel romance. These were the original character descriptions:

MONICA: Smart. Cynical. Defended. Very attractive. Had to work for everything she had. An assistant chef for a chic uptown restaurant. And a romantic disaster area.

RACHEL: Spoiled. Adorable. Courageous. Terrified. Monica's best friend from high school. Has worked for none of what she has. On her own for the first time. And equipped to do nothing.

PHOEBE: Sweet. Flaky. New Age waif. Monica's former roommate. Sells barrettes on the street and plays guitar on the subway. A good soul.

ROSS: Intelligent. Emotional. Romantic. Monica's brother. Suddenly divorced. Facing singlehood with phenomenal reluctance. A paleontologist. Not that it matters.

JOEY: Handsome. Macho. Smug. Lives across the hall from Monica and Rachel. Wants to be an actor. Actually, wants to be the next Al Pacino. Loves women, sports, women, New York, women, and, most of all, Joey.

CHANDLER: Droll. A wry observer of everyone's life. And his own. Works in front of a computer doing something tedious in a claustrophobic cubicle in a nondescript office building. Survives by way of his sense of humor. And snacks.

The descriptions were both great platforms and springboards from which strong characters could be developed. The final important factor was the casting. We had amazing luck in that all six of the people we wanted were available. Six really good-looking people who were funny. A lot of people were watching the show just to see these good-looking people. So much so that the writing was underappreciated. It took eight seasons for *Friends* to win an Emmy, which they deserved long before.

I had no idea we had six centers when we started. It was a plethora of talent and gave me much more latitude to craft scenes. Over the first four shows, we realized that this was an equal group. Each script already had three storylines, but the writers started revising to create a balance. It has never happened before or since with a cast that large.

Courteney Cox, or Coxenhammer, as I affectionately call her, was initially the most well-known member of the cast, mainly for her role on *Family Ties* and when Bruce Springsteen pulled her up onstage for his "Dancing in the Dark" video. She was not the funniest one in the group but grew into it and found her humor. They figured out how to write for her. Monica was the logical center. She was stunningly beautiful and was the connection between the other cast members. The show could have easily been called *Monica's Friends.* She knew everyone, and other than the coffee shop, Central Perk, her apartment was the meeting place. Monica was a late bloomer. From the outset, we see that her dating life is still hard:

MONICA

This is not even a date. It's not. It's just two people going out to dinner and not having sex.

CHANDLER

Sounds like a date to me.

Monica is sleeping with Paul the wine guy, who pretends to be impotent so that Monica will feel special as the one who restores his virility. When she goes to work the next day, a co-worker tells her that she slept with Paul because he told her he was impotent. Monica realizes that she was duped.

MONICA

Why would anybody do something like that?

Lily Tomlin

There were close to three hundred guest stars who appeared on *Will & Grace*. Here are just a few of them.

Sydney Pollack

Elton John

Gene Wilder

Glenn Close

Matt Damon

Bebe Neuwirth

Michael Douglas

Sharing a moment with then–vice president Joe Biden, who praised *Will & Grace* for how much the show had done to educate the American public on change and acceptance.

Bob Newhart and me at the DGA Lifetime Achievement Awards.

Chuck Lorre, my collaborator in crime.

In her earliest auditions,
Melissa McCarthy made choices
that weren't in the script.
Her instincts were remarkable.
Makes me so proud that
she's now one of the biggest
stars in the world.

Directing Melissa McCarthy and Billy Gardell in the "Happy
Halloween" episode of *Mike & Molly*.

I fell in love with the cast,
stayed for two seasons, and
also came back to direct the
series finale.

With Andrea Anders and
Jesse Tyler Ferguson, part of
the talented ensemble cast of
The Class, a show that should
have been a hit.

Cast of *Live in Front of a Studio Audience: Norman Lear's "All in the Family" and "The Jeffersons."* As co-producer Jimmy Kimmel told the audience, "Norman did so much for freedom of speech and inclusivity. We'd be way behind without him."

Cast of *Live in Front of a Studio Audience: Norman Lear's "The Facts of Life"* and *"Diff'rent Strokes."* Keep 'em coming, guys!

Directing the pilot of *Two and a Half Men* with Charlie Sheen and Angus T. Jones.

With Norman Lear. We now have 179 years of show business between us.

My bar mitzvah ceremony at the ripe old age of 47.

With Mom and sister, Laurie.

With Laurie at a Night at Sardi's event, which she founded to raise money for Alzheimer's research in honor of our dad. She also stole my earrings.

My daughters, Kat, Ellie, Maggie, and Parls at the DGA Lifetime Achievement Awards.

I came in last place in the Family Olympics in 2000. My daughters robbed me!

My wife, Debbie
Easton, and me
at a wedding in
England. She has done
so much for me,
starting with upping
my shoe game.

Posing with my wife, Deb,
for photographer
Annie Leibovitz

A portrait
taken by
the legendary
photographer
Arnold Newman
of me holding a
picture of my dad
in Studio 8H, where
Saturday Night Live
is shot.

ROSS

I assume we're looking for an answer more sophisticated
than "to get you into bed."

JOEY

Let's put it this way: Were you especially attentive last night?
Especially selfless and giving? You know, makin' that little extra
effort 'cause it was all about *him*?

MONICA

I hate men. I hate men.

We got a note from the network, asking, "Does she have to sleep
with him?" I said, "She has to sleep with him to have any emotional
investment and for the audience to care enough about the story."
We won that round.

In the pilot, Ross's wife has just told him that she's a lesbian:

MONICA

Are you okay, sweetie?

ROSS

I just feel like someone reached down my throat, grabbed my
small intestine, pulled it out of my mouth, and tied it
around my neck . . .

CHANDLER

Cookie?

MONICA

(explaining to the others)
Carol moved her stuff out today . . .

JOEY
Hey, you gotta get back on the horse.

MONICA
And speaking for all women, thank you for the livestock analogy.

Lisa Kudrow had guest-starred on *Cheers* as Woody's acting partner. She also had a recurring role as the ethereal waitress Ursula on *Mad About You*. That character was very similar to Phoebe—so much so that they created a storyline on *Friends* where they were twins, and they appeared together with Lisa playing both roles. Phoebe referred to Ursula as "her career-driven sister." Because *Mad About You* was an NBC show as well, Lisa's continued appearances as Ursula weren't a problem. It was also an advantage during the first season of *Friends* to have Lisa on another hit show.

Despite losing the role of Roz on *Frasier*, Lisa couldn't have been more professional about the whole thing. Although, when the *Friends* pilot was in production, I heard from someone on the show that Lisa said, "That fucking Jimmy Burrows is directing the show. Can you believe it?" We're really good friends now.

PHOEBE
I remember when I first came to this city. I was fourteen. My mom had just killed herself and my stepdad was back in prison, and I got here, and I didn't know anybody. And I ended up living with this albino guy who was, like, cleaning windshields outside Port Authority, and then he killed himself, and then I found aromatherapy. So, believe me, I know exactly how you feel.

(Pause.)

ROSS
The word you're looking for is "Anyway" . . .

Phoebe was the "outsider" character, the eccentric one. Marta and David were smart enough to know, and to agree with the fact, that if the rest of the group liked her, we'd like her. During the rehearsals, when they were sitting at the table as Rachel was cutting her credit cards, I told Lisa, "Play the scene sitting under the table. You're ditzy, you're different." It was a challenge for any performer, because under the table alone she had no one to play off of. When we did the scene in front of the writers, David said to me, "That's interesting, but I'm not sure it works." Lisa was worried that they would blame her, concerned that I wouldn't have her back, especially since she'd been replaced on the *Frasier* pilot. I immediately told the writers, "That was my idea. I told her to do it." After that moment Lisa knew that she could trust me and that I would protect her. It was the beginning of our longstanding friendship.

After *Friends*, Lisa starred in *The Comeback*, which she co-created with Michael Patrick King. She played Valerie Cherish, a former B-list sitcom star whose attempt at a return to a sitcom is simultaneously being shot as a documentary. They cast me as Jimmy the director. Lisa and Michael co-wrote the first episode. The turning point in the script is when Valerie realizes that she's not "it" anymore. "Please don't make me be the one that turns her," I begged. They didn't listen. They needed a character who tells the truth with no agenda. I played a sardonic guy who delivers pithy lines. Michael kept saying, "Jimmy, smile!" I replied, "I don't do that!"

After Valerie refuses to leave the stage when the scene is over and openly undermines Jimmy's authority by demanding more takes, I pull her into a side room and tell her, "You're not it anymore. You took a small part, you hit it out of the park. You can't ask for better than that." I was pretending that I was talking to one of my own daughters and I needed to be as honest as possible to keep her safe.

I found out later that casting me was Lisa's way of honoring me. "You know why your show got canceled?" I tell Valerie. "Because in the last season you had a chimp working at the law firm." When Valerie tells the camera, "By the way, everyone loved that chimp," I say off camera, "No they didn't." (I improvised that.)

I told Michael, "I think I'm too mean." He responded, "I want you to be that mean." They also gave me the moment of wisdom in the series finale. Valerie is nominated for the Emmy Award she's been waiting for her entire career, and at the ceremony she confides in Jimmy about her marital issues. I tell her with paternal concern, "This is important, but not as important as that. This is one night. A great night, but it's only one night. And if you do win, hold on to that Emmy and to everything else." I was connected to her both in character and in real life.

The part of Ross was written for David Schwimmer. I had worked with him in another pilot, called *Monty,* with Henry Winkler. David initially turned down the *Friends* job because he had a miserable experience on another show. He was hesitant to commit to a five-year minimum term, which all sitcom actors have to do. At the time, he was playing Pontius Pilate in a production of *The Master and Margarita* in Chicago. I called him and said, "You have to come and meet everyone." He was concerned that the show wasn't going to be collaborative and that his ideas wouldn't be welcome. We assured him that this experience would be different and it would be an ensemble.

Schwimmer is a great physical comedian. He's very smart and he's a good actor. He internalizes everything and turns out every beat. He has a specific style and can play hangdog better than anyone. He got a laugh in the very first scene by just saying hi—his inflection and his physicality tell you all about Ross in that one word. A theater-trained actor, David is also a co-founder of the Chicago-based Lookingglass Theatre Company, which still turns out amazing productions. When you start in theater you do everything: hang lights, make costumes, build sets. Like me, he has respect for every aspect of the production and the same respect for everyone on soundstage, gaffer, props, and wardrobe. He is also a talented director. He listens and hears everything. Once, when an extra came in one beat too early, we both heard it.

During the first season of *Friends,* he asked me if I would mentor him. He shadowed me, first on *Friends* and later on *Will & Grace* and other sets. I was as happy to teach him as he was eager to learn. He went on to direct ten episodes of *Friends,* other television episodes, a few movies, and lots of theater in both Chicago and New York. I once told him, "Schwimmer, you're the second-funniest person I've ever known." To this day, I've never told him who the first is.

Ross's predicament in the opening scene of the pilot is the perfect entrance point for Rachel:

ROSS

See, but I don't want to be single, okay. I just—I just want to be married again.

(At that moment, a woman in a bridal gown enters.)

CHANDLER

And I just want a million dollars!

Monica introduces Rachel to the group. When Ross attempts to hug her, his umbrella opens. He sits back down, defeated again. A moment of silence follows as Rachel sits and the others expect her to explain:

MONICA

So you wanna tell us now, or are we waiting for four wet bridesmaids?

RACHEL

Oh God . . . Well, it started about a half hour before the wedding. I was in this room where we were keeping all the presents, and I was looking at this gravy boat. This really gorgeous Limoges gravy boat. When all of a sudden—[to the waitress that brought her

248 • James Burrows

coffee] Sweet'N Low?—I realized that I was more turned on by
this gravy boat than by Barry! And then I got really freaked out,
and that's when it hit me: how much Barry looks like Mr. Potato
Head. Y'know, I mean, I always knew he looked familiar, but . . .
Anyway, I just had to get out of there, and I started wondering,
"Why am I doing this, and who am I doing this for?" [To Monica.]
So, anyway, I just didn't know where to go, and I know that you
and I have kinda drifted apart, but you're the only person I knew
who lived here in the city.

MONICA
Who wasn't invited to the wedding.

Jennifer Aniston—JA, as I call her—was originally in a holding
position when she auditioned, meaning that at the time she was
committed to another show, *Muddling Through*. We were auditioning other actresses but hoping that her show would not get picked
up. JA is the hardest type to find in comedy—she is both beautiful
and funny. She was able to play the basket-case runaway bride in
the open. As a neurotic Jewish woman, almost an early version
of Grace Adler, she could play the pathos of that role and still be
incredibly funny. From *Friends,* JA moved to a successful movie
career and back to television. She still calls me Papa, and it still
touches me.

Matty LeBlanc is one of the sweetest people I've ever met. He is
incredibly irreverent in person, but because he is so good-natured,
you can't get angry with him. It's a tribute to his skills that his character developed over the course of the series. He never played Joey
as the dumb guy, just as the incorrect guy, the "much smarter than
you think" guy, the one with the most growth potential, the least
number of rules, and who became the most empathetic.

A character can't evolve if it's not in the script, but you also need
an actor who can really show that growth. Matty was "the most improved player." He grew the most, because he paid attention to all

the notes and was the most willing to learn from the other five and from everyone else involved. As Joey, Matty always had to be ready on set to come in and punch up the ending of a scene with a complete non sequitur. In a scene that needed a funny ending, he could walk in the door to Monica's apartment and say, "You got a tweezer?" and get a huge laugh.

After *Friends,* NBC tried to spin off the Joey character into a new sitcom. The writing and the cast of *Joey* were not particularly good. But David Crane leaped over *Joey* and created the amazing *Episodes,* where Matty played a real-life exaggerated version of himself as the former *Friends* star. The concept and the execution were genius. I directed Matty again in *Man with a Plan,* where he played the smart guy. I agreed to do it because of him. He was the center, and the show ran successfully on CBS for four seasons.

Finding the right actor to play Chandler was tricky. Broadway actor Craig Bierko turned down the role. Jon Cryer was also up for it. He was in London and had to get up in the middle of the night his time and rehearse the part with someone on tape. The tape was rushed off to FedEx to be shipped overnight to Los Angeles. FedEx wound up losing the package. We never saw it.

Like Jennifer Aniston, Matthew Perry was also initially in second position, solely due to a commitment to another show. He had done a pilot for ABC called *LAX 2194,* about baggage handlers in the future, and was waiting to hear if it got picked up. Matthew had a very distinctive style. He was the smart, quick one. He brought the self-deprecating and the funny good-looking guy to the table. I turned down directing the updated version of *The Odd Couple,* which he co-starred in, because I thought he was playing the wrong character. Matthew would have been a much better Felix than Oscar. He would have been even better with Matty LeBlanc playing Oscar opposite him, given their already amazing onscreen dynamic.

We had an extraordinary run-through for the pilot. After five minutes of warm-up, we slowly dimmed the lights and had the actors start reciting their dialogue, without any segues or introductions. We wanted the audience to feel like they were actually in a coffee shop. There was the same electricity as during the *Cheers, Frasier,* and *Will & Grace* run-throughs: The audience immediately cared about these characters. They cared about Rachel's plight, and that Monica was sleeping with a guy who was lying to her.

As director, I am there to help create the ensemble, to do everything I can to foster a community among the company, and to train a new set of actors to behave as a group and respect one another. The first thing I did to facilitate this was to make sure the cast had every opportunity to become friends in real life. Before the show aired, I asked Les Moonves, who was then head of Warner Bros. Television, if I could borrow the corporate jet to take the young cast to Las Vegas. He liked the idea of taking the group to Las Vegas but wasn't crazy about lending me his plane. He eventually agreed.

I made a reservation for just the seven of us at Spago. I asked for the center table in the restaurant, where everyone could see us. I knew the show had a chance to really take off and told the kids, "This is your last shot at anonymity. Once the show airs, you guys will never be able to go anywhere without being hounded." None of them believed me. None of them had any money at that point either, so I gave each of them a couple of hundred bucks to go gamble. I laid out fourteen hundred dollars. If the math doesn't seem right, it's because LeBlanc had no idea how to play craps and he lost his two hundred dollars in seconds, so I gave him another two hundred. They went back to Los Angeles, the show premiered, they've never had a shot at anonymity since, and they each wrote me reimbursement checks for the money I gave them. I am very proud and humbled by what some people have called the Jimmy Burrows Curse, turning unknown actors into stars.

Other than the Reverend Jim's driver's-license scene in *Taxi,* the only time I kept the cameras rolling until the laughs stopped was on the seventh episode of the first season of *Friends.* In "The One with the Blackout," Monica, Phoebe, and Joey are in Monica's living room singing "Top of the World"; Chandler is stuck in an ATM with the wonderful and lovely Jill Goodacre (a place we'd all love to be); and outside on the makeshift terrace, a nervous Ross is working up the courage to ask Rachel out on a date. Right before Ross can ask the question, a cat jumps on Ross's shoulder. Ross starts running back and forth outside the apartment, trying to get the cat off him. We cut inside. Joey, Phoebe, and Monica are still singing, while you see Ross in the background with the cat. I told him to keep running until the audience stopped laughing. He had to run so much he lost his breath.

Speaking of animals, I generally prefer not to work with them. No disrespect and not to generalize, but they don't take direction very well. They don't listen to the director; they have their own trainers and wranglers who feed them so they'll perform on cue. On *Frasier,* Marty's dog, Eddie, refused to listen to me. But the only animal I ever really hated was Marcel, the monkey on *Friends.* I directed his first appearance. He wound up in the rafters. I told everyone who would listen, "When I come back to direct another episode, please, no monkey."

On *Friends,* it was the couch in the Central Perk coffee shop that became its own character. It's actually the first thing you see when the theme song plays, and at the end of the theme they're all on the couch with their backs to the audience. The couch also becomes a metaphor, as it connects everyone.

For the pilot, I had to decide where everyone would sit. There were four of them in the scene to begin with, so I put Matty in the adjacent chair, Courteney and Lisa on the couch, and Matthew up on the arm. When Schwimmer comes in, he winds up on the couch and Lisa is on the floor in front of the couch. JA is the last to enter, in her wedding dress, and she winds up on the couch too.

Set designers know what is required in a sitcom. There are angled walls so you can shoot faces. Sometimes I'll change pieces; I'll move furniture around. The TV in Monica's living room was already on a credenza between the bedroom doors. Back then, it was unique for a show to have the television against a wall and the characters facing it. As with Archie Bunker's set, the TV was typically placed downstage so the audience could see the actors' faces as they watched it. Our way worked just fine. I would open the door to Rachel's bedroom so we could shoot through. John Shaffner and Joe Stewart are production designers who have worked on so many sets. When I mentioned that the windows in Monica's apartment looked a little ordinary, they gave the living room the look of an artist's garret, with an artist's studio window that the Friends were always looking out of. Sometimes you just need to plant the seeds and let them blossom among brilliant minds.

The apartment was supposed to look like a once-grand residence that had been chopped into smaller pieces. Shaffner and Stewart put in a post and beam that separated the kitchen and the living room. The pillar and beam served as visual trim, an attractive background detail to subtly remind viewers of the space's forlorn elegance. I wanted the pillar in the master shots when people were coming in and out. It gives dimension to the apartment. After I was gone, so was the pillar, because no one could shoot around it. There was a pillar in *Wings,* which they took out. *Taxi* had a pillar where the pay phone was. On big sets, it gives dimension to the foreground and adds to the character of the environment. Even if you're looking at a single shot, it makes it more interesting.

One of my rules with a cast is "Work something until it works." I rehearse until actors are so skilled that it doesn't take much more effort for them to work with one another. The *Friends* group was very comically oriented, knew what was funny, and they worked very hard to develop the characters. It made me look great because they were so good. I had Lisa try so many different things to define Phoebe, including delivering her monologue alone under the table during the pilot. When Joey and Chandler take Ross to a hockey game to get his mind off the anniversary of the first time he slept with ex-wife Carol, a hockey puck hits him in the face. At the hospital, Ross has a bandage on his nose, and Joey has the puck. We were looking for a downbeat, a sad note. I said, "Hey, LeBlanc," and I motioned bringing the puck to his face. Matty got it right away. He held the puck in his hand and brought it to his face over and over like he was trying to re-create the moment that Ross was hit by it. Ross, in turn, was not at all amused. It worked because they were so great, both individually and collectively.

It took two episodes for me to get a shorthand with the cast. The six became real friends and would play poker in my dressing room. It was about bonding. They genuinely adored one another. A director and cast live for that kind of connection.

In "The One with the Thumb," Phoebe is given seven thousand dollars when she finds a thumb in a can of soda. It was such a great premise and peculiar subject. David and Marta found innocent little stories to do and never ran out of them. In "The One Where Nana Dies Twice," while going through his deceased grandmother's apartment with his mother, Ross is asked to climb over a dresser that is wedged in the closet to search for a dress to bury her in. A box full of Sweet'N Low packets that his late grandmother hoarded rains down on him. Later, at the cemetery, Ross falls into the open grave. From the moment in the pilot where Schwimmer's umbrella snapped open, I knew he was a great physical comedian.

I directed the first ten episodes of *Friends* in season 1 and came back to do five more later on, including a Thanksgiving show where everyone's plans go wrong and they wind up together. I directed Elliott Gould and Christina Pickles as Monica and Ross's parents and Morgan Fairchild as Chandler's mother. I did not get to direct Kathleen Turner as Chandler's father. That would have been fun.

I also directed the episode where Ross and Rachel break up; it was a two-parter. In "The One with the Morning After," Ross and Rachel have it out in Monica's living room, oblivious that the other four friends are trapped in Monica's room for the rest of the night, scared to make themselves known. I had six cameras on the group: two permanently in the living room, two in the bedroom, and two in the center that would go back and forth. That gave me four cameras on each set. There was a theatrical timing to the episode of shooting on two sets simultaneously, which had never been done on a sitcom before. Critical to the nature of the piece, each time Ross and Rachel said something, the camera setup allowed me to film the others' reactions in real time in front of the audience, without having to stop and reset.

Ross and Rachel never got back together on my watch. With Sam and Diane, I was in the writers' room with the Charles Brothers, plotting the arcs. The Ross and Rachel romantic roller coaster came from David and Marta. It was their creative baby to nurture, and I trusted their judgment. In "The One with All the Rugby," I directed Ross with his new girlfriend and future fiancée, Emily (Helen Baxendale). She was nice but not particularly funny. Schwimmer had no one to bounce off. It was like clapping with one hand.

In sitcoms and any type of romantic comedy, the funny is just as important as the chemistry. The off-again phase—the lull before the next on-again—has to be interesting and funny as well. We discovered that any new girlfriend for Ross needed to be as funny as Rachel. Often, you can't recast, because of tight shooting deadlines or other logistical considerations. We had the same problem with Kate Mulgrew, when she played Sam's romantic interest on *Cheers*. She had great chemistry with Ted and great acting chops but wasn't funny enough. Likewise with a pre–*Grey's Anatomy* Patrick Dempsey on *Will & Grace*. Bobby Cannavale was very funny, so we could bring him back ("Look, I'm a romantic. Call me old-fashioned, but I believe that when a guy takes another guy out, he should treat him like a lady"). You don't cast anyone to be a straw man, unless it's for one episode. You need someone who gets laughs. Sometimes you start an arc and it ain't working out, so you have to get rid of that person. If it's a day player, it's a quick goodbye.

The reverse is also true. If there's chemistry, the writers go to work to figure out some way of keeping the actor. You can see character arcs on comedies all the time. If Kelsey was not funny, he'd have been done after his four-episode contract to play Frasier on *Cheers*. If Woody was available, we would have kept him on as Grace's boyfriend. During the end of season 7 in *Cheers*, we created a sister for Rebecca, Susan. Marcia Cross was brought in to play her when there was no chemistry with the original actress. Sam tries to set up a three-way with the sisters and is in turn set up by them to think that Rebecca killed Susan. The chemistry was so good that we considered taking the relationship into the following year and having Sam marry Susan. We abandoned that idea in favor of other ideas we thought were even better.

Maggie Wheeler's Janice, Chandler's on-again off-again girlfriend, was not in the original permutation of the show, but she was so great, especially with that high-pitched nasal voice. Their relationship was atypical of sitcom romances. Chandler didn't like her but was nonetheless attracted to her. In "The One with the Candy Hearts," Joey begs Chandler to agree to a Valentine's Day blind date and to double with him. Joey's new girlfriend brings Janice. Neither is happy. "By the way, Chandler, I cut you out of all my pictures. So if you want, I have a bag with just your heads." Chandler is irate and yells at Joey in the bathroom: "Calm down? You've set me up with a woman I've dumped twice in the last two months!"

They drink too much champagne and wind up in bed together. When Chandler starts with "There's no way for me to tell you this, or at least no new way for me to tell you this . . ." Janice says that it's not over. "You seek me out. There's something deep in your soul that calls me out like a foghorn, 'Jan-ice, Jan-ice!' And you push me away and you pull me back, 'Jan-ice, Jan-ice!' You can't live without me, and you know it. You just don't know you know it." It was an interesting relationship for Chandler. They weren't in love, but they were attracted to each other. He was embarrassed by her voice. But for him to be locked in a scene with her was hysterical, because his reactions were so funny. Like Rhea Perlman and Dan Hedaya on *Cheers*, they were funny together. Janice got a lot of laughs. In a sitcom, if your guest actor can get commensurate laughs with the principal in the scene, it behooves you to keep that storyline going. If you find chemistry like that, you run with it. One of the reasons *Friends* holds up is that there are six different ways of coming at things. You know what each character's attitude about everything is. If a subject is brought up, you know how each character will react. Every show I've done has that. *Taxi* and *Cheers* had seven. *Will & Grace* had four. You knew the issue and the attitude toward each issue.

After the first season, the group sought my advice about how to renegotiate their contracts. I advised them to negotiate as a group and stay in lockstep financially. Negotiating with the six individually would have given the network leverage against each of them. Since it was clear that there were no subsidiary characters, it made sense to me for them to stick together. The show was a home run. If the network could pay six million dollars an episode to the group, you could only imagine how much money they were making. By negotiating separately and pitting them against one another, the network could have easily destroyed all the chemistry they'd developed. If you have equally talented people who become a family, you need to treat them that way. It's the right thing to do and it's also good business. In what made international news at the time, it became precedent for sitcom stars to be paid the same amount. After the second season, each of the *Will & Grace* stars also got paid the same amount for the duration of the show, for the same reason that the *Friends* stars did—they had all become equals.

I had to stop directing *Friends* during the second season because of other commitments; I was developing shows at that point and had an obligation to direct the shows that were coming out of my production company. I sat down with the *Friends* cast and said, "You're going to have other directors. Please listen to them and learn as much as you can. If you disagree, say something. You're all gifted and creative. You're all instinctive performers, you know your characters better than the director, but don't attack the director. Discuss." To Schwimmer and JA, I said, "You're also physical comics.

Pitch all the bits you want—it will make the show better." I wasn't trying to make them director-proof. I wanted to make sure that they didn't lose their sense of whimsy and creativity. I wanted to embolden them.

I told them, "Writers are very possessive of their work, and they have every right to be. You were out having dinner and they were still writing. You do the work as written and then you say, 'We have an idea.' Sometimes it will go in the show, sometimes it won't." If you tell an incoming director and writers what your bits are and how you feel about jokes, they will listen. Often, when Schwimmer was told something, he'd say, "Aha," and write it down. If he didn't like it, he wouldn't do it. Writers respected it. One of my few regrets in my career is that I didn't stay with those six kids, who are now amazing adults and good friends, for the entire ten-year run.

In May of 2021, the *Friends* reunion dropped on HBO Max. James Corden hosted the six stars seventeen years after the show ended on the main Warner lot, on a replica of the Central Perk couch. They were in front of the fountain where they shot the opening credits, which was excavated and moved from the Warner Bros. Ranch studio. They rebuilt the original set as a meeting place for the cast. The furniture was in storage, as were whatever tchotchkes the cast and crew hadn't taken home as souvenirs when the show wrapped in 2004.

James read off the remarkable statistics: "Two hundred thirty-six episodes; broadcast in two hundred twenty territories; TV's number-one comedy for six straight seasons, averaging twenty-five million viewers a week. Fifty-two million people watched the finale. The show has been watched over a hundred billion times over all platforms."

The group fell back into the rhythms that only real friendship enables you to do, reminiscing and reading from scripts, re-creating classic scenes. JA and Schwimmer talked about how they were crushing on each other at the time but couldn't act on those feelings because both were romantically involved with other people.

I was in the audience, sitting with Marta, David, and executive producer/director Kevin Bright, when they turned the cameras on me and then asked Matty about the first time the six met. He said, "It was on the pilot—we all came in and sat around the table. And I remember when we started, you could feel it, it was something special. And you know, Jim Burrows doesn't do crap. He probably craps, but he doesn't do crap."

I talked about the six of them. "I did a lot of pilots that year, and this was the last pilot I shot. These six actors were available—at the end of pilot season. We were lucky enough to get these six people. They were at the right place at the right time." They showed footage of my first day on set. Matthew said, "When James Burrows directed, he directed us to be together as friends. We knew not to mess it up with romance, and we became friends." JA said, "He made it a point to tell us that this is a special show, it will become extraordinarily successful. The six of you must take care of each other, support each other, be each other's allies, because this could be tricky when something like this becomes so big for people as young as we were at the time." Matthew added, "It's a little less special now that he hired us only because we were available."

I teared up. These were great people who would have triggered the parental instincts in anyone with any sense of warmth. I had a connection with these kids as if they were my own.

Within a year, I had back-to-back successes with *Frasier* and *Friends*. They were immediate hits, something I never had before. Broder negotiated the second great deal of my career: He asked for a royalty. While the Writers Guild ensured that writers of pilots would receive royalties, the Directors Guild did not provide for sequel payments for pilot directors. Because I had been getting so many pilots on the air, Broder was able to negotiate a deal where I would earn a small percentage of the revenues of any show that made it to series.

For many years, Broder saved six blocks of time on my schedule during March and April for me to direct pilots. Rather than waiting for studios to set their production schedules and hire me as a director, he sold my availability. Producers would call Broder and tell him that a pilot was picked up by a network and he locked them into one of the six blocks. It worked out well for me.

Ever since *Friends,* I've thought of the casts and writers of shows I've worked on as my brilliant kids. And I've always felt an obligation to writers I've worked with to help get a new show sold. The mentor in me wants to give them a push; the father in me wants to help my children. I can set up the template for a show and get the cast and crew going.

Speaking of kids, I want to mention my own family. I am a family man. Or, rather, the only man in a family of four daughters. I do the dishes. I make my wife laugh. Just not at the same time.

I treat my daughters the same way I have always treated actors and writers, or vice versa. With a lot of love, a lot of support, and a lot of expectations. As my girls grew up, it was important to me that they develop a work ethic and contribute to society as early on as possible. All four of my daughters had to have summer jobs from the moment they were legally able to work. They had to go to college, like I did, far away from home. The "no kids doing laundry on the weekends at home" rule that my parents set for my sister and me was passed down a generation.

It was very important to me that they each found their professional passion, something they were good at and that they loved doing, like I did. I wanted them to witness someone who enjoyed their work so much that they would feel entitled to that same joy.

My eldest, Kat, had no interest in the entertainment business. Her passion is design. She owns her own consulting business, helping designers translate their creative vision into market. She works with them on pricing, marketing, and margin targets. She is the commercial voice of reason for the creative. Not dissimilar to a director working with actors and writers.

Ellie had considered the entertainment business for a short time but realized that she only loved it because she loved me. She wound up co-founding and being the CEO of a mindful-meditation company that, pre-COVID, had more than seventy employees. I was very proud when her business was on the front page of *The New York Times*.

Maggie is a third-generation Burrows director. Trained at Yale, she has directed pieces all over the country, including being part of the Geffen Playhouse in Los Angeles. I've never proactively offered advice, but when solicited, I've told her that the most important thing is for theaters that hire you to hire you again. You don't want a moment; you want a career. You're building a life.

Paris, my youngest, came into my life when she was two and a half years old. She started riding horses at three and has spent most of her life around them, competing at a high level in high school and college in championship show jumping. She's currently training for the next equestrian Olympic games.

I've often reminded my girls that they should never go to bed angry and always work out their differences, because for the rest of their lives these are the only sisters they'll have. I'm very proud that my daughters are one another's closest friends.

Over the years they visited me on sets and became close to some cast and crew. I was a breakfast dad, because I made sure that I was around for at least one meal a day. Every morning, I had a rotation of different omelets and eggs, pancakes, waffles, and Cream of Wheat. I cut the fruit and sliced the green apples so they were brown by the time they were served. I didn't want my kids to ever feel like I was around less because I was working too many hours.

My former wife, Linda Solomon, was a great mother. She was very loving to our children and had the same expectations that I did. Her days would begin with making sure that everyone ate the breakfasts I made, to the point where I nicknamed her the "Breakfast Police." Once, she actually came to breakfast in a London police outfit and cap.

Sadly, she was ill for most of her life. She passed in 2004. I had my daughters spend more time with her than with me toward the end of her life, because I knew that I'd get more time with them later on.

I finally got some testosterone into my family with sons-in-law, Kat's husband, Adam Schatzow, and Ellie's, Simon Gluck. I have seen both of them do dishes. I now also have four grandchildren, Sophie, Theo, Luna, and Poppy.

I also owe meeting Debbie Easton, to whom I've been happily married for twenty-five years, and who (way too) many people refer to as my "better half," to my directing style. Debbie was a hairstylist on sitcoms.

A lot of show-night shoots go past two in the morning. I had a reputation of shooting quickly and efficiently—so much so that there were times during run-throughs that I'd have my car keys in my hand in anticipation of wrapping up. Seeing the car keys actually got a cast excited, because it became a physical representation that I thought they "got it."

As a mother with a baby at home, Debbie was trying to avoid working all night. She'd heard from a friend that Jimmy Burrows's shows wrapped early, so she applied to work on shows I directed. I first met her on the *Frasier* set. She walked up to me and made fun of my shoes, telling me that "they looked like Earth shoes." I told her that they weren't Earth shoes and walked away. Not a sitcom-like beginning, but it worked for us. We started dating during *Friends*. Our wedding reception was celebrated on the Paramount lot with more than four hundred guests. We had Wolfgang Puck catering and an In-N-Out Burger truck. Debbie has been a great mother, stepmother, "Dede" to her grandchildren, partner, and friend. The best word that I can use to describe our connection is "joyful." I always looked forward to going home. The happiness of my home life carried over into my work life, and as often as I could, I tried to help turn my working group into a family.

Mike & Molly & Chuck

MOLLY
Dinner was delicious. Good for you, finding a man who knows
his way around a kitchen.

MIKE
I know my way around a kitchen.

MOLLY
I meant cooking, not finding an Oreo in the dark.

he love-at-first-sight relationship between Mike Biggs (Billy Gardell), a Chicago cop who goes to an Overeaters Anonymous meeting and meets Molly Flynn (Melissa McCarthy), a school-teacher, started off with everything going for it, including a great cast, writer/producer Mark Roberts, and Chuck Lorre, a genius who created and produced some of the best sitcoms in history.

I fell in love with that group. I directed the first two seasons and then came back to do the series finale. On set, I am a hugger. And I have always, and still do, refer to everyone—regardless of gender, age, race, or sexual orientation—as "honey." At the very beginning, I told the cast, "Get together, run lines, have meals together. Find out about each other's families. Because if you don't like each other,

I'm not going to believe that you like each other, and neither will the audience."

Billy Gardell is one of the sweetest people I've ever met or worked with and is another example of a stand-up comedian who worked very hard to become a great comedic actor. His earnestness and geniality come across and connect with the viewers. I gave him his first job in a pilot called *Queens*. He was doing anything he could to get my attention, and he kept saying the one line he had in the script, "You'll have to leave, ma'am," louder and louder. I finally yelled back, "Stop broadcasting that goddamn line!" Other than Bob Newhart and Billy, whose comedy worked, and Jay Mohr, whose didn't, I don't think I've ever done a show with a stand-up as lead, because I prefer to work with a group of people who are actors. As a rule—which I am open to breaking depending on talent—I prefer actors who understand the importance of the ensemble and not those who need to be serviced. Also, Billy told me early on that he was a "pocket passer. I plant myself and I say lines. Don't make me throw." I came up with the term "Gardell blocking," where I'd start a scene with Billy on the couch and never move him.

Everyone in the cast had theatrical training, except for Billy, who was a mix of Jackie Gleason and John Candy. Billy quickly grew as an actor. As a stand-up comic, he had no fear of the audience, but he learned that he could act and play emotion. Week after week he got the audience to laugh. The more he got accustomed to the sitcom process and the more adulation he got from me, castmates, and the audience, the more confident he became.

Stand-ups run into trouble when they insist on trying to be the funniest guy in the room. Billy, as big a sports fan as I am, learned that the center is the quarterback. The center doesn't generate the big laughs. The reaction of the surrounding nuts is how they get their laughs. They have to throw the ball around.

Billy began studying a range of acting and comedy influences. I had him watch *Tonight Show* hosts Jack Paar and Johnny Carson and then study how Jack Benny and Carroll O'Connor could hold a pause. Their jokes became twice as funny because they were set up right.

During the second episode, I told him, "If you're number one on the call sheet, you have a responsibility to lead." I quoted an old phrase, saying, "'The fish stinks from the head.' If you come in and you're kind, giving, and caring and don't take yourself too seriously, that will spread through the whole set. If you're toxic, that will spread through the whole set. I hope you make the right choice." It's no surprise that when I introduced him to Ted Danson, I said, "Teddy, meet Billy Gardell, the second-nicest guy in television."

I worked hard with Billy because I saw his potential. I pushed him until he figured out his stage directions. When I told him, "Honey, you have to move this way so we can see your *punim*," it took him six months to finally ask me what *punim* (face) meant. I'm happy to report that Billy learned all his Yiddish phrases from me.

CBS wasn't sold on Melissa McCarthy as Molly. Chuck and I fought for her. Melissa was working on another level. She could do everything, from physical comedy to great emotional work. In her earliest auditions, Melissa made choices that weren't in the script. Her instincts were remarkable. We didn't discover her physicality on *Mike & Molly* until I had her sit on an ottoman and she went ass over teakettle. We were amazed at how committed and brave she was. Nobody knew yet how powerful she was in her performance. In the second episode, Molly mixes too much wine and cold medicine. Her take was hilarious. A year later she became a worldwide movie star. When producer Judd Apatow was testing *Bridesmaids* in front of audiences, they went crazy for Melissa. He went back to the editing room and added more footage of her to the movie, knowing she provided perfect and essential touches of comedy to the film.

Coming from theater and dramatic television, Melissa wasn't initially comfortable with multi-camera comedy: "Come in, stop, say the line here, and then go to the next thing." She always wanted to be in motion, telling me she was like a shark. She'd come through the front door and go through the living room straight into the kitchen, saying her lines without stopping. We had a fun banter as I tried to get her to say a line on her designated mark. "Honey, stand still," to which she would reply, "Don't your cameras have wheels? Honey, move the cameras!" Through our affectionate exchanges we found our creative balance.

During one scene, Melissa was sitting between Billy and Reno Wilson (Officer Carl McMillan). I told her to get up and leave. A couple of the writers didn't think it was appropriate for the scene to have her leave. I acquiesced to them. Melissa said, "I think I should be leaving." I told her, "Walk away in your mind." And that's the way she played it. Later on, she gave me a gift with a card with that direction written on it. She never forgot that moment.

The show was based in part on *Marty*, the Paddy Chayefsky teleplay starring Rod Steiger and Nancy Marchand and the later film with Ernest Borgnine and Betsy Palmer. It turned the story of two people who had given up hope of finding someone to fall in love with into a funny premise, and the audience connected with and rooted for the romance. Chuck Lorre, the executive producer, also was enamored with the idea of two people bonding over something they struggled with and how they supported each other through their struggles.

As soon as Mike and Molly fell for each other, the audience became more engaged in their witty banter and less preoccupied by the fact that they weren't very young or of a typical Hollywood nature (thin):

MIKE

All right, the dishes have been washed and dried. Oh, wait, there's one more dish. [hugs Molly] I think this one I'll just lick clean.

MOLLY

Mike!

MIKE
Want to go upstairs and burn off dinner?

MOLLY
I can't. I have like three hours' worth of papers to grade.

MIKE
Three hours! What am I supposed to do for three hours?

MOLLY
What did you do before you had a girlfriend?

MIKE
I didn't do dishes. I could tell you that.

Swoosie Kurtz, who played Molly's mom, Joyce, was a consummate professional. She knew all the ways of getting to a joke. We had a New York connection and a theater bond. Swoosie had never played a character like Joyce before—without filter, often vulgar. I encouraged her to get rid of any inhibitions. "Let her rip!" I said.

As Molly's sister, Victoria, Katy Mixon played ditzy well. She's also one of the best show-tune singers.

Louie Mustillo, who played Vince, Joyce's boyfriend, is one of my favorite people. I would tell him, "Louie, get yourself something to eat and plant yourself on the set." In one scene somebody fainted. I said, "Don't stop eating! Throw your lines from the sandwich." That was his character and he delivered beautifully. A sweet and playful man, Louie would ask me questions sometimes just to hear me say no. In "The Rehearsal," Vince needs a divorce from his wife, Francine, in order to marry Joyce. Mike and Carl accompany him to her apartment. Francine (June Squibb) turns out to be much older than Mike and Carl expected. In one of the funniest exchanges in the series, when Francine says, "You took my youth!" Vince replies, "I never saw your youth! The man who took your youth was wearing a powdered wig!" I told Louie to deliver that line with as much anger as he could. June Squibb immediately went on to co-star in *Nebraska,* for which she received an Oscar nomination.

I had never worked with Reno Wilson, who played Mike's police partner, Carl. He was another heat-seeking missile for comedy. He and Billy had been on an earlier show together called *Heist.* Cleo King, who played Carl's grandmother, was only four years older than Reno. Nyambi Nyambi was doing Shakespeare in the Park when we found him to play Samuel, the wisecracking diner waiter. Rondi Reed, who played Mike's mother, was part of the Steppenwolf Theatre Company, which creator Mark Roberts was a big fan of. She won a Tony for her role in *August: Osage County.*

We bonded as a group. Where in other workplaces familiarity may breed contempt, our familiarity bred even more affection. Billy started analyzing the small grunts I make on set, my subtle affirmations of yes or no, my "maaaaa"s, a soft sound I make that's been a shorthand for the crew for many years. It's a tone that has multiple meanings, from yes, no, I'm not sure, to not now, which everyone seems to understand. Billy then began to follow me around the set, exaggerating them into an Edward G. Robinson–type sound that became "MAAAAAAAA." Melissa had that embroidered on a blanket and gave it out as a gift to the cast at the end of the second season. It's still a term that connects us affectionately as a group. The blankets are nice too.

Bruce Springsteen and I are family friends (yeah, I know, it still amazes me too). Bruce said something to me that continues to inspire me: "Every show has to be the best show I've ever done." In his hometown gigs at New Jersey's Meadowlands, the ushers as well as the audience sing along to every song. Bruce and Patti's daughter, Jessie, and Debbie and my youngest daughter, Paris, are the same age and best friends. We got to know them through the horse world.

Bruce's youngest son, Sam, had aspirations of being a writer. I brought him to the *Mike & Molly* set. I introduced him as "Sam who's thinking about being in show business." He, Billy Gardell, and I were having lunch at Abe's after a run-through. Billy, who's the biggest Springsteen fan in the world, started talking to Sam.

"Where are you from?"

"New Jersey."

"Where in New Jersey?"

"Colts Neck."

"What does your dad do?"

"He's a musician."

"Really. What's his name?"

"Bruce Springsteen."

As I was watching this build to a crescendo, I thought Billy was going to explode.

My wife, Debbie, got Bruce and Patti to come to the show that night. They sat quietly backstage. When Chuck Lorre, who made his early living playing guitars on cruise ships, arrived on set, I said, "I need you for a second." He said, "I'm on the phone." I dragged him backstage. Chuck, who is never taken aback over anything, looked at Bruce and was dumbfounded. "Oh my God, it's you." It was the only time I'd ever seen him speechless. Without fanfare, I brought in each of the cast to meet him. Every person was more shocked and excited than the one before.

When Bruce did his Broadway show for the first time in 2017, Debbie and I met him backstage afterward one night and we went to see Rita Wilson, who was performing at Café Carlyle. We trudged uptown and, not surprisingly, Bruce and his entourage were ushered to the head of the line. Bruce looked at me and said, "You're finally here." I didn't know what he meant until I realized he wasn't talking to me. I looked behind me and there was Paul McCartney and his wife, Nancy. We were seated in a booth together, so we were all facing the stage, watching Rita, who started singing "Harper Valley PTA." She was terrific. I turned to my left and Bruce was clapping and singing, and I turned to my right and Paul was clapping and singing. To be clear, I was at Café Carlyle watching the Boss and the Beatle clapping to "Harper Valley PTA" sung by Rita Wilson.

I saw the Beatles in 1964 at the old Paramount Theatre in New York on 43rd Street. Steve Lawrence and Eydie Gormé opened for them. When Steve and Eydie came out and started singing, you couldn't hear a word, because the teenage girls were screaming for the Beatles. When the Beatles came out, you couldn't hear them either, because the girls were still screaming. Now I was actually sitting with Sir Paul, who was very sweet and humble and turned out to be a *Will & Grace* fan. I wondered whether anyone was trying to figure out who this bearded Jewish man and his Gentile wife sitting between Bruce Springsteen and Paul McCartney were.

I have directed more pilots for Chuck Lorre's shows than for anyone else. Like me, he prefers everything to come from character. He can have as many as six sitcoms on the air at once and he feels fully responsible for every one of them.

Dharma & Greg in 1997 was Chuck's breakout hit. He had certainly paid his dues, working for Roseanne, Brett Butler, and Cybill Shepherd, known to be three of the most difficult stars in television history. Jenna Elfman, who played Dharma, was coming off *Townies*. She had a kinetic energy. She knocked my socks off when she told me she was a backup singer for ZZ Top, my favorite rock group.

She played a free spirit who married a buttoned-down lawyer (Thomas Gibson). Chuck surrounded her with crazies. Susan Sullivan and Mitchell Ryan were Greg's white-shoe parents, and Alan Rachins and Mimi Kennedy were Dharma's former-hippie mother and father. Shae D'lyn was the roommate. They were funny but not breakout. It was a very complicated pilot to shoot, with twenty-two scenes in twenty-five minutes. There are generally eight to nine scenes.

Dharma worked for five years but was especially hard for Chuck to sustain because it was stunt after stunt. It was a cartoon show. I directed an episode with a canoe coming down a mountain. I said,

"Chuck, I'm not sure about this." He said, "Jimmy, it's a cartoon!" From that point on in our working relationship, whenever a scene was outlandish or cartoonish, Chuck gave me his shorthand: "Dharma!"

After *Dharma & Greg*, I did a pilot for Chuck, *Slightly Damaged People* (also called *Last Dance*), that was based on Liz Taylor's last marriage, to Larry Fortensky, about two alcoholics who meet en route to the Betty Ford Clinic. We needed a Liz Taylor or Judy Garland type. We had Gail O'Grady, fresh off *NYPD Blue*. But we both fell in love with Paget Brewster, and she was paired with David Keith, from *An Officer and a Gentleman*.

We shot in Acton, in the San Fernando Valley. In the opening scene, Paget is in a limo and David's in a pickup truck. She sticks her head out of the sky roof and flirts with him, then climbs into the pickup. They have sex and then meet the next day in rehab. Chuck and I both felt that it was too ephemeral, because Paget's character didn't seem like she had lived enough to be world-weary. The story should have been about an older woman with a guy who could draw her out. We felt that younger people just out of rehab would both go off the wagon again soon after. The story of two people struggling didn't succeed here, but it did later with *Mike & Molly*.

Sometimes talented actors aren't a good fit for their roles and need to be replaced. On the original *Two and a Half Men* pilot, Blythe Danner played Evelyn, Charlie and Alan's mother. In Chuck's mind, Blythe wasn't mean enough. Holland Taylor plays the archness and sternness the character required with more ease and facility. Blythe can play sarcastic but not dark. Like Lisa Kudrow wasn't the best fit for Roz Doyle on *Frasier,* Blythe wasn't exactly what the character of Evelyn required, and I knew that we had to replace her.

Chuck wrote the script with Charlie Sheen in mind, knowing his reputation would draw viewers in. He was essentially playing himself. In the pilot, you immediately forgive Charlie Harper's wandering ways and bad behavior, because he cares about his young nephew and takes him and his newly divorced and now-homeless brother in. Charlie Sheen was respectful to me. I also got to meet his father, Martin, whom I've always admired.

Jonny Cryer, with whom I've worked a few times, is a consummate professional and all-around nice guy. He always knows his lines and how to tell a joke. He was the ultimate brother, a great Abbott to Charlie's Costello. He was Will to Charlie's Jack. Marin Hinkle was terrific as Alan's ex-wife, as was New Zealander Melanie Lynskey as Rose, Charlie's literally wacky neighbor. Conchata Ferrell as Berta the smart-mouthed housekeeper was added later.

Angus T. Jones was Chuck's only choice to play young Jake. Chuck called me and said, "You gotta come over to CBS—I found the kid!" Angus was so unexpected in that there was something so natural about him. There was no acting in that kid. To find that kind of young talent is difficult and rare.

Working with kids has been a challenge for me. Their schedules are regimented by state-required school hours, and, more important, kids can't walk the creative or comedic plank, because they haven't usually gone through enough in their lives. They don't have experiences to draw on. But if they're good, they can grow into a role, and as they get older, they develop good instincts.

Most pilots are one and done. If it doesn't get picked up, you won't hear about it ever again. There are some major exceptions to that rule. People see gold nuggets, characters worth retooling, or characters worth saving and putting in other environments. *All in the Family* went through three pilots before CBS gave it the green light. Norman Lear kept tweaking Archie Bunker, whom he'd based on his own father. I directed two different pilots for two shows, *3rd Rock from the Sun* and *The Big Bang Theory.*

In the first version of *The Big Bang Theory,* Sheldon (Jim Parsons) and Leonard (Johnny Galecki), the two nerd geniuses, are out walking on the street and come across a young lady sitting on the curb, crying on the phone to her mother. They take her in and find out she's a prostitute. The story was going to be the three of them, but we couldn't find the right person to play her. CBS called Chuck and said the show wouldn't be picked up but, since they liked the writing, would he consider trying it again. Chuck reformatted it and added two more nerds, Howard Wolowitz and Rajesh Koothrappali (Simon Helberg and Kunal Nayyar). We waited for Kaley Cuoco, who was soon to become available from 8 *Simples Rules*. Kaley became Penny, the new neighbor from across the hall who Leonard was immediately smitten with, and it worked.

There was a moment onstage during the second shoot where Sheldon is explaining to Penny why he needs to sit in his requisite spot on the couch, which she is currently occupying: "In the winter that seat is close enough to the radiator to remain warm and yet not so close as to cause perspiration. In the summer, it's directly in the path of a cross-breeze created by opening windows there and there. It faces the television at an angle that is neither direct, thus discouraging conversation, nor so far wide as to create a parallax distortion. I could go on but I think I've made my point." The audience howled with laughter. Chuck and I looked at each other and smiled. It was a wordless exchange that something remarkable was happening that defied our expectations. That scene alone validated the do-over, giving us that second chance to generate a hit.

Johnny was the center and the heart of that show, starting with falling in love with the woman who's out of his league. Chuck told me that the audience had no concept of a lot of what Jim Parsons said and did. But you didn't need to. You understood the intent.

These guys are yearning for love and acceptance and never talk about it, but you constantly feel it. They'll never go out and have a real life. This was a show where the actors were not only funny but each played their own comedic instrument to get laughs: Sheldon was always cynical, Leonard always upbeat, Howard came from a sexual point of view, and Rajesh was the dumb one, or at least as dumb as a brilliant scientist could be. He couldn't speak to a woman unless he was inebriated, which is the smart way of saying drunk.

In 2021 I directed the pilot and the first few episodes of Chuck's *B Positive*, which was created, written, and developed by Marco

Pennette, a now old friend, with whom I've worked on a number of projects over the years. The premise is one of the darkest in television history: Drew (Tom Middleditch), a thirty-five-year-old divorced dad, learns that he needs a kidney transplant quickly. He eventually finds a prospective donor in Gina (Annaleigh Ashford, a brilliant Broadway performer), a good-natured, hard-partying former high school classmate. The twist is that Drew needs to keep Gina off booze and drugs for ninety days so she can qualify to be his donor.

An intriguing aspect of *B Positive* is that it's based on Marco's real-life story about needing a kidney transplant in 2013. He got a donation from his mother's best friend's daughter. She had to lose forty pounds so she could donate. The *B Positive* storyline was modified from weight loss to detoxing.

The key to the show is Annaleigh's performance. Gina serendipitously runs into Drew years later and remembers him as "the only guy in high school that I didn't sleep with." The flaky Gina is humanized when we see that she works as a nursing home bus driver, ferrying the patients to and from the hospital for treatment. She explains to Drew that she was in a car accident and was supposed to be dead. She says, "I really believe I was saved for something, and this is it." The comedy grows out of that relationship, not despite the severity of the situation but because of it. When Drew tells her, "You have to stay clean," her response is "I've been clean for three days . . . just not in a row." It's an *Odd Couple*–type relationship between the uptight Drew and the free-spirited Gina.

I told Annaleigh, "This is a mixed forum, it's an amalgam. Your subtle gestures may not look fine for the studio audience, but at home it will work great. But you also have to be aware of the audience. If they laugh, you have to wait and not say your next line. Even though I'll still go to the other actor for a reaction shot, you have to be able to play the laughter and react to it."

When we originally shot the pilot, in the last scene—the tag—Gina shows up at Drew's doorstep with a suitcase. "I'll take you up on your offer of moving in." When Drew asks why, she replies, "Because a guy is after me because I owe him a lot of money." When Drew inquires how much, she replies, "The kind of money they break your legs for." Chuck, who is as adept at creating and protecting characters as anyone who has ever worked on sitcoms, said, "Don't waste that moment. We can do an entire episode about Gina moving in."

Because no audiences were allowed due to COVID, the second episode was a "block and shoot," where we staged the scene and filmed it. We introduced the group that was in dialysis. It was very similar to *Cheers*—the same way people sat around a bar talking, here people sat with tubes coming out of their veins as they spoke, as well as people sitting on a bus. We had veteran sitcom actors Bernie Kopell, who was Siegfried on *Get Smart* and Doc on *The Love Boat,* and Linda Lavin, who starred for nine seasons in *Alice* and had an impressive career on Broadway.

Linda is another member of the rarefied group of heat-seeking missiles for a joke. No matter what is in the script, there are multiple ways she will make it better. I go back with Linda to my first years as a sitcom director on a 1976 episode of *Phyllis,* "Widows, Merry and Otherwise." When I shot the *Sean Saves the World* pilot, Linda played Sean Hayes's mom. During a scene, I told her, "When you cross over, just pick up the ashtray and put it in your purse." In one second, I turned her into a kleptomaniac and gave her character specificity. She played it beautifully.

Chuck's fertile and creative mind has made him one of the most prolific and successful sitcom creators and producers in the business. Our collaborations combine clever premises with smart scripts and talented casts. I look forward to our next show together.

Behind the Scenes,
More Favorite People,
and Near Misses

KAT WARBLER
Look, all I'm saying is he sounds like a guy who doesn't
like you as much as you like him.

LINA WARBLER
Ugh, yes he does!

KAT WARBLER
Okay, you always say that. And then when they dump you,
you're like, "Oh my God! I can't believe he stole my Jetta!"

LINA WARBLER
Oh. That one did come as a shock.

THE CLASS

When you direct a sitcom, you're serving two audiences: the studio audience and the home audience. Both need to be entertained. Neither needs to know what is really going on behind the scenes. Most people don't want to see how the sausage is made. They just want to eat and enjoy. As they should. But every process beyond the stage is complex and integral to the success of the show.

During a sitcom season, the most important night of the week is show night, when everything is performed on camera before the live studio audience. I'm very animated on a set. I'm listening, I'm moving, I'm laughing. It's a play. You have to keep rolling. You are part of the entertainment.

On a modern sitcom taping, if something doesn't work, or if the

writers and director decide it can be better, the joke will be rewritten and the scene reshot. If something isn't funny, I'll try nine ways
to make it funny. I'll change the straight line to get more ideas, or I'll
find a funny position for the actors. During tapings, the writing
team generally watches the performances on the monitors, where I
am off alone, pacing. I still walk behind the stage and listen. I am
focused and watching with my ears. My ultimate litmus test is the
spoken word. In my head, the dialogue and the delivery need to be
funny enough to also make for a great radio show.

When I first started directing sitcoms, it took me a few years to
find my groove on multiple fronts. I learned how to place and move
the cameras, which is a skill a lot of television directors still don't
learn. By the time I had become comfortable with three cameras,
Taxi introduced four. It took me ten shows to get comfortable using
all four, but with the fourth camera, I was a kid at Christmas. With
only three cameras, sometimes you missed covering the joke, which
in a sitcom is devastating. Four cameras enabled me to get more
coverage and additional shots, which made for a better show.

While earlier in my career I stayed up late agonizing over marking the script to correspond to each of the three cameras. Now, I no
longer plan ahead. Instead, I come to the set with no preconcep-
tions about where people should be placed. I'm doing my home-
work with the actors; this way they get to give input. I now rehearse
a couple of times. I block the scene twice, but then it's pretty much
what I am going to shoot, unless the scene or dialogue changes significantly.

Generally, the cameras are brought in on the fourth day of the
shooting week, Thursday. Cameras have to be pointed at actors before they start speaking, and as soon as it is finished—not the dialogue, but the laugh in response to the dialogue—the cameras pull
over to focus on the next scene. That dance has to be pre-thought
during the week. It can take forever, and actors get bored and lose
momentum. I've developed incredible speed in camera blocking,
running through the script with the crew, substituting dialogue with

my signature Yiddish gibberish *"Chubdta chubdta."* I know I'm doing it again on Friday. I'm not concerned that I won't get the shots.

In a movie, where the camera is placed drives how the story is told. In a sitcom, the story has to initially work without cameras. Once it does, you bring in cameras to enable the home audience to see the play. In a sitcom, the cameras are technically covering the play. The technical aspect is the truth. It doesn't come from cinematic creativity; it comes primarily from getting all the jokes, the business, and the sight gags on camera. The sitcom director's primary job is to make sure the frame of the camera sees what is about to happen.

Unlike movies, where the director is king, television, especially a sitcom, is an incredibly collaborative form of media. In its optimal version, everyone has input and suggestions flow from writer to actor to director to crew. I don't think like a movie director, and on a sitcom it's actually counterintuitive. The camera is not a character on a sitcom; it is a pair of eyes capturing the action. While that is a different focus—pardon the pun—you still have to think about keeping the cameras moving and not locked down. There is artistic merit to moving a camera. We're not just filming a play. It wakes the audience up too.

Also, in a movie there are big moves that happen to a character. In a sitcom, there are deliberately smaller moves. A movie character's evolution is much quicker. In a sitcom it takes longer to give the character all their dimension. You have to draw it out over at least five years. The other important aspect for a director is to always allow yourself the surprise. Ninety percent of comedy happens when you don't see it coming.

Musical knowledge has informed my listening and rhythms. Stagecraft has informed what I do on television. I've always been a theater rat. I film theater. A lot of directors do two or three passes for coverage. I prefer to keep it going, again like a Broadway show. My directing philosophy has always been that I'm filming a play but not necessarily a play that's going to be in front of a theatrical audience; I approach it more like an informal workshop. I know there will be two hundred fifty people laughing in the bleachers, but I also know the actors have to play the reality of the moment both to the cameras and to the audience and find the sweet spot somewhere in between.

If you're filming a play, the actors are playing for the television audience, not the live one. Their reactions have to be less than what they'd be in the theater; they don't have to reach as far back. In the theater a small gesture doesn't work as well as a big gesture. The twentieth row has to see what the second row sees. In television those gestures do work. Some of the most important direction I've ever given sitcom performers was "Don't push." There's a camera that gets the close-up shot, so when you edit it together, you get the reaction that you need. In theater you can't see the tears from the fifteenth row. For what I do in television, everyone is in the second row. By dint of my cameras, everyone is in the same spot. I can capture the poignant moments. I'm aware that the reaction shouldn't be too big, despite the two hundred fifty people in the audience.

Directors, writers, and actors learn so much from an audience, which is why the audience must be cultivated, nurtured, and protected. The best way to protect the audience is by protecting the joke. Sometimes an actor will stumble on the joke, and I will react quickly, shut it down, and back the scene up. I will not let an audience hear a joke unless it works. I don't want to lose the spontaneity or the momentum. You also have to be careful of an audience that just won't respond to the comedy. In that case, you know it's the audience and not the writing. Performers often intuitively play the material harder to appease an unresponsive audience, so they have to be monitored, because when that pushing gets in front of the home audience it looks exaggerated.

If you're not facile with cameras, moving them is more of a challenge. A lot of directors bring the actors in, sit them down, and shoot them talking. They may rely on camera coordinators to do the technical work that they should be learning to do themselves. Those shows are easier to shoot but not realistic. In real life, people move around. The audience senses the difference before they actually realize it.

It takes a well-oiled machine to work behind the cameras. On a new show, I will defer to a writer who wants certain people on the crew, but I will always have my core team of camera operators, grips, and lighting and makeup people. I've developed my own ballet of cameras that catch everything. My rules are simple: If you're pointing the camera at somebody and they're not reacting, you're on the wrong person. Don't spend time on the wrong shot. After you land great actors and writers, make sure to also have a talented crew behind the camera. I've worked with the same crew for almost three decades, and no one gets flustered. After *Taxi*, I hired and took crews with me. Assistant directors Dale White, Caryn Shick, Doug Tobin, Richie Silva, and Ben Weiss; directors of photography Johnny Finger, Kenny Peach, Tony Askins, and Gary Baum; camera operators Lance Billitzer, Ed Fine, Travers Hill, and Glenn Shimada: They've been with me for more than twenty-five years. They all take copious notes during rehearsals, and they know where to look and when to get pickups while we are rolling. All these folks have been integral to my successes.

The large pedestal cameras are not so easy to move, and it is a hard skill to master quickly. The grip is a dedicated technician trained to operate the camera dolly, which is a wheeled cart. They place, level, and move the dolly track and push and pull the dolly. A good grip will let you know if you don't have a good shot. A camera operator and camera assistant are usually riders. I had three guys on each camera—one who looked, one who adjusted, and a dolly grip who moved the camera. On *Cheers*, one camera followed every person who came into the bar, in order to make the bar look grand. The dolly men are grips too. It is hard to train someone on the fly to get to the right marks. On a *Cheers* episode, when a dolly grip got sick, I pushed the dolly for the scene myself.

You have to think at least three shots ahead and know where

everything needs to be five minutes from now. Generally, in the four-camera world, the middle—or B and C—cameras in the center shoot the wider shots, and the far cameras on either side of B and C—A and X—shoot close-ups. The fourth camera was christened X early on because D sounded too much like B and had the potential to be more confusing than helpful on a hectic and noisy set.

In my world, rules are made to be broken if it will get you to the best-quality shot. I will have a C camera cover a close-up shot because it will look better. No camera does the same assignment 100 percent of the time. I can have a camera focusing on the actor who is talking, then I'll move another camera that I know won't be used in the edit so that the second camera covers the ensuing action, as the first camera is now covering something else.

Newsreeling is a type of shot I prefer: If I back up to an earlier line, the camera has to stay on that person, but I'll use another camera to get a reaction from other people, shooting all over the set to capture what is happening. It's an improvisational form of shooting. Chuck Lorre hates pans, because additional music must be created to accompany them, which is both expensive and time-consuming. My compromise with Chuck is what my crew and I now refer to as a *Mike & Molly* shot, starting with a wide shot and slowly pushing the cameras in.

The worst thing you can do on a set with a live audience is call "Cut." The minute you cut, you have to bring back the hair, makeup, lighting, and set-dressing teams. The scene crashes. Time, momentum, and audience energy are lost. I don't cut anymore. If an actor flubs a line, I just softly say, "Bababa" (as opposed to "Maaaaa"), and the actors back up to the last usable line. Any problem that is immediately fixable is not really a problem, so I'm careful not to make the audience think that anything's going on that is not de rigueur. If we have to do a scene change, I yell, "Reset." The actors freeze, and cameras get into different positions. The sound mixer plays Rimsky-Korsakov's "Flight of the Bumblebee," now best known as the theme

from *The Green Hornet,* which signals to the audience that something fast-paced is about to happen. On *Will & Grace,* Sean Hayes
would pantomime playing the violin as the audience heard the
music.

On *Cheers,* we would shoot one take and then get shots that I
missed or add new jokes, which are called "alternates" or "alts." Occasionally, we would do a scene again. A typical show took a maxi-
mum of two hours to shoot. Now a show generally takes four hours.
On *Will & Grace,* jokes would be rewritten multiple times and
scenes redone until the team couldn't think of anything more. With
great writing the cast not only doesn't panic, they get excited, because they know what is coming next will be even better. A typical
Friends taping ran between five and six hours. They'd have a second
audience waiting to replace the first one, which would grow fa-
tigued from being around for so long. I don't think the extra time
makes a difference; you know while you're shooting in front of a live
audience whether you have it. And you always have the safety of the
editing room to make any additional changes before the show airs.

On *Cheers,* I looked through every camera viewfinder as I was
blocking. After a while, I'd ask each camera guy what they saw. I
can now tell whether the shot is good. Before monitors, only the
camera operators could see whether they were getting their shots,
because they were the only ones who see through their viewfinders.
Each camera sits on a gear head with control wheels. The wheel
you control with your right hand moves the camera up and down;
the one that your left hand is touching moves the camera from right
to left. I could look at the camera operator's hands and see if the
wheels came to a nice, finessed completion. If the wheels were still
moving, I knew that they didn't have the shot yet. I could see
whether the wheels of the dolly were still moving, which also told
me that the camera was not ready to capture the shot. Both would
precipitate a "bababa."

There is a device called the quad split monitor, which allows you
to see what each of the four cameras is looking at any given mo-

ment. It wasn't available in the 1970s when we shot on film. We didn't even have a video assist, which is a video camera in a film camera that allows you to see what is coming through the lens in real time.

On *Will & Grace,* technology advanced to the point where the video assist came off the cameras and was put in on a monitor. A television screen was divided into four smaller ones: A and B on top, C and X on bottom. It helped me with blocking scenes. Early on, when a show was shooting, I never let anyone except the editor look at the quad. I didn't want writers to worry about the filming and lose focus on the piece being performed in front of them. I would also avoid it and, like Abe, would either close my eyes or go backstage to hear the dialogue being delivered. I'm listening to see if the instruments are being played correctly. A lot of directors take photographs first. I make a recording. I'm listening for characters that grab you, that you immediately invest yourself in and care about. There has to be some form of empathy. That comes before and gets you to the comedy.

I eventually yielded and allowed everyone, including myself, to watch the quad, primarily to avoid any problems with cameras. The writers congregate in what is called "the video village," which houses all the recording equipment, as well as a couple of quads and program feeds. Some directors feel pressure to be closer to the writers instead of the actors. The writers' group will always give me suggestions, but I still separate myself. Now when I block scenes, I have a quad, but I'm always in front with the cast, available to support the actors. If I was any closer to the actors, I'd be in the scene I was shooting.

On *Will & Grace,* I had access to a smaller camera with its own separate monitor, which was attached to a PeeWee dolly. It was always available as a backup in case one of the four cameras malfunctioned, but I also utilized it as a fifth camera during certain instances, where I had more than the four principals on the set or was filming a large gathering, like a wedding. It was not very maneuverable, but

I could use it for close-up shots, and it would free up the other cameras for other shots.

Once shooting is done, you have to edit the show to get it ready for the television viewers. Editing on sitcoms is much different from on movies. In a sitcom, you know while you're shooting in front of a live audience whether you have what you need. With live audiences, you ride that laughter. As a director, you put your imprint on the show when you first rehearse the actors. Your contributions will get through the process and make it onto the show. On a pilot, I'll spend more time with the cuts, but generally I don't spend a lot of time editing, for three reasons: first, because I shoot a show the way it should be cut; second, because when I'm done shooting, I am working on the next week's show; and third and most important, because I've always worked with strong editors.

Editors come to the shoot. They watch and they listen, which is also great training to become a director. When there's no audience, the editor decides what take to use and the script supervisor marks it. When there is an audience, a good editor pays attention to everything from the audience response to the glint in an actor's eye, and that will guide them in terms of what and where to cut.

The director's cut is more important in a movie because the story can be shaped by the editing. That's really hard to do in a sitcom, where you have put on a play and the audience is reacting to what you have put on. In a movie you don't know how the audience will react until the preview screening. By the time a sitcom has been filmed, we've already told our story to a live studio audience and their reactions shape how the story will be edited for presentation to the television viewers. During my early years I looked at cuts together with the writers but usually acquiesced to their opinions regarding what to keep.

On *TMTMS*, Doug Hines was the editor. He used a three-headed Moviola, one of the first machines for motion-picture editing, and looked at what all three cameras shot at once. When he cut, he'd mark the actual film with a black X. Then he and the associate producer would literally cut and paste the clips together to form the final show. Now it is all done on an Avid machine. During our first season of *Cheers,* our editor was Andy Chulack; then came Andy Ackerman, who later went on to direct *Seinfeld.* Peter Chakos trained on *Cheers* and then worked on *Will & Grace* and *The Big Bang Theory.*

On *Will & Grace,* creators/executive producers David Kohan and Max Mutchnick cut most of the episodes. The twenty-eight minutes shot were cut down to a twenty-two-minute show. It's all about finding the right cuts to not hurt the rest of the show. When the show was in the can, we had incredible laughter. You can't change what the audience laughed at; you can only shorten it. Having said that, one of the unwritten rules is "No good joke goes unwasted." We're always on the lookout for an SOS, a joke or a piece of business that won't make it into the final edit but can be saved for "some other show."

During the 1990s and early 2000s, I also gave priority to directing shows I was developing. I formed another production company, Three Sisters Entertainment (after my daughters, not nuns), to create and produce sitcoms. I later changed the name to Three Princesses and a P, to include my fourth daughter, Paris, whom everyone calls P.

Jamie Tarses ran my development company for two years. She was smart and creative. She worked on *Friends* as a network executive and helped nurture NBC shows. When I worked on *Dharma & Greg,* she was running ABC. She was part of a group that was trained by Tartikoff. These were Brandon's "kids"; they were "Brandonized." They had strong opinions, were really smart, and let the creative people do their work without a lot of interference. When I said I was going to develop shows, Broder said, "Partner with Jamie." Like their father, Jay, she and her brother, Matt, also created shows. Gary David Goldberg named the *Family Ties* sister, Mallory, after her sister.

I quickly realized that I didn't like developing shows from the point of concept/idea. It wasn't in my wheelhouse. Instead, I like taking someone else's fully baked script and building upon that. I prefer to enter the creative process later on in development.

Paul Simms sent me the script for *NewsRadio,* an ensemble show about a New York City radio station. The premise of the pilot was literally based on his work on *The Larry Sanders Show* with Garry Shandling, where on the first day of his new job he was told to fire the guy he was replacing. There were two scenes in the pilot, and I was able to shoot it in an hour and fifteen minutes. The *Friends* cast came to watch. There was a lot of smoke and mirrors with some gold nuggets in that pilot. The set was unwieldy, but I found ways to make it work. Dave Foley, while a great comedian and character actor, was not the leading man we needed. He wasn't a center and never had the romantic chemistry with Maura Tierney that would have likely made the show a hit and at the very least was a missed opportunity.

It was a talented cast but not a cohesive ensemble. Everyone was playing in different worlds. Stephen Root was the wealthy station owner, Andy Dick was the gofer, Khandi Alexander was one of the news anchors. I had a great time working with Phil Hartman. We did a wonderful episode where he tries to quit smoking and slowly unravels ("I coughed up something that looks like escargot this morning. I guess that's a good sign"). He was a great sketch comedian with a big heart, who had acting chops and was very inventive.

Ray Romano was originally cast as the station handyman. He wasn't right for the part and was replaced by Joe Rogan. Ray managed to recover quite nicely. A great life lesson is that talent and perseverance will take you places, and while it's difficult, try not to be discouraged when you lose or don't get a job because you're not right for the part.

My friends Fred Barron and Marco Pennette created *Caroline in the City,* about a cartoonist. It was inspired by the creator of the *Cathy* strip, Cathy Guisewite, and was about a woman who struggles through the "four basic guilt groups" of life—food, love, family, and work. They were able to get Lea Thompson, a movie actress who was doing television for the first time. The skill sets between acting in movies and sitcoms are different, especially when it comes to being funny. Lea was very talented and was able to adapt. She was a good center and was supported by a funny group: Eric Lutes, Malcolm Gets, and Amy Pietz. It was a medium success. I directed twenty-one of the ninety-seven episodes. Lea and her husband, Howie Deutch, are still good friends of mine. Our daughters, Paris and Madeline, have been friends since the age of four. On Thursday nights in 1998, I was producing four sitcoms on NBC: *Union Square* (which was also created by Fred and Marco), *Conrad Bloom, Caroline in the City,* and *Will & Grace.*

Joe Pantoliano, aka Joey Pants, is a natural actor and good friends with Danny DeVito. He was great on *The Fanelli Boys,* a pilot I directed about Brooklyn brothers who move back home with their mother. The cast also included Ned Eisenberg, a pre–*Law & Order* Chris Meloni, and Andy Hirsch. Ann Guilbert, who played Laura Petrie's best friend on *The Dick Van Dyke Show,* played their mother. The show was developed by Terry Grossman, Kathy Speer, Barry Fanaro, and Mort Nathan, the team who had worked on *The Golden Girls.* I thought that Grossman and Speer sounded like a German architectural firm. Turns out there actually is a structural engineering firm with the same name in Glendale.

I got to work with Judd Hirsch three times after *Taxi,* more than I've worked with anyone as a lead on different shows other than Kelsey Grammer. *Dear John* was my second collaboration with Judd, an ensemble comedy, similar to *Taxi.* Judd played a New York City teacher who is part of a divorce support group. Ed. Weinberger developed it based on a British show. It was during the Writers Guild strike in 1988, which meant there were no script changes because writers couldn't be on set. I had enough time to work on nuance. I got to develop all the fun business with Jere Burns, where he put his leg over the chair to sit down. Jere always wore a jacket. I told him to button the jacket when he sat down and to unbutton it when he stood up, just to be contrary and counterintuitive. It was a subtle direction but helped with his character development.

The combination of Bob Newhart and Judd in *George & Leo* was almost as easy as "bring 'em in, sit 'em down, and let 'em talk." Bob played George, a demure bookstore owner whose son (Jason Bateman, another bonus for me), was marrying the daughter (Bess Meyer) of the shady Leo (Judd), from whom she's been estranged for ten years. The two of them killed. Bob continues to play one type of character and plays it better than anyone else. Judd had to make the adjustment. Here he's not dealing with a crazy, he is the crazy one. He got to play a different color.

Superior Donuts was developed for television for comedian Jermaine Fowler. It was based on the stage play by Tracy Letts about despondent Arthur Przybyszewski, a former 1960s radical who owns a run-down donut shop in Chicago, with Fowler playing his energetic assistant Franco, who wants to update the establishment with lively music and healthy menu options. Mike McKean starred as Arthur on Broadway.

Jermaine had great ideas that he would pitch. We shot the pilot with the lead role played by Brian d'Arcy James, who played King George in the original production of *Hamilton*. Les Moonves didn't like him. We thought, who was a more natural choice to play a Polish man than Judd? We reshot. Jermaine held his own with Judd. We added Katey Sagal to the cast as a cop, as well as Maz Jobrani, as a local businessman who is buying up all the property in the gentrifying area. He was a John Larroquette–like, acerbically funny character. You can set out to do a dark show, but you need funny to get people in the car with you.

The drama of it worked. It was *Cheers* in a donut shop, although the humor often felt like it was secondary to the drama. When the audience didn't laugh, the writing team insisted that the material was funny and wouldn't change the jokes. Audiences need to be woken up and surprised. Tracy Letts came to our first reading and stayed for the network's notes session. He said, "How do you guys listen to this?"

Michael Patrick King came to me after *Sex and the City* with *2 Broke Girls,* a show he co-created with Whitney Cummings. Whitney was very funny and pitched a lot of great ideas. Kat Dennings and Beth Behrs played the leads, two waitresses who start a cupcake business. Kat was already known for *The 40-Year-Old Virgin.* Kat's acerbic persona, the tough character with the heart of gold, would have played great on *Taxi* or *Cheers.* Beth's character was based on Michael's idea that she be the daughter of a Bernie Madoff–type, adjusting to her new life without any money. They had great chemistry. I had seen Jennifer Coolidge in Chris Guest's *Best in Show.* When she came onstage as the flashy, curvy Polish upstairs neighbor, the audience went crazy. She has that very feminine body and plays ditzy well like Catherine O'Hara.

Michael and I not only worked well together, we always had fun. We shot the pilot until two in the morning. In the original plot, Kat's character, who works at a diner, has a second job as a babysitter for the newborn twins of a wealthy and self-absorbed Tribeca couple. Michael kept trying to make the scene work. I said, "You're going to cut the scene. It's hilarious in the coffee shop." We shot that scene over and over again until he relented. He's as tenacious as he is talented. When I came back in season 5, I got to work with George Hamilton, who played a rich producer that was based on Robert Evans. He was so funny. Michael asked me, "How am I going to get rid of George in this scene?" I responded, "Helicopter." Through the magic of sitcoms, we had the sound of a helicopter, a spotlight, and a ladder drop down.

We did a similar scene on *Will & Grace,* when Stan comes to pick up Karen. Special effects allowed the audience to imagine the helicopter. On another *Will & Grace* episode we actually had a helicopter. Grace is saying goodbye to someone on a pier and the rotors are going. I made them hoist the chopper—I needed the effect of it being started up.

I enjoyed directing the pilot for *The Neighborhood*, which was based on creator Jim Reynolds's real-life experience about when he arrived in Los Angeles and moved into a black neighborhood in Altadena. Max Greenfield and Beth Behrs play the white couple who move into the neighborhood, and Cedric the Entertainer plays Calvin, the set-in-his-ways next-door neighbor. Jim, who is white, and who came off *Big Bang*, is looking at the show from the perspective of how white people would see it, and Cedric is focused on how the black audience would see it; they would meet in the middle. Cedric was terrific. He has a great presence, is very creative, and is strong-willed and very protective of his ideas. As adamant as he was, he was also the consummate professional and willing to incorporate other good ideas.

Henry Winkler is one of the sweetest and most talented people you'll ever meet. We go back together to our childhood. We grew up on the same block on the Upper West Side. I was friends with his older sister, Bea. I got to direct him twice. *Monty* starred a post–*Happy Days* Henry as a conservative, Rush Limbaugh–type television talk-show host, with his wife, Fran (Kate Burton), and two liberal sons, Greg and David (David Schwimmer and David Krumholtz). Krumholtz is another heat-seeking missile for comedy.

GREG
I have an announcement to make everybody.
Gina and I are getting married.

MONTY
No, you're not. This is not a democracy. I didn't spend all this time and all this money molding my son's future for him to throw it away on Gypsy Rose Lee. You are going back to law school and you are returning to the mother ship!

In the original version of the script, Monty's daughter brought home her lesbian girlfriend. America and DreamWorks weren't ready for that in 1994. It was later changed to Monty's son who stopped studying law in order to become a chef. The politically corrected version didn't have the edge that it started out with.

I also directed Henry in the pilot of *Beverly Hills S.U.V.* Larry Wilmore wrote a great script about used-car salespeople. We thought that by dint of Henry being in it, it would attract interest. Sadly, we had a lead that was not likable.

Cindy Chupack, who later worked on *Sex and the City*, wrote a great script called *Madigan Men*, about a famous widowed architect (Gabriel Byrne) who lives with his son and whose eccentric father comes from Ireland to live with them. I went to New York a few days early to meet with Gabriel, who was starring on Broadway in *A Moon for the Misbegotten* with Cherry Jones and Roy Dotrice. We were scrambling to find someone good to play the father, until Gabriel suggested Roy. John Hensley was very good as the son, Luke. Gabriel was great at comedy and could throw away lines perfectly.

Another male-bonding-centered show was *The Secret Lives of Men*. Peter Gallagher, Bradley Whitford, and Mitch Rouse played divorced men trying to figure out their postmarital lives. It was my second show with the brilliant Susan Harris and the beginning of my close friendship with Peter. In the show, Peter's character, Michael, is at a restaurant, waiting to have lunch with his ex-wife, Marcy (Harley Jane Kozak). The script called for him to build a small house out of breadsticks, like Lincoln Logs. I thought, "Eh." I said to Peter, "Since she's late, start eating the breadsticks, and have fun eating them." He puts one in his mouth and pushes it in. She shows up and he starts gagging. During the notes session, producers Paul Junger Witt and Tony Thomas turned to Susan and said, "He didn't do the thing with the Lincoln Logs." Susan replied, "What he did was funnier." Like Gabriel, Peter is a talented, great-looking actor who's very funny and similarly doesn't get a chance to do enough comedy because he's so adept at dramatic roles. He was great on Broadway as Sky Masterson in *Guys and Dolls*. Not only could he sing, but he understood that role—a man who expects to live alone his whole life and loves it, until a woman unexpectedly comes into it and he falls deeply in love for the first time. Not the easiest role to get right.

Jason Bateman and Paula Marshall played co-workers with great chemistry in *Chicago Sons*. Sadly, the show didn't really explore the romance until the end of its thirteen-episode run, missing the potential for the *Cheers* Sam and Diane connection. From the first time I directed him in the pilot of *Valerie,* I knew there was something special about Jason. He has amazing presence and comic timing. He's also brilliant in dramas like *Ozark,* where he also executive produced and directed many episodes. Like Teddy, Jason has the gift: extremely talented and good-looking. He's a center. You feel comfortable with Jason, as if he were one of your best friends. I can say that both professionally and personally, because he actually is one of my best friends. I love him.

It's a lot easier to entertain as a director than as an actor being seen on television. As a director, I get a lot of scripts, so I don't have to act or appear on camera or look great all the time (although I think I look great most of the time). I get to work my wiles in the background. I don't have to change my personality. The audience, however, expects their favorite characters to be the same way they were in the last sitcom they were in. It's a harder sell.

Unless you have a distinctive quality or a unique set of skills, it's difficult for an actor to repeat success in the sitcom world. Very few actors have been able to replicate their successes, especially as a center. Teddy Danson made it work with *Cheers, Becker, The Good Place,* and now with *Mr. Mayor.* Bob Newhart was able to do it multiple times because of his unique presence and style. Ted Knight followed *TMTMS* with the short-lived *The Ted Knight Show* (and way too many *Love Boat* episodes) but then had a seven-year run with *Too Close for Comfort.* After *Seinfeld,* Jason Alexander and Michael Richards didn't work as centers, but Julia Louis-Dreyfus is an incredibly strong center. She did *The New Adventures of Old Christine,* which didn't get great ratings but won her a Lead Actress

Emmy, and then starred in *Veep,* which was a huge hit, and more Emmys followed. It happens occasionally and is a tribute to great acting and great writing.

Sitcoms burn through characters and performers more quickly than any other art form. There is only so much elasticity a character and a performer have, especially one who's great at it. A sitcom, especially a successful one, is not only demanding, it exposes you more than any other form. Film actors are exposed for ninety minutes once or twice a year at most, while sitcom actors in a twenty-two-episode season over five years are exposed for at least sixty hours. There is a lot of that actor in front of people's faces. Even in television drama, you're a cop, lawyer, or doctor. You're playing in the same creative colors. In comedy, the colors are different even though you don't realize it, because the characters are often so distinct and individual, which is what makes them successful and often iconic.

On sitcoms, actors are musicians who each play a specific instrument. The audience may not like the piece that they are playing, but they love the instrument. It's hard for an audience to get used to anyone playing a new instrument, which is why it's especially hard for a performer to become a new character after endearing themselves to the audience with an established one. In the same vein, being beloved is often a double-edged sword. Sitcom stars can become prisoners of their own success. There's the Hollywood joke "Jamie Farr to block," which references the actor Jamie Farr, *M*A*S*H*'s cross-dressing Corporal Max Klinger. He became so recognizable in that role that it was virtually impossible for him to work again. No one could see beyond his beloved and iconic character. That's when you wind up as a regular on *The Hollywood Squares.*

If I don't have to spend too much time helping an actor develop a role—which is usually when a great script meets a great performer—I can concentrate on the overall show and work on nuances. I don't have to spin my wheels. As you probably know by now, I try to be a great collaborator. I can take a wonderful script and improve upon it. I can also often turn a fair script into a good show, but no one can turn that good show into a great show. Lipstick on a pig, a Band-Aid on a bullet hole—pick your metaphor. Weak writing is more often than not the reason a show doesn't make it. A sitcom will stay on the air until the studio pulls the plug. I'll use what I call "smoke and mirrors" to try to make something work. If I'm making too many suggestions, then I know there are some real holes in the lifeboat. I've never stayed on a show where the writing wasn't strong enough to support it. That's a recipe for disaster, because weak writing means that the characters can't grow and develop, which means you end up with very unhappy actors.

Sometimes, success breeds a dangerous sense of arrogance. An actor starts swinging the hammer, but in actuality they don't necessarily have the goods to swing that hammer, because their previous success was less about their skills and more about the writing and the directing. A few shows into the season, the false confidence makes them think that they can do everything on their own, and that's where problems occur.

Teddy Danson never went on a show and said, "We're going to do it my way or not at all." He was secure and self-confident in his ability. I still wonder whether I could have averted the acrimony between the co-stars if I had stayed on *Laverne & Shirley.* I also realize that a lot of the discord comes from the person who's complaining and what they really want or need. Do they want to play together, or do they want and/or need to continue complaining for reasons that have nothing to do with the show?

I like developing characters that the audience feels like they had a hand in creating. The icing on the cake is then turning performers into stars. That was *Cheers, Taxi, Friends, Mike & Molly, Will & Grace, NewsRadio,* and *Night Court.* I've worked on shows where there were only one or two stars and endeavored to create an ensemble around them. I rarely get mad. Camaraderie and kindness are not just the right thing to do, they are the tools for success for any smart director. Harmony among cast members always translates to harmony on the set and on the TV screen. I'd like to think I have magical powers to take a person who is bent out of shape at being part of an ensemble and get them to work and play well with others. But it's not only about what I do; it's also about the makeup of a person who wants to be either a star or part of an ensemble. Ensemble members who succeed and break out are more likely to become stars and stay stars if they're team players, because success is based on work, not on a contract.

This idea that people who are difficult are worth it is a myth predicated on the belief that acting involves some mysticism, that it's magic and not a craft. It is a craft, and everyone is doing their job. No amount of brilliance is worth having to pull teeth to get there. There is simply no place for anyone acting like a prima donna on my set. Back when I was starting out, I had neither the balls nor the gravitas to fully set the tone, so I tolerated a lot of bad behavior. If an actor was surly, I dealt with it. Now, you don't want to fight with me, or anyone else on my set, or piss me off. I won't get angry, I'll just shut down.

In recent years, I've had a "fun clause" provision, so to speak, on every sitcom I've worked on, an understanding with networks and producers that I can unilaterally walk away from a project if I'm not having fun. I've only walked away once, from a show called *Men Behaving Badly*. It was based on a British show of the same name and was about two of the sweetest men you ever saw, Gary and Dermot (Martin Clunes and Harry Enfield), who did horrible things. The execution of that premise worked because the two leads were sweet, so you forgave the bad acts. The first mistake in the American version was casting Rob Schneider with Ron Eldard and Justine Bateman, who played Ron's girlfriend. Rob was neither sweet nor did he know how to play a sweet character, so it became a show about a malevolent guy doing malevolent things. No one could connect with that. Rob and Ron never got on. Occasionally, the producers would say, "Rob's in his trailer and he won't come out. Can you talk to him?" The vitriol got so bad that during a taping, in front of an audience, the cast "walked through the show," saying their lines with no emotion. They tried replacing Ron with Ken Marino, but people found it very difficult to work with Rob. I was done.

In sitcoms, you can only play the hand that you're dealt. You can never bluff the audience. Sometimes there is lightning in the bottle; other times there's just a dead fuse. There is no more nurturing of an audience. Networks have much more of a hair trigger now than they did years ago. If the numbers aren't there immediately for a show, networks won't invest in the future—they'll call time of death, pull the plug after a handful of episodes, and replace the show with one waiting in the wings.

There should be a neon sign over each sitcom production saying LUCK, because without it, you can have the best writing in the world but get the wrong time slot. You can have the best leads but weak chemistry between them. Another one of my very few regrets was with a 2006 show, *The Class*, which I thought was an extraordinary piece of writing by David Crane and Jeffrey Klarik.

It was about a group of third-graders reunited twenty years later by pediatrician Ethan (Jason Ritter), who met his fiancée in that class and plans a surprise party. She comes in and dumps him. The chemistry and dynamics of all the people reuniting was amazing.

Jason inherited his father's brilliant comic timing. John Ritter was one of the greatest physical comedy actors that ever lived and a wonderful human being. The cast also included accomplished actors Lizzy Caplan, Jesse Tyler Ferguson, David Keith, Andrea Anders, and Jon Bernthal.

I made the same speech to CBS that I had earlier made to NBC about *Will & Grace:* "Please, just let us sneak into town." I wanted a less popular time slot, which would allow us to build an audience.

They promoted the show and it tested well, so they started to promo the hell out of it. It got a big ratings number the first week, and then the second week it dropped. I knew that would happen.

What almost always happens is that the perception of the show changes when the network sees that lower number the following week. That kind of thinking has always upset me. It was a great show. It had some early flaws, which we fixed, and David and Jeffrey did an excellent job of uniting the cast. It was the lead-in to *How I Met Your Mother*. If it had been scheduled behind that show, people would have come to it slowly. Putting it on at eight o'clock and promoting the hell out of it got people to the dance who wouldn't ordinarily have come, but it didn't establish the core audience who really would have liked the show, and it prevented a slow-but-steady word-of-mouth building process.

We did nineteen wonderful episodes of *The Class* before CBS canceled it. It almost makes me cry over what a hit it could have been. If networks knew what they were doing, there'd be nothing but hit shows on the air. It drove David and Jeffrey away from network television. They went to Showtime and did the hit *Episodes* with Matty LeBlanc. David is one of the best writers of comedy and one of the nicest human beings. He ran the *Friends* writers' room for ten years. He was there for every show, pitching wonderful ideas. He has a great sense of story and empathy. He would never settle on a joke. Instead, you had to keep pitching until he loved it. I can say the same thing about Jeffrey. A great writing partnership is the same as acting. It's all about talent and chemistry. It's the spinning of ideas off each other; you have to have the same sense of humor and be completely comfortable with the other person. You can't buy it at the store. It has to be there.

At its worst, the sitcom process is tantamount to the biggest roller-coaster ride you've ever been on. But at its best, you get to work with the most talented artists and greatest people on both sides of the camera. Everyone watching at home is connected to the energy onstage and the energy that emanates from the studio audience. When it works, there is community and camaraderie for both the studio audience and the one at home. It is one of the most exciting and energizing forms of entertainment. And on show night, there are two hundred fifty people in the audience roaring together with laughter. I am often the person laughing the most and the loudest on a set.

Will & Grace

JACK
I am a platinum-star gay.

GRACE
Gaysplain, please.

WILL
Gold-star gay has never been with a woman. Platinum: haven't
been with a woman and were born via C-section.

JACK
Hence, I have never touched a vagine.

WILL
It's all going to be in his book, *Men Are from Mars,
Who Cares Where Women Came From.*

When asked about same-sex marriage in a *Meet the Press*
interview in 2012, then–vice president and now-president Joe
Biden said, "I think *Will & Grace* probably did more to educate
the American public than almost anything anybody's ever done so
far. People fear that which is different. Now they're beginning to
understand."

That was, and still is, one of the proudest moments of my career.

In its best incarnation, television is one of the most important
platforms for creating awareness and advancing understanding between people, race, gender, and culture. People don't fear what or
whom they know and understand, not only in their community but
also in their own families. The path to understanding and aware-

ness becomes even smoother if you can take a serious subject and approach it by layering a sensitive discussion with laughter.

Between 1996, when Congress passed the Defense of Marriage Act (DOMA), defining marriage as a union between a man and a woman, and 2011, more Americans supported gay marriage than opposed it. Finally, in a 2015 Supreme Court ruling, same-sex marriage was legalized nationally. The lesbian, gay, bisexual, transgender, and queer (LGBTQ) community has gained much acceptance over the last forty years, and television comedy, in particular, contributed to that.

The first gay character in a sitcom appeared on the short-lived 1976 comedy *The Corner Bar*. Shortly thereafter, in a first-season episode of *All in the Family*, "Judging Books by Covers," Archie learns that his drinking buddy, a former pro-football player (Philip Carey), is gay.

Back in 1977, Jay Sandrich brought me a three-quarter-inch tape of the pilot he had just directed, *Soap*. Susan Harris had created and written a beautifully funny parody of soap operas, with Billy Crystal co-starring as Jodie Dallas, a gay man and the first gay father on television. Sitcoms were dealing with gay family members and friends and people struggling to come out decades before anyone else was willing or able to publicly address the topic.

Before *Will & Grace*, I directed a number of shows and episodes that featured gay characters, including *The Bob Newhart Show*, *Phyllis*, *Taxi* ("Elaine's Strange Triangle," for which I won an Emmy), and *Cheers*. All of these episodes were cutting edge in their time. But while they offered increased awareness, tolerance, and support for the gay characters, shows never went as far as having gay characters as leads. Audiences weren't given the ability to get to know these characters on a weekly basis, where they could view the world through their perspective.

Ellen was a relatively ordinary sitcom for its first three seasons. Then, in 1997, in a revolutionary move, Ellen DeGeneres came out, both in real life and in her sitcom persona. *Ellen* became the first show to have a gay main character. Ellen Morgan's as well as Ellen DeGeneres's coming out became international news, with Ellen on the cover of *Time* magazine and Oprah Winfrey guest-starring as her therapist. Ellen tried to change the perception of the show, which is always extremely hard to do. I've often said that Ellen knocked down the door in terms of the audience accepting gay characters, and we, as *Will & Grace,* waltzed through it.

David Kohan and Max Mutchnick (whom I will refer to as the Boys, not only for brevity but as an expression of genuine affection) met in Beverly Hills High School in a musical comedy class and have been friends and writing partners ever since. When *Mad About You* was ending its successful run, NBC asked the Boys to come in with a new kind of young-love story. They wrote a pilot about four couples. Warren Littlefield, who was then NBC's president, said, "I don't like the pilot, but I like one of the couples, Will and Grace."

I first read the *Will & Grace* pilot script in November 1997. My initial reaction was "Oh my God, this is really good. This dynamic is incredibly well-handled." It was funny as well as smart and timely. The Boys had captured a genre and a group of characters that no one had ever seen on television. They had a finger on the pulse of doing a gay show in a straight kind of way—pairing Jack, an over-the-top gay man, with Will, a more moderate "straight" gay man.

I told Warren that I really wanted to direct it. It had a distinctive voice the way *Cheers, Friends,* and *Seinfeld* did. The project went away for a while, then Broder said it was still out there and NBC was going to do it. I jumped in and helped move the process along.

The pilot had a number of attitude jokes, particularly between Will and Grace. An attitude joke is a line that's made richer and funnier because of the character saying it. It's the Norm entrance. It's a bon mot, not a hard joke. By Norm saying it, the laugh is enhanced. I immediately saw a symbiotic relationship—two people who could finish each other's sentences. The laughter came not necessarily from a funny line but in showcasing the synergy between the two. People who are close draw an audience in. The core relationship has to be funny:

GRACE

The psychic knew I had issues with my mother, had relationship problems, and that my best friend was a gay man.

WILL

You just described half the women in New York City!

As always, when I get a script, the first thing I look for is great writing. Again, it's not the concept the attracts me, not the idea, it's the execution of the idea. I want to know how the writers are drawing the characters and what these characters say to me and to the audience. I immediately wanted to meet the creative voices who wove the interesting tapestry about these two best friends. I met David and Max at Walter's Coffee Shop. While they thought that they were auditioning me, I was auditioning them. I liked them immediately, told them that I was going to direct the pilot, and then stuck them with the check.

Will & Grace may have started out as high concept, with two gay men at the center of the show, but it quickly became a love story where the two people can't consummate the relationship sexually.

In the very beginning, you see a man and a woman talking on the phone. They are clearly close friends. They start talking about the show *ER,* and there is a deliberate reveal about Will. When Grace asks Will if he is jealous that she is with a man, he responds, "Honey, I don't need your man. I've got George Clooney." When Grace says, "Sorry, babe. He doesn't bat for your team," he says, "Well . . . he hasn't seen me pitch."

As we defined the characters, we also crafted their surroundings accordingly. When it came to the layout of the set, Will's apartment had many small corners, and I took advantage of every one of them.

We knew that we needed the kind of apartment that a gay man and an interior designer living together would have, where there would be much attention to detail and everything would be impeccable. The television was in the small reading room off the living room. There was a love seat for two people. A few episodes later, I had the love seat replaced with one that sat three. Sean Hayes asked, "Won't the audience notice?" "Honey," I replied, "if they notice the new love seat, then we have much bigger problems."

In the pilot, Grace is about to marry her boyfriend, Danny, whom Will hates. We only see Danny's legs in boxer shorts walking away. We don't need to see him; we just need to establish his presence to advance the narrative.

There was initially a scene where Will goes running down to the courthouse to talk Grace out of the marriage. I told the Boys, "We've seen that scene already. Maybe instead you want to do one where they get very angry at each other."

"Don't marry Danny," Will emphatically tells her. "This guy's not enough for you. I mean, you're passionate and you're creative and beautiful and perfect. And this guy . . . he's not funny. He doesn't know what your favorite flower is. He's passive-aggressive. The man high-fives you after sex. You're so afraid you're never going to get married, you can't even see how wrong he is for you. Think about it. If you really believed he was the one, would you be asking me for my blessing?" An angry and hurt Grace tells Will to go to hell and leaves.

Will feels bad and goes to Grace's office. Karen tells him that Grace went to city hall to get married. Grace shows up at Will's office in her wedding dress and in tears because she couldn't go through with the marriage. We got that dynamic rather than the typical courthouse confrontation. The Boys considered and took my suggestion, and that was the beginning of our long working relationship. I saw how all they cared about was making the script better. Where Glen and Les Charles became my brothers, Max and David became my sons.

At the end of the pilot, Grace is still in her wedding dress as Will consoles her:

WILL

Sweetie, remember in college we saw that French film about a man and a woman that were perfect for one another, but they kept missing each other. And in the last scene, they meet on a plane, because that's the way it was destined to be. Remember when you said, "That's gonna be me." Gracie, you're just in the middle of your movie. Danny was a plot point, a nice, decent, postcoital high-five-ing plot point. There's still time, you know. Go get some Raisinets.

GRACE

I like Red Vines.

WILL

Whatever you want. The point is, it's not over if your movie's going to have a happy ending. You just have to see it through.

At a bar later, they let the other patrons believe that they just got married. Will toasts his new "ball and chain" and they are prompted to kiss, after which Grace asks, "Anything?" To which Will responds, "Sorry, nothing."

The characters were named after philosophers in Martin Buber's book *I and Thou*. Buber talks about the various types of relationships you have with people and with God. In order to have that relationship, you need the will to go after it and the grace to receive God. Philosophy major David thought these were complementary things. "If we ever had a love story with two complementary people, these would be great names because the two of them together are so good." It's a good thing he never saw *The Sorrow and The Pity*.

The creators of the show generally do the early casting, then I sit with them for the last three or four choices and we consider them together. Eric McCormack was the first person we were set on. We loved him and knew he would be perfect for the role of Will.

We already knew about Debra Messing. She had done the sitcom *Ned and Stacey,* which lasted for two seasons. Her first reading was held in the den of my house. NBC asked us to see Nicollette Sheridan as well. Nicollette was pretty and had shown some skills. But once Debra came into the room, there was no question that she and Eric had chemistry together. They were finishing each other's sentences during the audition. Teddy and Shelley, Kelsey and David, and Jennifer Aniston and Schwimmer all had that. I take no directorial credit for any of that chemistry. It was fully there between them from the get-go.

We had two choices for Jack: Sean Hayes and Alexis Arquette. Jack is based on a man in New York who slept with everyone. By casting Sean, who looks fairly innocent and sweet, we didn't go to the dark side and therefore the character became much more appealing:

JACK

Judge said I gotta spend the next two weeks picking up trash.

WILL

At least this trash won't call you the next morning.

There is something very genial about Jack. He's a lonely guy, as is Will. But he knows that, as close as they are, they will never be a couple.

At the beginning of the second season, during the opening scene, Eric is dressed in a nice suit. Sean enters wearing a fancy jacket and shirt. I don't know from costumes. Max is the one who loves to do the "rack checks." But when I saw Jack, I immediately yelled, "Cut," in front of the audience. I explained to Max and David and to the wardrobe people that Jack needed to look as innocent as possible, to balance out his lascivious side. We changed up the wardrobe and had Jack in his signature sweater vests, jeans, and Converse Jack Purcell sneakers—a physical representation that at his core he is sweet and almost childlike. I try to always see what the audience sees and hears.

Unlike the Brothers, who were my contemporaries, the Boys were a generation younger than me and brought a needed wisdom and perspective, both on lifestyle and pop culture and social and cultural issues, that I didn't have. They got the gay and camp humor that drove the show. They were living it and helped me hear the music I needed to understand the comedic value of the new sounds. Between takes during the pilot, Debra came in in an outfit and Max changed the joke for the scene, telling Sean to say, "Oh, here comes Sporty Spice." I looked at Max quizzically, not knowing what this new reference was. He said, "Trust me, it's going to get a big laugh." It did. Jack and Karen famously bumping stomachs in that early episode came from things the Boys saw in their own lives.

Will and Grace are Jupiter and Mars. The challenge was to make sure that we structured the show to allow for the humanity to rest on that foundation. By having Will like Jack and Grace like Karen, the audience would like them as well, and the language could get as sharp and funny as we wanted. Will could say: "Jack, you're not shy around men. You'd hit on the pope if he drove a better car," and "Okay, here's the plan. Call Dorothy. Tell her to meet at the Yellow Brick Road. When you get to the end of the road, you'll see a man. Ask him for a brain."

From the outset, we played Will's style and subtlety against Jack's high energy:

JACK
You don't even know me that well. Why would you
assume that I was gay? . . . Most people that
meet me don't know that I'm gay.

WILL
Jack, blind and deaf people know that you're gay . . .
dead people know that you're gay.

JACK
Grace, did you know I was gay when you met me?

GRACE
My dog knew.

The formula was similar to that of *Cheers,* where the audience connected with the supporting characters through Sam's affection for Cliff, Norm, and Frasier, so the audience got into the show through those perceptive windows. Initially, the audience connected with Jack by dint of Will's affection, and with Karen via Grace. The through lines of developing connection through affection are important components of this and every successful show.

The audience loved the pilot. The Boys and I went to the network and I strategically asked, "Please put this show in a time slot where we don't have to prove ourselves." NBC agreed and put it on Monday night at nine-thirty, so we had some breathing room to build an audience. We initially got low ratings, but after a while people started telling their friends that there was this kind of a funny show with these unexpected characters that was worth watching. I have always liked to sneak in quietly, especially with a show with no star and no high concept, just a simply good comedy.

Will & Grace is a fairy tale, literally and figuratively. It's not grounded in the same reality as other shows. There are realistic aspects about it, like the relationship of Will and Grace, but the characters could insult each other affectionately, say anything euphemistically, and could get away with it, because there's something innocent about those four people that makes them all likable, despite their flaws. That was the genius of that show, and it took the network until the middle of the first season to fully realize it. To their credit, they were always supportive and never had any reservations about airing a "gay" sitcom.

The heartbeat of the show was Max and David—Max because he is gay, and David because, although heterosexual, he was "married" to Max for twenty-five years as his best friend and creative partner. They both made sure that Max's story as a gay man was heard. We were all concerned with how the characters were portrayed and what they did. Every attitude. We didn't want to do anything to demean the characters, especially the gay ones. Max was the most protective. He'd write something and then, when he saw it in rehearsal, would say, "I don't want a gay man doing that."

I told Eric McCormack the same thing I'd told Teddy Danson sixteen years earlier: "Don't try so hard to be funny. You're the center—react. Don't hit the lines too hard. Throw them away."

Since the set had different levels, with a few steps up to the kitchenette, Eric would stand in the kitchen, making it his "Captain Kirk" station, planning his cooking based on how long his scene was, and changing it if the scene changed. He could do the same speech the exact same way each time if he chose to. By deciding how he'd be placing a sandwich on a plate, he developed his timing. The more involved he was in making coffee and not looking up, the funnier the lines would be. After a while I'd say, "What're you making, honey?" I was always hungry after shooting those scenes.

NBC saw that the show was about four human beings, two of whom just happened to be gay. The greatness of the show was that it was about funny people living their truth. From the beginning, Don Ohlmeyer, who was then running NBC, and Warren had our backs. My job was to corroborate the Boys' vision. I wasn't going to dilute anything in that script. Our show snuck in under the radar, but the media reviews were good. When there were new executives, I would get the occasional "Aren't there too many gay jokes?" I would respond, "If not here, then where? If not now, then when?"

Each character was likable, with rough and sharp edges. Jack was over the top, but we could get away with it because he played against Will, a gay man who was fairly conservative. Grace was a neurotic Jew—who in syndication still is a neurotic Jew—but she was played with pathos and vulnerability by Debra Messing, a very funny comedian.

Grace's less-than-competent assistant, Karen ("Sorry I'm late, but I got here as soon as I wanted to"), was the hardest part to cast. Megan Mullally originally read for Grace, but when she read for Karen, we knew we had our cast. Karen was a rich, pill-popping, boozing woman, who Megan played with incredible vulnerability. She knew and acknowledged that her life was terrible in many regards but never in a self-pitying way, and the audience gave her a lot of play: "Marriage is a series of moments. Waking up in the morning, smiling at each other across the kitchen table, hiding jewelry together and blaming the maid. Then firing her and watching her cry as she loads her one tattered suitcase into the back of the cab. You know, couples' stuff. . . . God didn't give me the ability to play piano or paint a picture or have compassion. But he did give me the ability to crack a walnut with my hoo-ha!"

WILL

Karen, tell Grace she should fire you.

KAREN

Grace, tell Will he should redirect his anger at his mother, where it belongs.

Jack and Karen had a very interesting relationship. They were two outrageous characters that adored each other. They didn't have the serious bond that Will and Grace had. They were people from different planets who hooked up and clicked. To quote Alice Roosevelt Longworth: "If you can't say something good about someone, sit right here by me." There had never been a sitcom relationship like Jack and Karen's before. We exploited it. Jack was a foil for

Karen's nastiness, and both were great foils for Will and Grace. You could do the weirdest things with them.

Karen's character wasn't fully developed until the second episode. Max said, "Okay, Jack brings a tassel that Grace left at the house back to the office, so he meets Karen." This thin line of plot allowed for the two characters to meet and for me to direct the tummy touch, which became so important to the characters and the show. Karen and Jack touching bellies viscerally and metaphorically defined the characters as both cutting-edge and outrageous. It was followed with a recurring bit of Jack and Karen slapping each other hard, followed by hugs. The popularity of the two characters exploded.

Jack and Karen slapping is farce; Jack's entrances and nipple-pinching are farce. They were tethered by the sobering elements of both Will's struggle to exist in a world where gay men aren't completely accepted and Will and Grace's relationship. Part of the effectiveness of the racy lines is that they were delivered with innocence. Karen could say, "Take me to Jewdorf Goodman, you big dancing butt pirate"; "Sorry I'm late. I wanted to make sure I missed most of dinner"; and "I love you like the mother I had committed against her will"; the same way Carla Tortelli could on *Cheers*. When Grace asks, "Can you imagine me in a three-way?" Karen replies, "I can't imagine you in a two-way!" You know how sad their lives are, but it makes you love them even more. They can get away with it. It's incumbent on Karen to talk that way. No other character could do that outrageous a joke.

The beauty of Karen's character was that, like Louie De Palma and Carla, she was capable of rare moments of affection and warmth. In "Swimming Pools . . . Movie Stars," her stepson, Mason, is competing in a swim meet. She arrives late, drink in hand, and exclaims, "Lord, I can't believe I'm at a public pool! Why doesn't someone just pee directly on me!" When Jack tells her that Mason had said, "I know why she's not here, she doesn't really like me," she sits the young man down and says, "Listen, I'm not very good at this kind of thing, but I am so very proud of you. I probably don't tell you often enough, but I do care about you. As a matter of fact, you're the best little boy any mom could have. And if you think that I don't like you, you're wrong. I love you." When Jack then explains that the boy she is talking to is not Mason, Karen says, "Well, how the hell am I supposed to know what they look like wet!"

It really moved the audience to see her as fully human and vulnerable. The balance of the four characters' defining qualities allowed us to say a lot of outrageous things, but we were always forgiven. We never got criticized. The audience knew we were more alike than we were different. Everyone on some level understood what we were saying. We had politically incorrect moments, rescued by other sweet and tender, more responsible moments.

Megan has a beautiful voice and can sing her ass off. We always had to remind her that when she played Karen, she had to sing like Karen would, the same way we told Bebe on *Cheers* that Lilith couldn't dance like Bebe could in real life. Twice we let Megan go all out. Her beautiful rendition of "The Man That Got Away" still resonates in my head. Deb could also sing, and we got a laugh out of her high soprano. Initially, when we were developing Karen's character, we would have her voice go up higher each episode, until we found that high register that literally registered with the audience. It's very different from her own voice, which oftentimes throws people off when they meet her.

In "Homo for the Holidays," Jack feels extremely uncomfortable when he has to come out to his mother, Judith (Veronica Cartwright). Grace says, "Jack, this isn't going to be as hard as you think. On some level, your mother has to know you're gay. I mean, she has met you, right?"

When Judith arrives for dinner at Will's apartment, there is nervous tension. When Judith says, "Jack, honey, I'm worried. You haven't said a thing about my bangs," Jack responds, "They're a little short, but they'll grow in. Mom, I have something I want to say to

you. I've kept this from you for a long time, and that's wrong because it makes it seem like I'm ashamed of something I'm not
ashamed of. I want you to know who I am, because I'm proud of
who I am. . . . Mom, are you wearing Chloe?"

Will yells at Jack, prompting him to stay focused:

JACK
Mom, I'm gay.

JUDITH
Oh.

GRACE
Okay, so he's gay. He's still the same little boy who gave you
highlights for the first time.

KAREN
Honey, I think you're missing a silver lining here? When you're old
and in diapers, a gay son will know how to keep you away from
chiffon and backlighting.

Jack feeling uncomfortable is what made him so likable. During
the first season we got great reviews, including "clever, quick, and
somewhat subversive." We received some criticism that Jack was
too stereotypical, and we started giving him more dimension. His
entrances were always a "moment." A lot of times he'd come in on a
Lenny and Squiggy setup. I had him cartwheel, back in, enter on
hands and knees. We put a stop on the door, so once when he
slipped in, the door closed by itself. Sean would spend the weekends rehearsing and embellishing the entrances, and I would spend
extra time on set rehearsing with just him, figuring out different
permutations. Even in physical comedy, there's a small story that
you must pay attention to.

I directed him in *Sean Saves the World*, and later on he was brought in to help save *The Millers*. Sean is a great producer. He and creative partner Todd Milliner formed Hazy Mills and produced the NBC drama *Grimm*. They're conceptual, smart guys who always have a creative iron in the fire. Sean also co-hosts the *Smart-Less* podcast with Jason Bateman and Will Arnett, both of whom I've worked with, respect, and like very much. The three of them are great together.

While we straddled the line with dialogue and gestures, we never crossed it. We came up with euphemisms for sex and each of the body organs. It was like the 1940s suggestive aspects of comedy. The audience could say, "Oh, that's a reference to the penis." Your brain is rolling the balls into the holes. A large part of the reaction is "I can't believe they just said that."

Michael Patrick King wrote the episode "Will on Ice." Everyone was afraid of him except me. Michael is very attached to his ideas and is very passionate about everything he writes. He is a strong, wonderful, and creative presence in any room and has an amazing wit. He is a brilliant writer and knows exactly what he wants. I would later work with him on both *The Comeback* and *2 Broke Girls*. I've spent time with him and his partner, Craig. *Sex and the City*, which he executive-produced, had been filmed but had not yet debuted when he came to *Will & Grace*.

In the original version of the script there was no story, just jokes. I had to tell Michael, "You have to create a story for them." Even after the success of *Sex and the City*, he'd still drop back in during a taping to randomly pitch new jokes after we shot scenes. Some writers work all day to see a pathway to new jokes; Michael could pitch off the top of his head. He crafted a joke where Grace enters and says, "I just came from having a Belgian wax." When Will asks what that is, she replies, "It's a wax that hurts so much that I treated myself to a waffle." (Similarly, when Macaulay Culkin guested, Billy Wrubel pitched a joke where Macaulay gives Karen a twenty-dollar bill and says, "Go get yourself a wax, I like a clean work space.")

We did things I had never done before, that had never been

done on any show prior. The show became a machine gun for topical and pop-culture references. When Will expresses that his biggest regrets include giving up the role of Kenickie in his high school production of *Grease* because he was afraid to jump off the car during "Greased Lightning," and asks whether a day goes by where he doesn't think about it, Grace glibly responds, "God, I hope so!"

Unlike others, many of whom I admire—including and especially Norman Lear—I have never done an overtly political show. I never proselytize. My mind doesn't work that way. The genius of *Will & Grace* is that the leading man happens to be gay. The essential relationship is based on two simple things: love and living your truth. We tried not to overplay it. When my daughter Maggie was in the seventh and eighth grades, I drove carpool on Thursdays. We'd load up the car with kids and, on the way to school, all these thirteen- and fourteen-year-olds would want to know, "What's on *Will & Grace* tonight?" We were reaching young people before any prejudices were instilled in them.

As a result of our efforts, audiences grew comfortable with gay characters. They didn't think about the fact that the characters were gay. That was the point: It wasn't a gay show, it was a show about people. This was indicative of what was going on not only in Los Angeles but all around the country. At that time, 25 percent of the country would refuse to watch *Will & Grace*, because it starred two gay characters. But the other 75 percent would give the show a chance. We thought if we could get those people to watch the show once, they would come back because it was so funny.

So while we never set out to make a gay show, we did set out to make a show with universal themes. A romantic comedy with an insurmountable obstacle. Will and Grace were each other's soulmates in every way but sexually. During the first season, we tried to manipulate the audience into believing that Will and Grace might become a couple, that his gayness would go away, or that he would take the magic pills and become straight and marry Grace. There's that kiss at the end of the pilot, as well as one during the last episode of the first year, just to get the audience to say, "Whoa." We knew it would never happen, but we wanted to get that part of the audience to watch as if they thought it might. Once they watched the show, that no longer mattered. They were hooked because the show was funny and outrageous.

After two seasons, we realized that this wasn't just a hit sitcom, it was a social movement. I cared very much about the cultural impact of the show. Our ratings went up after our Emmy win. We got a lot of letters and emails from gay people who told us that the show made them realize they weren't so different and helped them come out. By laughing at them and with them, we normalized them. The fact that they could see someone who looked like them on television every week, with healthy friendships, living their truths, gave people from the rural South to Egypt hope and made them feel both less alone and less invisible.

One of the amazing benefits of being both a hit and a social statement was that so many major celebrities wanted to be guest stars. We accommodated every one of them. There were close to three hundred guest stars, which included Hollywood legends. In a stroke of genius, we cast Debbie Reynolds as Grace's mother, Bobbi. Debbie was an entertainer with a million stories. She was our first guest star and was the consummate professional. She had the driest, most perfect delivery. When Grace was getting married and her father wasn't feeling up to giving her away, Bobbi said, "Just put a pastrami sandwich and a *TV Guide* under the chuppah and he'll find his way."

All the gay icons came on the show: Patti LuPone, Bernadette Peters, Madonna, J-Lo, Sandra Bernhard, and Lily Tomlin. When Cher guested, Jack initially thinks she's a Cher impersonator and starts coaching her on how to be more Cher. When he finally realizes it's the real Cher, he faints.

Molly Shannon was great during both incarnations of the show.

Molly is an actress who performs without a net. She will commit to the most outrageous things, and she does them believably. She's unafraid to do anything comedically. A lot of her attitudes are made up, and she created a lot of the physical business she did on *Will & Grace*. I watched her like an East German diving judge, grading her at nine or ten. It was like working with Cloris Leachman all over again.

Michael Douglas was hysterical as a gay detective, and Glenn Close was terrific as an eccentric celebrity photographer who shoots Will and Grace for a family portrait. I knew her because her daughter was also an equestrian.

I was a fan of Gene Wilder and a little intimidated by his talent. He played the heretofore-unseen senior partner of Will's law firm. It was actually his last on-camera acting role, and he won an Emmy for it.

Gregory Hines was very funny, classy, and one of the greatest dancers of all time. We were able to show off his footwork, doing a little "shim sham," on the show. We had wanted to do interracial romance before it was acceptable. As Will's other boss, Ben, he dated Grace. We also had Taye Diggs as James, another one of Will's boyfriends.

In "Steams Like Old Times," Will regularly visits the elderly Clyde (Richard Chamberlain), bringing him food and talking to him. Will wonders about growing older and wonders what his life is going to be like without a partner. Will is scared that he is going to become Clyde—only to learn that Clyde is straight. It was great to reconnect with Richard. People couldn't get over the fact that Dr. Kildare was in the house. He was a heartthrob. In *The Thorn Birds*, he co-starred with Rachel Ward and was a leading man who couldn't come out.

In "A Chorus Lie," Matt Damon played Owen, a straight man who pretends to be gay so he can sing in the gay chorus and go to Europe for free. Jack, realizing that he's straight, tries to trap him:

JACK

What gym do you go to? Why haven't I seen you at the clubs? And who have we slept with in common?

OWEN

I work out at home, I'm allergic to smoke, and I'm in a long-term relationship with my high school boyfriend.

JACK

Name?

OWEN

Ben.

JACK

I know him.

OWEN

No you don't.

JACK

How do you know?

OWEN

He told me you don't.

It was one of my favorite episodes. The whole concept was so great. When Jack's initial ruse doesn't work, he enlists Grace to seduce Owen. We shot a great scene with Matt and Debra fooling around on the couch. Matt was as sweet as could be.

Some of our most famous stars were so used to being the center of attention that they had to adjust to being part of an ensemble. We nurtured egos. I told each guest in the most respectful way possible that they needed to keep up with the cast. On the show, they were the guest star, not *the* star. Almost all of them rose to the occasion.

Most of them weren't used to an audience. I warned each guest star not to get lost. The cast played at 50 percent during rehearsal and saved the high energy for the tapings. "In taping they'll blow you away. Don't be intimidated. Don't lay back. Otherwise, you'll disappear." Those that I knew, I didn't have a problem with. With others, I was more assertive. "You're in our house, play by our rules, and you'll have a great time."

Out of all the guest stars, my personal favorite was director Sydney Pollack, who played Will's father. I admired his directorial work, from *Three Days of the Condor* to *Tootsie,* but he started his career as an actor. David Kohan had worked for Sydney, so he approached him, and he was willing to play with us. His comedy was so unexpected.

John Slattery played Will's estranged brother, Sam, on two episodes, in which he and Grace have sex. Karen tells Grace that she's using Sam as a substitute for Will, and Jack tells Will that Grace is using Sam as a surrogate for Will. We would have had John back, but he went on to star on *Mad Men*. Sam was later played by Steven Weber.

Minnie Driver was a delight as Lorraine Finster, Stan's mistress. You could see the level she played it at. I got to work with John Cleese again when he played her father.

In "Will Works Out," Jack gets thrown out of his gym because, after three years, they discover he's been using someone else's membership. When Grace mentions that Will has a thirty-day guest membership pass to their gym, Jack grabs it. Will is demonstrably upset. He tells Grace that he doesn't want Jack at his gym with people he does business with, that it would reflect badly on him because Jack is "such a fag." Jack overhears Will and shows up the next day in a macho outfit. In a very masculine pose, he says "faggot" a few times. We used it because we thought that, while derogatory, it was appropriate in context, that gay men had the right to say that about one another. The network called and said we lost a couple of sponsors because of it, but, God love 'em, they told us to keep doing it. In the vernacular of *Will & Grace,* that word was okay.

Grace had more boyfriends than Will because we were sensitive to the fact that a significant portion of the audience was still uncomfortable seeing two men dating. When Will did have a boyfriend, we cast actors like Bobby Cannavale as Vince and Patrick Dempsey as Matthew, not necessarily expected choices.

Bob Odenkirk had signed on to play Grace's boyfriend Nathan. We had our first table read and Bob's performance was off. Years later, he explained to me that he and his wife had just had a baby, and he was exhausted because the baby kept him up all night. In his pre–Saul Goodman days, he had no significant acting creds, so we didn't know how good he could be, but if he couldn't step up right away, we couldn't go through two or three days and have him not get there. We decided to replace him. We postponed that taping and I called Woody Harrelson, who was terrific.

Harry Connick Jr., whom I affectionately call Hesh, played Grace's boyfriend, then husband. He also guested on *Cheers,* playing Woody's cousin, who was infatuated with Rebecca. It was the only *Cheers* show where I brought the piano downstage near the jukebox, because if you're gonna cast Harry, he has to play. And he was funny too. Working with him was one of the great times in my life. The minute he was cast on *Will & Grace,* I had a piano brought onto the soundstage as well. I couldn't believe what he could do with those two hands. One time we had a problem with the lights and stopped shooting to fix them. I turned to Harry and just said, "Go." He played for twenty minutes. He was kind enough to give my daughter, Paris, a music lesson—something she will likely never forget.

Harry could do a joke. He was sexy, handsome, and half Jewish, a perfect match for Grace. To have those four cast members was sheer heaven; to have someone else who could play in that sandbox, soak up both the energy and the fun was amazing.

While not the right fit for the role of Charlie and Alan's mom on *Two and a Half Men,* Blythe Danner was perfect as Will's mother. She has a wispy voice and an addlepated delivery that no one else can do. Alec Baldwin could go from drama to comedy with equal aplomb better than anyone else, with the possible exceptions of Kelsey Grammer and John Lithgow. You could just look at Alec and start laughing. As Malcolm, the character with the mysterious past and Karen's current love interest, he confronts and tries to threaten Jack:

MALCOLM

I know two ways to get a guy to call me friend. One is to attach his nipples to a car battery. The other is to buy him a fine Italian suit.

JACK

Do I have to choose?

When Malcolm first meets Karen and is smitten by her, he is holding ice cream in a paper bag. Will says, "Your package is dripping." Malcolm responds, "What can I say, I like her."

We had a lot of fun with Kevin Bacon. I knew him from when he was a waiter at the All State Café, which was my Cheers in New York City. When I had a house in Millbrook, New York, we became regulars at the bar of the Old Drovers Inn in nearby Dover Plains. Kevin came in with his wife and fellow great actor, Kyra Sedgwick. I went over to him and said, "We have something in common: the All State Café." We exchanged numbers. When Jack was stalking Kevin Bacon on the show, I called Kevin and asked if he'd make an appearance as himself. He was happy to be on. Jack interviews to be Kevin's assistant:

JACK

First film, *Animal House.* Character's name in *Footloose,* Ren
McCormack. Number of films of full-frontal nudity, four;
number of films with full sidal nudity, three; number of
films with rear frontal nudity, priceless.

KEVIN

Wow. Impressive. The rest of you can go.
You know nothing about me.

I knew Daryl Hall from Millbrook as well. I spent a lot of time
on his porch. That's how we got Hall & Oates to guest-star in "The
Definition of Marriage," where Karen hires them to "sing and pick
up dirty plates."

In season 6, the Boys pitched the idea of doing a live show. The
ratings were starting to wane a bit, so we were looking for any opportunity to put something new into the mix. In 2004, Jeff Zucker
was the head of NBC. He was all about supersized episodes.

In the first episode of the eighth season, "Alive and Schticking,"
we learn that Karen's dead husband, Stan, is still alive. The garbage
bag of ashes they scattered was really "dirt and Rice Krispies." Will
says, "It's all convoluted and doesn't make sense. It's like the contract you sign when you marry Tom Cruise."

We did two shoots—one for the East Coast and then, three
hours later, one for the West. Everyone was nervous, especially me.
I rehearsed those episodes more than any other, especially with
cameras and shots. There was a moment where Sean and Deb were
laughing so hard while doing their lines that they almost broke. It
was nerve-racking for them but wonderful for the audience.

I retain how a show is cut in my head. I rehearse and review at
least six times to get into the rhythm of how it's going to go. It's
muscle memory. I never sit still very long. On a taped shoot, I have
a clicker in my hand—I'm too old to snap. When I click, it's the
tech guy's signal to cut from one camera shot to another. I know

that the line before the cut is going to be a big joke, so the camera cuts on my interpretation of the joke.

I was nervous for the entire half hour. I wasn't used to it. There were multiple monitors to follow the action, including a monitor for the program and a monitor showing the next shot. I had my editor, Peter Chakos, with me as an extra pair of trained eyes, to help look at everything.

Clearly, I could never do live sporting events. I wouldn't know which monitor to look at. Al Michaels, the veteran NBC sports-caster, is one of my closest friends. I'm one of the few civilians who was ever allowed to spend four *Sunday Night Football* games in the truck. I watched director Drew Esocoff and producer Freddie Gaudelli and was amazed at how they do it, with so many people talking in their ears. The pacing was just insane. I talked to them at halftime and at the end of the game, but I never interrupted them during the game.

The live show was so successful that we did another one, "Bath-room Humor." The entire episode takes place in Karen's bathroom during her celebrity star-studded birthday party. It was mostly slap-stick and the four spraying one another with powders, our version of the food/pie fight.

During a live show there's nothing you can do when something goes wrong. We had one incident during the second live show for the West Coast. In the planned scene, when Karen opened her medicine cabinet a hundred bottles of pills fell out. The East Coast version went exactly as planned. During the second show, there was trouble getting the knot out of the bag that contained the pill bot-tles inside the cabinet. There were twenty seconds of struggling before they cascaded out. Eric ad-libbed, "They can do special ef-fects on *King Kong,* but they can't get the pills out." The audience loved it.

After eight successful seasons, we wrapped up *Will & Grace.* In the finale, Will is married to Vince, and Grace is married to Leo. After a big fight and estrangement, they have a subsequent reconciliation, and almost two decades later Will's son and Grace's daughter meet in college, fall in love, and get married. We were able to put a bow on it, tying everything together in a satisfying conclusion. I liked this ending because having their kids meet perpetuated the myth of Will and Grace. I also loved that Megan and Sean sang "Unforgettable."

I've learned over the years that people hate last episodes, especially with sitcoms, because you're depriving them of something they love. They're emotional, but there's also a pissed-off-ness from every human being that you're taking away the characters on the show who became their friends and the people in real life that they watched it with. No more *Cheers, Will & Grace, Seinfeld,* or *M*A*S*H.* The audience will find ways to dispute the ending. You can't win. The Yankees won a lot of pennants, but you knew there would be more Yankees next season. But there will be no more *I Love Lucy* or *The Dick Van Dyke Show.*

And then . . . eight years later, we got something you almost never get in the entertainment business: a second chance. Hillary Clinton is partially, if not completely, responsible for the *Will & Grace* revival. Max called me and said, "The band's getting back together again; we hope you're in." Debra was a die-hard Hillary supporter and had spoken to Max. They wanted to do a piece about getting out the vote for the 2016 election. I said yes as soon as he asked.

The set was still available. It was stored at Emerson College in Boston, Max's alma mater. He paid for it to be shipped cross-country and reassembled. We tried to keep it as secret as possible. I directed in the basement of a soundstage at CBS's Radford studios. The moment we sat down to read, I thought, "The magic is still here. It hasn't left. It's crazy. These guys have not lost a beat, and they look almost exactly the same."

We invited guests, including Norman Lear, without telling them what they were coming to see. When the curtain went up, the audience went crazy. The spot went viral and was trending. In every episode, when Jack walks into Will's apartment, he takes something out of the refrigerator. I told Sean, "When you open the fridge, say, 'Why does everything in here look ten years old?'" It was funny and poignant to see him crossing the stage again, strutting like a peacock. Bob Greenblatt, then-president of NBC, asked us if we wanted to do a show again. We thought there was life in the old gang. As soon as we got the commitment, I said, "You can go homo again."

According to my rabbi, David Wolpe (every sitcom director needs a great rabbi): "Coincidence is when God wants to stay anonymous." Ten years ago, he asked me to do the appeal on Yom Kippur. I had to ask 2,500 Jews for money. I never worked harder on a speech in my life and was never so scared:

"I'm sitting at home, curled up on the couch with a good book and a glass of wine, when the phone rings. I do not screen the call, I answer it. . . . It is the rabbi, asking me to do the appeal. It is one of the few times I would have preferred a telemarketer. Now, saying no to a rabbi is tough enough, but saying no to this rabbi is impossible because of who he is. And he does control the time the shofar is blown. We talk. Someone says yes. I think it was me. It must have been me, because unless this is a dream, I'm up on the bimah, trying not to be nervous so I don't have to calm myself by imagining the congregation naked."

People ask me why I finally agreed to do it. I tell them the story of the old Jewish man who is walking down Lexington Avenue in New York City with a package in each arm. Another man, obviously lost, comes up and asks if they are in front of the Chrysler Building. The old man asks him to hold his packages. He then raises his arms up and says, "I don't know!"

I also used the Brothers' line about being bar mitzvahed at forty-seven and losing my hair at thirteen. We had a successful appeal.

On September 28, 2017, *Will & Grace* was back on the air. It was crazy to hear actors read and feel like nothing had changed in ten years. We had to deal with the fact that fans already had one reality in their heads. Shows have been playing with timelines since the days of radio. If you're old enough to remember *Dallas,* the popular character Bobby Ewing (Patrick Duffy) was killed off at the end of the eighth season. Audience demand for him was so great that they had to bring him back. The opening episode of season 9 had him coming out of the shower as if nothing had happened, as if the prior season was a dream. Our season 9 was similarly going to revise the universe. We didn't want to go into reboot with Will and Grace both having children, as we had previously ended the show. Instead, we felt that the show would be better served not by them bringing up kids but by them once again bringing up each other.

In the fourth episode of the new run, "Grandpa Jack," Jack is visited by the grandson he didn't know he had. Skip (Jet Jurgensmeyer) is the child of Jack's estranged son, Elliot (Michael Angarano). ("Like Will's hair, they had a falling-out years ago.") Elliot and his wife, Emma (Natalie Dreyfuss), whom Jack has also never met, are in New York to drop Skip off at the upstate Camp Straight Arrow, a "deprogramming camp." They believe Skip is "broken," because Skip thinks he might be gay.

Will and Jack go to camp to rescue Skip, and Jack explains to Skip that the camp cannot fix him because he's not broken. He responds to Skip's confusion:

JACK

Of course you're confused. So let me tell you a story about another young man who was once confused, a young man who grew up to be a model citizen and today is proud of who and what he is. People adore this man not only because of his good looks and dynamic personality but because of his open, loving heart.

SKIP

Will?

JACK

No, not Will! Will's a fat lawyer. How does that guy make an impression on everyone? I'm talking about me. It was hard for me once too, but believe me, it gets better.

SKIP

I don't see how.

JACK

Skip, you are going to be invited to so many good dinner parties. And there's something else. When you get older, you'll understand that there's the family you were born into and the family that you choose. And the family I chose . . . Well, it doesn't get any better than that.

SKIP

But what do I do now?

JACK

I don't know. Your hero, Will, he didn't really think this through. You're just going to have to be really strong.

SKIP

It's hard being me sometimes.

JACK

I know, but I'm going to be there for you as much as I can, and when I'm not, I want you to picture me in your head looking at you like I am right now and saying, "You are exactly who you're supposed to be."

Reboots are tricky. They don't always work. As creators, you have to be very protective of the integrity of your franchise. While my wife, Debbie, and I were in Millbrook, Mary Tyler Moore had a house nearby. She invited us over and told me that she and Valerie Harper were doing a movie of the week, and they wanted to know if I would direct. I read the script and I couldn't see the appeal of watching those characters again, despite how beloved they once were. I politely declined. We had kicked around the idea of a *Cheers* spin-off with Cliff and Norm, but we didn't think they made a show. We tried the Tortellis. It was funny, but it died. The Brothers said that *tortelli* was an old Italian word that meant "It was Jimmy's idea."

A reboot that worked is *The Conners,* the revival of *Roseanne.* The people don't look too different, and the writing and acting are extraordinary. Every line is perfectly thrown away.

Will and Grace were now in their fifties—older and more mature. They both wore reading glasses. Jack was in "the second decade of his thirties." A lot more life and opportunities had passed them by. When they're in the Statue of Liberty, Grace says, "Think of all the stories, milestones, men who have disappointed us." We were still very protective of the original eight seasons. We didn't want anything we did in the reboot to compromise that.

Max and David set the bar very high for the second incarnation. The sophistication of the writing blew me away. To be able to go out on top twice was a wonderful feeling. The second incarnation was a much more polished platform. While the stories were still very funny, they were also more thoughtful and layered. We initially got overtly political but pulled back to find a balance. In "The Return: 11 Years Later," Will and Grace both wind up in the White House, as Grace is hired to redecorate the Oval Office and Will brings Jack to meet a gay congressman he's been corresponding with. We then toned it down. The Boys were very skilled at crafting emotional and funny stories that dealt with both the characters' evolved relationships and gay issues.

The second generation had a lot more stunts. Arduous, yet fun to shoot. One of my favorite episodes involved Grace and Karen being trapped in the automated shower. Poignant moments were balanced against broad slapstick. It had a Lucille Ball/Vivian Vance vibe—actually more of a direct rip-off, but we don't apologize for it, especially since we did a full-on imitation of *I Love Lucy* later on. Shooting was challenging, and we had to pre-shoot a lot, because once the two were in the shower, it took too long to dry them off and redo their hair. Also, we wanted the flexibility to add to the script once they were in the shower. We then had artful editing.

The stories in the second incarnation were better because we had to justify a way to bring the series back. We went for the heart. "Who's Sorry Now?" was an episode that came out of Max's soul and loins. Will and Grace read their college love letters to each other: How Grace was in love with Will and never realized that he was gay. How his being gay broke her heart. Grace finds a thick letter from Will from decades earlier that she'd never opened and reads it:

GRACE

I'm the worst person in the world. I read your letter.

WILL

Come on inside.

GRACE

I can't go inside. I don't deserve to go inside, I'm horrible.

WILL

If we never let horrible people in our apartment,
we'd never see Karen.

GRACE

That's true. How did I not read this letter? I mean, you went
through so much after you came out, and I wasn't there for you.

WILL

We don't have to talk about it.

GRACE

No, we do. I have to. You were tortured and I never even thought
about that. I got to the part where you write, "Grace, I don't want
to be gay, I just wish I was normal." Oh my God. Will. It broke my
heart. And then the part where you said that you were thinking
about hurting yourself. I mean, is that true? Sweetie?

WILL

It was a long time ago.

GRACE

Look, this might be thirty years too late, but I just got smart in the
last hour. You're right, I didn't think about your pain. I only
thought about mine, because that's the way the story of the gay
guy and the straight girl is always told, isn't it? He broke her heart.
Poor her. But you were just being who you are and you were
scared to death that the world was going to find out and
hate you for it.

WILL

Wow. You did get smart.

GRACE

And you were right. I am sorry for not being there when you
needed me most. And I am so, so sorry that I never said this to you
before. Now, the fact that you are a gay man did not ruin my life.
It made it so much better.

WILL

Mine too.

That type of show had never been done before, seeing the an-
guish from the gay man's perspective. Before that, it was always
about the poor woman.

We also addressed the #MeToo movement. Grace confronted her father, Martin, now played by Robert Klein, about how she was sexually abused by his late best friend when she was fifteen and was scared to tell him at the time. Martin breaks down and cries. He asks his daughter how she got through the trauma. "Well, you just kind of split yourself into two people. The person it happened to and the one who gets through the day. And then you grow up and your life gets bigger. And that stuff gets smaller." The now-enraged Martin says, "I'm not going to visit that bastard in the cemetery. I never want to hear his name again. He's dead to me!" to which Grace responds, "Well, he's dead to everybody, Dad."

When Debbie Reynolds, who played Grace's mom, passed, we thought about Will's mother getting together with Grace's dad. Blythe came back, and she and Robert were terrific as a couple. Will leaves his law firm, first to partner with Grace in her design business and then to teach full-time at Columbia Law School. When a fellow gay professor, Paul (Barrett Foa), flirts with him, the consistently principled Will is uncomfortable, because he finds out his colleague is married with a child. When Paul presses Will to have a drink, Will says, "No! You have a husband and a baby, and not just any husband and a baby but a husband who clearly loves you and a baby who arguably has the greatest legal mind of any baby in our time." When Paul says that two guys can make their own rules, Will emphatically responds, "No, we don't. I don't. We spent all these years saying marriage is marriage and love is love. Till we were blue in the face. And now that we finally have what we were fighting for, we say cheating is not always cheating. I mean, that just seems like . . . cheating."

We did shorter seasons during the second run. By the third year, the ratings were down; NBC was in disarray. They were changing leadership much more frequently than during our first run. Our champion, Bob Greenblatt, was gone, so we knew that it was time to wrap again. With the pressure off, we were able to play more and have more fun, including lots of inside jokes. Nick Offerman,

Megan's husband, played a famous chef who seduces both Will and Grace. When he makes a play for Karen, she says, "So not my type." Will and Grace pull each other's hair in the kitchen and drag each other onto the floor, an homage to Sam and Diane, and to myself. There are only a few great moves in comedy. It's my job to disguise them and to freshen them up each time they're used. Only part of the audience will understand the subtext, the inside joke, of these bits. It's like the Schopenhauer joke in *Cheers*. You're winking at that part of the audience that gets it, giving a kiss to loyal audience members.

Similarly, we paid homage to Jack Benny's classic "Sí Sy Sue" routine that he did with Mel Blanc, "the Man of a Thousand Voices," including Bugs Bunny. Benny asks Mel a few questions, and he keeps answering with "Sí," "Sy," and "Sue." In "Dead Man Texting," Jack's fiancé, Estefan (Brian Jordan Alvarez), and Karen have a fight for Jack's attention during his birthday celebration at a fancy restaurant, which ends with both of them falling into the pool in the center of the dining room. A distressed Jack dresses down his drenched friends:

JACK
Do you realize how much this fighting hurts me?

ESTEFAN
Sí.

JACK
And how does that make you feel?

ESTEFAN
Sigh.

JACK
And if Karen hadn't paid them off, what do you think the restaurant would have done?

ESTEFAN
Sue.

JACK
Exactly.

Karen and Will are in a quiz runoff (a "Jackoff") to see who will be Jack's best man.

JACK
Will, this question is to you. In the fall of aught eight, I had a brief but torrid affair with a certain redhead. Tell me his name, where we met, and what food he threw at me when I told him I met someone else.

WILL
Dick, dock, duck.

JACK
That is correct.

David Schwimmer played Noah, a single father famous for his Twitter personality, in "The West Side Curmudgeon." We didn't let the audience know ahead of time who would be playing the role. When Schwimmer walked out onstage, the audience went crazy. In "Filthy Phil," Jack opens a bar called Queers, "Where everybody knows you're gay, and they're always glad you came." The Boys begged me to do a cameo as the co-creator of *Cheers*. I was sitting in the new bar at the end of the episode, saying, "I don't get it."

Since Debra looked so much like Lucille Ball, we always thought about doing a tribute to *I Love Lucy*. Max took the lead on that. John Quaintance wrote the "We Love Lucy" episode. It was the first time Lucie Arnaz and Desi Arnaz Jr. had given anyone permission to re-create scenes from the show; Lucie even agreed to a cameo appearance.

Max and David picked out the three episodes they wanted to emulate: "Lucy Does a TV Commercial," aka the Vitameatavegamin episode; "Job Switching," aka the chocolate factory; and "Lucy's Italian Movie," aka the grape-stomping episode. The costume changes were massive. We first shot the interstitials (the wraparound segments). Then we shot the Vitameatavegamin segment on one day and the chocolate factory on the next. It was a complete team effort.

We started out with Deb and Eric as Lucy and Ricky and Sean and Megan as Fred and Ethel and then mixed it up, with Deb and Sean doing the chocolate-factory scene, Megan and Leslie Jordan (as Karen's nemesis, Beverley Leslie) doing the grape-stomping routine, and Deb re-creating Vitameatavegamin. Deb, Sean, and Megan each took turns playing Lucy, Fred, and Ethel. The scenes were very complicated and fun to stage, and the crew from hair, makeup, costume, and production design, most of whom had been together since the show began, stepped up to meet the challenges of logistics and time.

Everyone had to put in 110 percent. Like the "Old-Fashioned Wedding" episode on *Cheers* and "The Innkeepers" on *Frasier,* there was so much more work that needed to be done, and it wound up being worth every extra minute of preparation, effort, and care we put into it. I was nominated for an Emmy for that episode. If I won, I would have thanked the three people who directed the original episodes, Marc Daniels, William Asher, and James V. Kern, because I copied all their camera angles.

In the final episode, we find out that the sad picture on the wall next to the fireplace in Will's apartment—which had been hanging there for the entire series, the same way Geronimo did in *Cheers*—is not actually Will, as Jack and Karen had previously referenced. Will says, "Okay, for the last time, that is not me. It's a painting my mother gave my father. But he didn't like it because he thought it was too gay. . . . My mistake."

I liked the ending of the reboot more than the one in the first run, because Will and Grace end up together. They move out of their Upper West Side apartment for a house in upstate New York, where the pregnant Grace and the adopting Will are going to raise their soon-to-be-born babies together. As they are about to leave Apartment 9C of 155 Riverside Drive in Manhattan—the place Jack referred to as "the apartment that sex forgot" and Karen described as a "poorly decorated crack house" but that was home for decades—for the last time as residents:

WILL

Are you ready for this?

GRACE

Hundred percent no.

WILL

You're going to be great. We are going to be great!

Will and Grace have an intense and enviable connection. They will always be able to finish each other's sentences. Together, they're a complete human being. I will always be happy about the two of them ending up together.

It was such a seminal moment when we were first on the air, but the reasons we were popular then were different than for the second incarnation. We weren't groundbreaking anymore. Streaming was much more prevalent, and gay people on television and in popular culture had become the norm. But it was great to have a denouement, another opportunity to tell stories that were important to us and our hearts and the larger community. We will be in the lexicon.

To my knowledge, I'm the only director who's directed every episode (246) of a long-running show. *Cheers* will always be my favorite because I was the co-creator, but *Will & Grace* is a close second. I wasn't giving up that protective influence. I was having fun and cared a lot about the show and the team.

I was fifty-eight when *Will & Grace* debuted and was seventy-seven for the reboot. I felt like Norman Cousins, who, to combat a crippling illness, developed his own laughter-driven therapy, which involved watching a lot of comedy. "I made the joyous discovery that ten minutes of genuine belly laughter had an anesthetic effect," he said. The hours of laughter that I got on *Will & Grace* added years to my life. I got a little nervous before every show night, but when the audience laughter resonated in my head and my heart, and I got to connect with and feel responsible for it, I couldn't think of anything else that I wanted to do at that point in my life or any other place that I wanted to be. While too many people in their seventies were relegated to their version of a rocking chair, I remained in the director's chair, where I laughed so hard I broke the footrests.

At the CBS Radford studios, where we shot the first eight seasons, there's a plaque outside the stage that says: THE HOME OF WILL AND GRACE, THE LOVE THAT DARED SPEAK ITS NAME. It's a reference to the famous quote about same-sex relationships. The ultimate-taboo plaque is meant to commemorate how special it was to have a show that celebrated the ordinary in the lives of underrepresented people. It was a poignant celebration of what we all had worked so hard to achieve years earlier.

In a 2015 interview about same-sex marriage, the late great Supreme Court justice Ruth Bader Ginsburg said: "When I was young, people who were gay did not say who they were. They would disguise what they were. But in recent years, people have said, 'This is the way I am,' and others looked around and we discovered it's our next-door neighbor, we're very fond of them. Or it's our child's best friend or even our child. . . . So many people recognized their own biases when they saw it with somebody they cared for, that they respected." I think that television comedy helped drive that familiarity.

I've seen the Broadway show *Hamilton* twice (don't be jealous). Deb and I met playwright Lin-Manuel Miranda backstage (okay, you can be jealous). He was incredibly gracious. We also met then–vice president Joe Biden. He was warm, good-natured, and affectionate. Very down to earth and genuine, and taller than you would think.

I introduced myself. "I'm Jim Burrows. I directed every episode of *Will & Grace*. And what you said about *Will & Grace* on *Meet the Press*, that our show was seminal in the gay-rights movement, meant everything in the world to my two partners and me." The vice president put his hands on my shoulders and said, "Let me tell you a story. When I was twelve years old, my father took me downtown where we lived in Delaware. I was walking along with him, and I stopped because I saw two men kissing. I didn't know what to make of it. I turned to my dad, and he said to me, 'Joey, they're in love.'" I was so moved by that story, and so was he. He's told that story a lot since, especially at rallies, but I had never heard him tell it before that moment. His father was right. When society really understands and cares about one another, that's when change and acceptance come about.

EPILOGUE

DIE WITH YOUR BOOTS ON

In 2015, I was working on a show called *Crowded,* which was written by Suzanne Martin, with whom I'd worked on *Frasier.* It was about kids who move back in with their parents. During that time I started counting the number of shows I had directed. I opened my diary, which began with *The Mary Tyler Moore Show* in 1974. Once *Taxi* started, I was doing almost thirty shows a year. During pilot season, if I shot six pilots, I had usually read around twenty scripts. I never thought about how hard I was working, because I was working on great shows with great people. And I loved it. Also, being able to hear an audience laugh at material I created makes me really happy. I reached the thousand mark on *Crowded.* The crew surprised me with a cake. Each member got dressed up for the occasion. When I mentioned it to Sean Hayes, he immediately said, "That's a special!"

An All-Star Tribute to James Burrows aired on NBC in 2016. Sean and his producing partner, Todd Milliner, got the casts from *Will & Grace, Cheers, Big Bang, Taxi, Mike & Molly, Frasier,* and *Friends* to appear onstage and share stories. Sean and Jason Bateman called me "a teacher, a mentor, and friend," and introduced a video montage. It was a joyful and emotional evening for me, to see colleagues and friends and share my milestone with a collection of people I'd worked with and cherished over the years. Bruce and Patti Springsteen appeared on tape, where Bruce explained that he'd done at least a thousand concerts, each of which were at least three hours long. He congratulated me for working "almost one-fifth as hard as we do." Funny. It was truly an amazing night.

In 2019, I got an email from Jimmy Kimmel, saying that he and Norman Lear were going to do live versions of the original *All in the Family* and *The Jeffersons* episodes and that there was only one person they wanted to direct them. I replied, "I'll see if Spielberg is available." Actually, I responded as quickly as I had to any other project I've ever been offered. I said I'd like to do the *All in the Family* episode. They responded, "We want you to do both." I wasn't going to pass up the opportunity.

Kimmel is so passionate and reverential about how he grew up watching all these sitcoms and how they influenced and inspired him. He's really funny in the throwaway kind of way. He could have easily been a sitcom star and still can. He also has a brilliant comic irreverence. With a name like Kimmel, it's a shame that he's not Jewish.

Norman's shows are so impactful and enduring in part because, in his words, "I only know one way to approach the subject matter of any show. I would always tell the writers, pay a lot of attention to the news, what's going on in the world, what's affecting you and your kids, your neighbors, and your soulmates. Listen to their problems, and the material for the shows will evolve from the world we are living in. That's what motivated everything we did."

They had already cast most of the parts for the two shows. Woody Harrelson was Archie Bunker, and Jamie Foxx was George Jefferson. Marisa Tomei was cast as Edith Bunker. Wanda Sykes was cast as Louise Jefferson; Anthony Anderson as Henry Jefferson; Ike Barinholtz and Ellie Kemper as Mike and Gloria Stivic; Will Ferrell, who also co-produced, and Kerry Washington as Tom and Helen Willis, one of TV's first biracial couples; Justina Machado as Florence Johnston, the Jeffersons' maid; Jovan Adepo and Amber Stevens West as Lionel and Jenny Willis Jefferson; Stephen Tobolowsky as Mr. Bentley; and Jackée Harry as Diane Stockwell.

The Jeffersons, which ran from 1975 to 1985, is a spin-off of *All in the Family,* which aired from 1971 to 1979. The two shows' living room sets were re-created side by side on a soundstage at the Sony Pictures lot. The idea of ABC's Wednesday-night special *Live in Front of a Studio Audience: Norman Lear's "All in the Family" and "The Jeffersons"* was to do two episodes back-to-back in a ninety-minute special. "Henry's Farewell," the *All in the Family* episode that introduced George Jefferson, was followed by "A Friend in Need," *The Jeffersons'* first episode.

I was nervous enough doing the live half-hour shows on *Will & Grace*. This was an hour-and-a-half show live on television. It takes a lot of work, and as I said before, I was totally out of my comfort zone. I marked my script book and planned on multiple rehearsals.

Everyone was incredibly deferential. We had eight days of rehearsals. Not everyone could come in at the same time. With so many famous stars, everyone had other commitments. Norman hired a bunch of great stand-ins.

I had a lot of chances to focus on nuance, because there were no script changes. We did it verbatim from the original script. We got to say the word "Heeb," but we had a challenge with using the N word. Norman fought tooth and nail with the network to not bleep it. He lost that one. I told Jamie, "You have to take a breath before you say it. If you don't, they'll bleep early and they'll cut out your lines before the N word."

Jimmy spoke to the audience during the rehearsals: "Norman did so much for freedom of speech and inclusivity. We'd be way behind without him. Some of the jokes are going to be shocking to you," he warned the crowd, noting the irony that certain words are no longer acceptable on TV, yet "now you can have dragons burning naked women at the stakes."

From Monday to Wednesday, we went on camera. Everyone was there. I was in the control booth, which is still alien territory for me, surrounded by a lot of people who didn't know whether I could do it. We had a great assistant director, Marty Pasetta. He asked me whether I needed help with my cameras. I told him about my first *Mary Tyler Moore* episode and the similar gracious offer from John Chulay and my similarly grateful declination, determined that I had to do it myself.

I did share the direction with Andy Fisher, who is Jimmy Kimmel's resident director. Andy directed the interstitial pieces and I directed the two live performances. We made a great team.

We had three live audiences on three nights. I knew the show backward and forward. My assistant director and technical director knew where the camera cuts were. The technical director was pressing the buttons to get to the next shots. I had twenty monitors in front of me. The actors were out there on live television.

We did the scenes over and over. Tuesday's run-through was good. Wednesday's was terrific. On Tuesday, Jennifer Hudson sang *The Jeffersons* theme song, "Movin' on Up," and brought down the house. It took a while, however, for *The Jeffersons* episode to get going. Jamie suggested that we should go to commercial after Jennifer's song. It was a great idea. It made the pacing of the live show work.

I'll always do a line run-through before the final show. The cast as well as the writers were in the room. Since some of *The Jeffersons* cast was in the first episode as well, everyone was there. I wasn't planning on making a speech, but the mood and the energy compelled me. I got up and said, "I loved working with you all. I've worked with a lot of people but never with as many preeminent people in one room. Remember this moment for the rest of your lives. Norman and Jimmy brought us together for something really special that has never happened before. I've never done an hour and a half of live television. And I've never worked with someone older than me who also knew my father."

Everyone was nervous. Actors have mechanisms for dealing with it. Even for stand-up comedians, like Wanda and Jamie, who are used to live performances, this was unique. When you're memorizing lines that you didn't write, you have to keep thinking about what is next.

During the live shoot, Jamie Foxx lost his line. He said, "It's live. Everyone sitting at home thinks their TV just messed up." I jumped out of my chair. I didn't know what I was going to do. Woody was in the background, and you could see from his expression, "This is live, right?" Jamie immediately recovered, and the audience wildly applauded. To this day, I'm not sure whether he "went up"—losing his place on purpose—or actually flubbed. Regardless, he has incredible stage presence.

When we were working on *The Jeffersons,* Marla Gibbs, who originated the role of Florence the wisecracking maid, was supposed to play Mother Jefferson. Jamie came to me and said, "You have an iconic black actress here, and she's playing a part that she didn't make iconic. It would be great if she could come back in the role she defined." We talked to Norman. Norman made that change and cast Fran Bennett as Mother Jefferson. When the front door opened and Marla came in, the audience went crazy. It is now an iconic moment in television history.

There were a couple of entrances in the show that I had to prepare for in anticipation of the applause. When the door opened for Marla, I was ready to cut to Jamie. In circumstances like those, I'm out of my element. On a taped sitcom, you can wait for the applause and adulation to subside naturally and edit later. I leaned on Marty for help. He cautioned me to wait for the applause on Marla and guided me as to when to move on.

In another scene, when George tells Jenny to come out of Lionel's bedroom, he thinks that she is naked. She has a quilt, a duvet, around her. She takes it off, to reveal that she is fully clothed. During the East Coast airing, I cut too soon and missed the comedic reveal. When we did it for the West Coast, three hours later, I fixed the one bad camera shot I had.

I made sure everyone got an entrance, so the audience could applaud for each of them individually. It was something I assiduously cut out of other shows because we thought it broke the fourth wall. On *Will & Grace,* every time Megan entered, she got wild applause. We'd tell the audience, "Sit on your hands. Laugh at her jokes, don't applaud." When guest stars played themselves, we'd allow it.

Everyone was so happy after the show. Both casts went to *The Jeffersons'* living room to celebrate. Norman and I sat on the couch. Jamie started singing *The Jeffersons* theme, and we all joined in.

There's so much adrenaline after that kind of performance. I was so thrilled that this show went well that, at that moment, I wasn't going to ever leave my comfort zone again.

With Norman at ninety-seven and me at seventy-eight, I said that we had one hundred seventy-five years between us. I didn't think I'd ever have a moment like that again. When Jimmy and Norman put the next one together, I was working on the last episode of *Will & Grace,* so I had to bow out. Hopefully, there will be more of these live re-creations in the future.

As of this writing, I've just celebrated my eighty-first birthday, a time when most people have already retired. By Norman Lear's standards, I still have a lot of work to do. I still love the adulation and that my talents remain in demand. The work keeps me sharp and youthful.

I was older before I got my first shot at directing television. Thirty-five is a tough age to start—today it's more like twenty-five. For those ten years before, though, I was honing my craft. It may have hindered me getting a gig. If a thirty-five-year-old came to me for career advice today, I'd ask, "What have you been doing?" If they said, "Theater," I'd say, "You have a shot in the business." If they were an assistant director, I'd say, "Go to an acting class and learn what acting is about so you can talk to actors." If a twenty-five-year-old came to see me for advice, I'd say, "Go get a job anywhere in show business." I worked on *The Patty Duke Show* for five weeks, then on *O. K. Crackerby!* I was a production assistant on the *Ford Presents the New Christy Minstrels* show. When I worked with Mary Tyler Moore, Grant Tinker said, "Go run lines with Paul Sand." I did anything and everything. All of it informed my later work as a director.

See if you like what's going on. Get close to the stage. If you're asked to do an errand, pay attention, learn. If you're a writer's assistant and you pitch a couple of jokes in the room, maybe you'll get a script assignment. Find a way to get yourself in. If you're around the scene of a crime, it's a lot easier to figure out who the murderer is than if you're not. If you're in the business, things will happen.

Go learn your craft. Get an iPhone and a cast. Use a single camera. Shoot something you're proud of. Then show the film to someone who will show it to someone else. Try to shoot your piece in front of a live audience. Those who ultimately watch it won't be as moved as they would be if they were watching actors making people in front of them laugh because of the communal nature of the audience. A comedy onstage will always be in demand.

Be prepared for rejection. Get used to the word "no." Even smart people say no. It's easier and safer to say no in this business, because you'll be right 98 percent of the time. But, oh, that 2 percent! ABC said no to *The Cosby Show,* NBC said no to *Roseanne,* and Tom Selleck turned down the role of Indiana Jones. I passed on both *Seinfeld* and *Designing Women.* I didn't see the potential of either at the time. It happens.

Also, get used to getting fired. That too will happen. Other opportunities will present themselves.

If you're going to work in comedy, study comedy. Figure out who makes you laugh and why. If I'm on a busman's holiday and watching a sitcom, I look for something I've never seen before. Study other directors' work. They may be competition, but they're your teachers as well. The modern era of great sitcom directors includes Barnet Kellman, Pam Fryman, Andy Ackerman, Mark Cendrowski, Jamie Widdoes, and Lenny Garner.

I adore Larry David, who's a genius at tying two disparate plots together in ways you'd never anticipate. I marvel at Bob Newhart, Richard Pryor, and Dave Chappelle because of how each performs their comedy in a totally different way from anything I've ever seen. Eddie Izzard is the smartest comic I've ever watched. Simply brilliant. The history professor telling jokes that you would never think of. Making the world funny.

The most important thing is to be fully prepared once you get your foot in the door, when you get your shot at directing. Work on what makes you laugh and smile. If you're lucky enough to be part of a hit, it will inevitably become harder to imitate the formula and tell continuing stories. Always maintain your quality. If you don't continue to do A to A+ quality work, people will flee. As you become successful, the standards will always get higher. You can neither slack off nor screw up. Believe in your work and protect it. Die with your boots on.

In the last five decades, I've attended the "funeral" of the multi-camera sitcom at least a dozen times, and it always seems to come back to life. Sitcom success has been on a roller-coaster ride in terms of popularity since its inception. I started in the limelight of *The Mary Tyler Moore Show.* In the early eighties, the sitcom died an awful death, and *Cheers,* followed by *The Cosby Show* and *Seinfeld,* created a renaissance.

Sitcoms are still relevant. On a multi-camera show, everyone is there on show night, because somewhere in the next two hours they will all be onstage. All the writers are there, to make any updates or revisions. And, just as important, a live audience is there. Multi-camera is a form that is certainly funnier than single-camera. In single-camera, you only have to make the writer laugh. In multi-camera, you have to make the audience laugh.

The sitcom will always exist in some form, because people need great character-driven stories that make them laugh and think together. It's a hybrid form, theater and film, with the live audience as guide. You're filming a show for the audience at home so that they can experience what the theater audience experiences. There will never be a substitute for live theater.

I'm often asked whether television comedy has changed over the years. Its popularity is ultimately subject to the quality of the shows, their longevity, and audience tastes, which are always changing. While sitcom episodes are now a few minutes shorter—and the audience attention span may also be shorter because of the Internet, PDAs, and social media—if you do a funny show, it will find its audience. The world has changed drastically, but there is one constant: People will always need to laugh. Now more than ever. You have to make sure they hear the joke, they see the joke, and that your cameras cover the joke. And, hopefully, the joke is funny.

I relish contributions from my actors and from my writers. I have a vision, but it gets done in a collaborative process. Actors walk the plank for me because they know I will catch them. They may get wet, but they'll never drown on my watch.

I still believe that kindness is the most important currency you can trade in, in business and in art. It brings out the best in everyone on all levels and provides the best possible outcome. What I believe I owe my success to is my way of making everyone in the lifeboat feel like they're keeping everyone else afloat. It requires trust, skill, and luck. I always try to have a calmness, an integrity, and a sense of how to get the ensemble to work together. Every actor must support the others and communicate. That is how creativity is maximized.

In 85 percent of acceptance speeches I've given, I've started with saying how lucky I am. Theater was a job for me. Television became my passion. This is what I do, and this is what I love. I want the real laughs. That is why I was put on this earth, to be a heat-seeking missile for the jokes and to bring out the best in others. It's tough to play with the form. But if it ain't funny, it ain't flying.

And that is my story, so far. Thank you for reading and thank you for watching. To the extent that I have made you and your family and friends laugh, I'm honored, grateful, and humbled.

Acknowledgments

Wow, I enjoyed reading this book. Can't wait to read the acknowledgments . . . What? I'm the one who has to write them? Can't I just acknowledge everyone who played a part in my life and career and be done with it? No? Okay, here goes . . .

To all the actors who put up with me and my insecurities while I was learning my stagecraft. I bless you for listening and not questioning me on my blocking and motivation or why we were in places like Framingham, Massachusetts, or Jacksonville, Florida, doing numerous *Odd Couples* and *Forty Carats*. To all the actors who put up with me and my insecurities while I was learning what I was doing early in my TV career. To Mary, Ed, Valerie, Gavin, Ted, Cloris, Betty White, Bob Newhart, and Suzanne Pleshette: I am eternally grateful that you didn't burst my bubble when I was calling "action" in a very tremulous and shaky voice. Sometimes the "ion" didn't even come out.

To Mary Tyler Moore and Grant Tinker, for taking a flyer on a kid from the comedy side of the tracks, and to my dad, for building a big house on that side.

To Jay Sandrich, who took me under his wing and taught me the ins and outs of navigating the sitcom genre and who became a lifelong friend.

I was blessed with the best words any director could want. I got to be in a room and hear Jim Brooks pitch entire scenes off the top of his head for a bunch of cabbies. The brilliant Glen and Les Charles and I took a trip that started in a taxi garage and ended up at a bar—a bar that inspired David Angell, Peter Casey, and David Lee to spin off a character for eleven years. I had coffee at Central Perk with Marta Kauffman and David Crane, two writers of impeccable skill who juggled six characters and three stories every week. I got to work with the incredibly talented and prolific Chuck Lorre many times and am flabbergasted at his ability to keep the sitcom alive. I also got to share the outrageous wit and amazing delicacy of Max Mutchnick and David Kohan on a groundbreaking show. I can't acknowledge all the other wordsmiths, but believe me, I was enormously blessed.

I still miss Brandon Tartikoff, who was not only one of my best friends but was also a network executive who let us be. To be able to do *Cheers* at NBC under Grant and Brandon was a charmed experience. I'm not sure that if others were in charge we would have made it.

To all the actors who put up with me and my insecurities on the shows that became our home and made us a family. I bless you all for enjoying the ride with me. Judd, Tony, Danny, Lu, Jeff, Chris Andy, and Carol . . . Teddy, Shelley, Kirstie, Rhea, Nicky, George, Ratz, Kelsey, Woody, and Bebe . . . Kelsey, Jane, David, Peri, and Mahoney . . . Jen, David, Courteney, Lisa, Matthew, and Matt . . .

Billy, Melissa, Reno, Swoosie, Katie, Nyambi, Louie, and Rondi . . . Eric, Debra, Sean, and Megan . . . and so many others. Please do not be offended if your name was not mentioned, but these are the end credits—I love you all.

Thanks to Norman Lear, for shining the light for all of us, and to Norman and Jimmy Kimmel for getting me out of the house to have fun at eighty-one directing the live re-creations of Norman's iconic shows, the latest of which are *The Facts of Life* and *Diff'rent Strokes*. Keep 'em coming, guys!

Thanks to Bob Broder, my agent and my friend. He is so powerful that they just call him Broder or, in crisis mode, Darth Broder. We've worked together since the seventies, and he has guided me through thick and thin with sage advice and love.

My appreciation to all my doctors who took my calls and replied, "Take two aspirin and call me in the morning with the ratings." And to my lawyers, especially Mr. Hoberman, who took my calls and billed me for them.

To my wonderful crew, many of whom were with me through thick and thin, thank you for your expertise and your ideas about how to make each show look and feel better.

Thanks to Eddy Friedfeld, whose passion for sitcoms is even greater than mine. He led me through this process like he was James Burrows and I was a fledgling actor. Gratitude to Mel Berger, who put the deal together with aplomb. To Pamela Cannon, editor extraordinaire, who steered me through this process with a velvet hammer. And especially to my loyal right-hand lady, Chris Connor, the most intrepid and diligent assistant a person could ever want.

To all the other actors who will have to put up with me and my insecurities in the future, let's just cut to the chase and have fun.

Then there is my family. First my friends—yes, they are family; thanks for being my friends. My wonderful sister, who has been supportive for all these years. My dad, who still inspires me and who I so wish could have seen what happened to his little boy. My mom, who got to see some of what happened, thanks for the nurturing. My wonderful daughters, who put up with my bad jokes at home only to roar at the good ones on TV. And to my wife, who has pushed me to do things I didn't want to do, like write this book. Thanks for the shove and, dare I rhyme, love!

Thank you for taking this journey with me,

CHEERS!

Photo Credits

INSERT 1

Page 1: All photos courtesy of James Burrows

Page 2: All photos courtesy of the Metropolitan Opera Archives

Page 3: Top: From the author's collection; middle and bottom: Courtesy of James Burrows

Page 4: Top and middle: Courtesy of James Burrows; bottom: From the author's collection

Page 5: All photos courtesy of James Burrows

Page 6: Top: *The Bob Newhart Show* copyright © 1977 Twentieth Century Fox. All rights reserved; middle: Courtesy of James Burrows; bottom: From the author's collection

Page 7: Top and middle: Photo stills from *Taxi*—Courtesy of CBS Studios; bottom: Courtesy of James Burrows

Page 8: Top: NBCU Photo Bank/Getty Images; middle: Photo by NBC; bottom: © 2022 Nina Barnett Photo by Nina Barnett

Page 9: Top and middle: © 2022 Nina Barnett Photo by Nina Barnett; bottom: Courtesy of NBC

Page 10: All photos courtesy of NBC

Page 11: Top: NBCU Photo Bank/Getty Images; middle and bottom: © 2022 Nina Barnett Photo by Nina Barnett

Page 12: Top and middle: © 2022 Nina Barnett Photo by Nina Barnett; bottom: From the author's collection

Page 13: Top and top middle left: Courtesy of James Burrows; bottom middle left: Art Streiber/NBCU Photo Bank/NBCUniversal via Getty Images; middle right: Photo by Terence Patrick/2022 Warner Bros. Entertainment Inc.; bottom: Vince Bucci/Getty Images

Page 14: Top: Walter McBride/Getty Images; middle and bottom: Trae Patton/NBCU Photo Bank/NBCUniversal via Getty Images

Page 15: Top and middle left: Chris Haston/NBCU Photo Bank/NBCUniversal via Getty Images; middle right and bottom: Trae Patton/NBCU Photo Bank/NBCUniversal via Getty Images

Page 16: Top: Chris Haston; middle: Chris Haston/NBCU Photo Bank/NBC Universal via Getty Images; bottom: Ron Galella/Getty Images

INSERT 2

Page 1: Top: Chris Haston/NBCU Photo Bank/NBCUniversal via Getty Images; middle: Gary Null/NBCU Photo Bank/NBCUniversal via Getty Images: bottom: Chris Haston/NBCU Photo Bank/NBCUniversal via Getty Images

Page 2: Top left: Chris Haston/NBCU Photo Bank/NBCUniversal via Getty Images; top right: Photo by Chris Haston/NBC; middle right: Courtesy of James Burrows; middle left and bottom: Photos by Chris Haston/ NBC

Page 3: Top: Bruce Glikas/Getty Images; middle: Photo courtesy the Television Academy; © 2013 Television Academy; bottom: Alberto E. Rodriguez/ Getty Images

Page 4: Top: Kevin Winter/Getty Images: middle right: Monty Brinton/Getty Images; middle left and bottom: Licensed by Warner Bros. Entertainment Inc. All Rights Reserved.

Page 5: Top and middle: *Live in Front of a Studio Audience* courtesy of ABC/ Sony Pictures Television; bottom: Licensed by Warner Bros. Entertainment Inc. All Rights Reserved.

Page 6: Top: Chris Delmas/Getty Images; middle and bottom: Courtesy of James Burrows

Page 7: Top: Kevin Winter/Getty Images; middle: Howard Wise/DGA; bottom: Copyright © by Terry Corrao

Page 8: Top: Courtesy of James Burrows; middle: Annie Leibovitz/Trunk Archive; bottom: Arnold Newman/Getty Images

About the Author

JAMES BURROWS has directed more than one thousand episodes of sitcom television and has earned eleven Emmy Awards and five Directors Guild of America Awards. His five-decade career began in theater, stage-managing on Broadway and directing regional theater. In 1974, he began his television career, directing episodes of *The Mary Tyler Moore Show, The Bob Newhart Show,* and *Laverne & Shirley.* He became the resident director on *Taxi,* then co-created the beloved classic *Cheers,* directing 243 of the 273 episodes, as well as all of the 246 episodes of *Will & Grace.* He has directed the pilots and multiple episodes of *Frasier, Friends, Mike & Molly,* the pilots of *Two and a Half Men* and *The Big Bang Theory,* and hundreds of other shows, where he has nurtured and mentored some of television's biggest stars.